The Academy of International Business

Series Editors
Academy of International Business
Michigan State University
East Lansing, USA

Rudolf Sinkovics
Alliance Manchester Business School
University of Manchester
Manchester, UK

Olli Kuivalainen
Lappeenranta University of Technology
Lappeenranta, Finland

The Academy of International Business – AIB-UKI Chapter book series is dedicated to publish cutting-edge research in International Business (IB) that is of contemporary relevance and at the cusp of conceptual and empirical development. The socio-political environment within which IB activity takes place is reconfigured and transformed with tremendous speed. This book series seeks to close the time-to-market of new findings and offer a solid evidence base and frameworks that helps to understand these changes. Each of the editions curates the work that exists under a special IB theme, bringing together advances by leading authors in the field.

More information about this series at
http://www.palgrave.com/gp/series/14246

Agnieszka Chidlow • Pervez N. Ghauri
Thomas Buckley • Emma C. Gardner
Amir Qamar • Emily Pickering
Editors

The Changing Strategies of International Business

How MNEs Manage in a Changing Commercial and Political Landscape

palgrave
macmillan

Editors

Agnieszka Chidlow
Birmingham Business School
University of Birmingham
Birmingham, UK

Thomas Buckley
Management School
University of Sheffield
Sheffield, UK

Amir Qamar
Birmingham Business School
University of Birmingham
Birmingham, UK

Pervez N. Ghauri
Birmingham Business School
University of Birmingham
Birmingham, UK

Emma C. Gardner
Birmingham Business School
University of Birmingham
Birmingham, UK

Emily Pickering
Birmingham Business School
University of Birmingham
Birmingham, UK

The Academy of International Business
ISBN 978-3-030-03930-1   ISBN 978-3-030-03931-8   (eBook)
https://doi.org/10.1007/978-3-030-03931-8

Library of Congress Control Number: 2018964107

© The Editor(s) (if applicable) and The Author(s), under exclusive licence to Springer Nature Switzerland AG 2019

This work is subject to copyright. All rights are solely and exclusively licensed by the Publisher, whether the whole or part of the material is concerned, specifically the rights of translation, reprinting, reuse of illustrations, recitation, broadcasting, reproduction on microfilms or in any other physical way, and transmission or information storage and retrieval, electronic adaptation, computer software, or by similar or dissimilar methodology now known or hereafter developed.

The use of general descriptive names, registered names, trademarks, service marks, etc. in this publication does not imply, even in the absence of a specific statement, that such names are exempt from the relevant protective laws and regulations and therefore free for general use.

The publisher, the authors, and the editors are safe to assume that the advice and information in this book are believed to be true and accurate at the date of publication. Neither the publisher nor the authors or the editors give a warranty, express or implied, with respect to the material contained herein or for any errors or omissions that may have been made. The publisher remains neutral with regard to jurisdictional claims in published maps and institutional affiliations.

This Palgrave Macmillan imprint is published by the registered company Springer Nature Switzerland AG
The registered company address is: Gewerbestrasse 11, 6330 Cham, Switzerland

Contents

Part I Risky Business: Multinationals, Governments and Political Risk 1

1 Legitimacy and Institutional Governance Infrastructure: Understanding Political Risk from a Chinese MNE Perspective 3
Xia Han and Xiaohui Liu

2 Applying Theory to Understand How Multinational Firms Address Brexit 27
Saad Laraqui and Bert J. Jarreau

3 Bureaucrats in International Business: A Review of Five Decades of Research on State-Owned MNEs 49
Asmund Rygh

Part II Paths to Performance and Current Perspectives on Emerging Markets 71

4 Contextual Transfer Barriers, Social Interaction, and Innovation Transfer Performance 73
Olivia H. Kang and Pao T. Kao

vi   Contents

5   **Equity Ownership Strategy in Greenfield Investments: Influences of Host Country Infrastructure and MNE Resources in Emerging Markets**   95
    Ahmad Arslan, Jorma Larimo, and Desislava Dikova

6   **The Value of Local Externalities in Country-of-Origin Clusters: Evidence from China**   117
    Berrbizne Urzelai and Francisco Puig

7   **Acquirer's Country of Origin and Target Firm's Performance**   135
    Jinlong Gu, Yong Yang, and Roger Strange

8   **Human Rights Reporting of BRIC and Non-BRIC MNEs: An Exploratory Comparative Analysis**   157
    Stefan Zagelmeyer

Part III   International Small (but) Mighty Enterprises and Entrepreneurs   175

9   **The Role of Culture in Responsible Business Practice: An Exploration of Finnish and Russian SMEs**   177
    Maria Uzhegova, Lasse Torkkeli, and Maria Ivanova-Gongne

10   **The Internationalization of Born-Digital Companies**   199
    Ioan-Iustin Vadana, Lasse Torkkeli, Olli Kuivalainen, and Sami Saarenketo

11   **Technological Disruptions and Production Location Choices**   221
    Lisa De Propris and Diletta Pegoraro

Index   241

Notes on Contributors

Ahmad Arslan is a senior research fellow (International Business) at the Department of Marketing, Management and International Business, Oulu Business School, University of Oulu, Finland. Previously, he has worked in academia in the UK and Finland as a senior lecturer, assistant professor and researcher. His core areas of research interests include cross-border mergers and acquisitions, emerging economies, foreign market entry strategies, internationalization of small firms and multinational enterprises' (MNEs) strategies. His earlier research has been published in prestigious academic journals such *as British Journal of Management, International Business Review, International Marketing Review, Scandinavian Journal of Management, Journal of Strategic Marketing, Journal for East European Management Studies and Journal of Global Marketing*, among others. Moreover, Ahmad has also contributed several book chapters to edited handbooks addressing different international business and strategy topics. Finally, he is an editorial board member of two academic journals (*Journal of East-West Business* and *International Journal of Export Marketing*).

Lisa De Propris is Professor of Regional Economic Development at Birmingham Business School, the University of Birmingham, in the UK. She has expertise in manufacturing, industry 4.0, technological change, clusters/districts, creative industries, regional economic development, industrial policy and European Union (EU) regional policy.

Desislava Dikova is Professor in International Business at Vienna University of Economics and Business Administration, Austria. She previously held academic positions at the University of Groningen, the Netherlands and King's College London, the UK. She earned her doctorate degree from the University of Groningen, the Netherlands. She is the editor-in-chief of the *Journal of East-West Business* Associate editor of the *European Management Review,* Senior Editor of the *International Journal of Emerging Markets* and is a member of the editorial boards for the *Journal of International Business Studies, Journal of World Business, Journal of International Marketing and*

viii   Notes on Contributors

Management and *Organization Review*. Desislava's research is focused on the international behaviour of multinational companies; she examines their foreign market entry-mode choices and the subsequent performance of foreign subsidiaries in transition economies. In addition, Desislava studies the competitive behaviour of firms with respect to the types of innovation investments and their cross-border merger and acquisition activity. Her research has been published in highly ranked international journals such as the *Journal of International Business Studies*, *Journal of Management Studies*, *International Business Review*, *Journal of Business Research*, *Journal of International Marketing*, *Journal of International Management* and others.

Jinlong Gu is a research assistant and a tutor at the University of Sussex Business School, UK. He holds a PhD in Management from the University of Sussex. His research interests include cross-border acquisition, firm internationalization and location.

Xia Han is Lecturer in International Business at Alliance Manchester Business School, Manchester University, UK. Her teaching and research interests include emerging market multinational enterprises (EMNEs), global political economy and political risk management. Her research addresses the implications of home-country institutions for EMNEs' post-entry performance. She also looks at political risk management strategies of EMNEs.

Maria Ivanova-Gongne is a university teacher in International Marketing, Åbo Akademi University, Turku, Finland. Her research interests include business-to-business marketing management, particularly the aspects of business interaction, managerial sensemaking and culture in international business-to-business relationships and networks. Her work has appeared in international top journals such as *Industrial Marketing Management*, *Scandinavian Journal of Management*, *Journal of Business and Industrial Marketing* and *European Management Journal*.

Bert J. Jarreau is a collegiate travelling professor at the University of Maryland University College Europe in Kaiserslautern, Germany. He is a scholar-practitioner whose professional experience includes information technology leadership roles across diverse industries including non-profit association, government and industry (information services, automotive and real estate). He teaches organizational behaviour, marketing and international business strategy in the MBA programme in Germany and the UK. His research focuses on international business strategy. Bert holds a Doctor of Management from the University of Maryland University College.

Olivia H. Kang is Assistant Professor of International Business at the Department of Business Studies, Uppsala University, Sweden. Her research covers the development and transfer of innovations in multinational firms, and the strategic management of innovations. Olivia's recent research covers the factors that impact the knowledge transfer with specific interest in the social innovation development process.

Notes on Contributors   ix

Pao T. Kao is Assistant Professor in International Business at the Department of Business Studies, Uppsala University, Sweden. His research interests lie in understanding how firms strategically manage their internationalization process in the face of changes in market, institutional and technological environments. Kao's articles have appeared in *Journal of International Entrepreneurship, Journal of Management and Organisational History* and *Progress in International Business Research*.

Olli Kuivalainen is Professor of International Marketing and Entrepreneurship at the School of Business and Management of the Lappeenranta University of Technology, Finland, and also Professor of International Business and Management at the Alliance Manchester Business School, University of Manchester. His main research interests include internationalization of small and medium enterprises (SMEs) and international entrepreneurship, and marketing and technology management. He has published in journals such as *Journal of International Business Studies, Journal of World Business, International Business Review, Journal of International Marketing, International Marketing Review, Technovation* and *Journal of International Entrepreneurship*.

Saad Laraqui is a collegiate travelling professor at the University of Maryland University College Europe in Kaiserslautern, Germany. He teaches leadership, organizational behaviour, finance, strategy and international business in the MBA programme in Germany, Italy, the UK and Bahrain. His research focuses on foreign direct investment (FDI), activities of multinational enterprises (MNEs) and economic integration. Laraqui holds a PhD in Finance and International Business from Rutgers University.

Jorma Larimo is Professor of International Marketing at the University of Vaasa, Finland. He is the Vice Dean of the School of Marketing and Communications and Head of the Doctoral Programme of Business Studies at the University of Vaasa. His areas of interest include small and medium-sized enterprise internationalization and foreign entry strategies of multinational enterprises, especially foreign direct investment, mergers and acquisitions, and international joint venture strategies and performance. He has edited six books addressing various aspects of international business. His research has been published in well-ranked academic journals including *the International Business Review, Journal of International Business Studies, Journal of International Marketing, Management International Review, Journal of World Business, Journal of Global Marketing, Journal of East-West Business* and *Journal for East European Management Studies*. Larimo has also contributed book chapters to several edited books.

Xiaohui Liu is Professor of International Business at Birmingham Business School, the University of Birmingham, UK, and Visiting Professor of School of International Business, Southwestern University of Finance and Economics, China. Her main research interests include knowledge spillovers, human mobility, innovation and the

x   Notes on Contributors

internationalization strategies of firms from emerging economies. She has published widely in journals such as *Strategic Management Journal, Journal of International Business Studies, Research Policy, Entrepreneurship Theory and Practice, Journal of World Business, Organization Studies, Strategic Entrepreneurship Journal, British Journal of Management* and *International Business Review.*

Diletta Pegoraro is a PhD student at Birmingham Business School, the University of Birmingham, UK.

Francisco Puig is an associate professor in the Department of Management of the University of Valencia, Spain. He is the coordinator of the research group GESTOR (Organizational Geostrategy: Clusters and Competitiveness). Puig's research focuses on the intersection between Location-Strategy-Performance.

Asmund Rygh is Lecturer in International Business and Management at Alliance Manchester Business School, University of Manchester. He holds a PhD in Business and Economics from BI Norwegian Business School, Oslo, and an MA in Economics from the University of Oslo. His research takes a corporate governance perspective on international business, considering issues such as the internationalization of state-owned enterprises, corporate finance and internal governance in multinational enterprises. His research-in-progress is also exploring further issues such as the links between corporate governance and corporate social responsibility. His publications include articles in journals such as *Global Strategy Journal, Management International Review* and *Business and Politics*, among others.

Sami Saarenketo is Professor of International Marketing at the School of Business, Lappeenranta University of Technology, Finland. His primary areas of research interest are international marketing and entrepreneurship in technology-based small firms. He has published on these issues in *Journal of World Business, International Business Review, European Business Review, European Journal of Marketing* and *Journal of International Entrepreneurship*, among others.

Roger Strange is Professor of International Business in the University of Sussex Business School, UK. He is a former president of the European International Business Academy (EIBA).

Lasse Torkkeli is an associate professor at LUT School of Business and Management. His areas of expertise are related especially to the internationalization of small and medium enterprises (SMEs), their networks and partnerships, as well as the role of dynamic skills and culture in international business. He has published research articles in both conferences and international academic scientific journals, such as *Journal of International Entrepreneurship, European Management Journal* and *International Journal of Procurement Management.*

Berrbizne Urzelai is a lecturer and team-coach at the Department of Business Management, University of the West of England, Bristol, UK. She holds an International PhD (Hons) in Economics and Business Management, on the research line of Entrepreneurship, Innovation and Territory (University of Valencia). Her research focuses on foreign direct investment (FDI), country-of-origin clusters, social capital and agglomeration economies.

Maria Uzhegova is a junior researcher at LUT School of Business and Management. Her research interests focus on the firm's international business relationships with specific emphasis on the small and medium enterprise (SME) internationalization, business ethics and sustainability. She has previously published in the *Journal of East-West Business* and *International Journal of Multinational Corporation Strategy*.

Ioan-Iustin Vadana is a PhD student and junior researcher since 2016 at School of Business and Management, Lappeenranta University of Technology, Finland. His areas of expertise are related especially to the internationalization of born digital companies, mostly their value chain, and business model, as well as the role of online strategy on international performance.

Yong Yang is Reader in Strategy at the University of Sussex Business School, UK. Before joining Sussex, he worked at the University of Essex and Brunel University.

Stefan Zagelmeyer is Reader in Comparative and International Business at Alliance Manchester Business School, University of Manchester, UK. His research focuses on international business strategy, comparative business and management, international human resource management and business and human rights.

List of Figures

Fig. 1.1	The moderating effect of Chinese MNEs' legitimacy with the host government on the relationship between Chinese MNEs' perceived level of political risk and host-country institutional governance infrastructure	19
Fig. 1.2	The moderating effect of Chinese MNEs' legitimacy in host-country regulated industries on the relationship between Chinese MNEs' perceived level of political risk and host-country institutional governance infrastructure	20
Fig. 1.3	The moderating effect of Chinese MNEs' legitimacy with host-country public on the relationship between Chinese MNEs' perceived level of political risk and host-country institutional governance infrastructure	21
Fig. 2.1	Relationship-specific advantage dynamic process model	37
Fig. 3.1	Reviewed studies over time	51
Fig. 4.1	Results of qualitative data	85
Fig. 6.1	Externalities by location mode. (Source: Own elaboration)	128
Fig. 6.2	Externalities by entry reason. (Source: Own elaboration)	128
Fig. 10.1	Internationalization aspect of digitalized (Internet-enabled) firms	204
Fig. 10.2	Sample classification of the born-digital companies	209
Fig. 11.1	GDP and trade (annual percentage change and ratio). (Source: Our elaboration from WTO statistics)	228
Fig. 11.2	Trend of the KOF globalisation index. (Source: Our calculation with KOF data (Gygli et al. 2018))	229
Fig. 11.3	Developed economies: FDI outflows, annual 1970–16 (as percentage of GDP). (Source: Our elaboration from UNCTADSTAT)	229

List of Tables

Table 1.1	Correlation matrix	15
Table 1.2	Measurement model and CFA results	16
Table 1.3	Discriminant validity	17
Table 1.4	Result of regression analysis	18
Table 4.1	Descriptive statistics and correlations	82
Table 4.2	Results of OLS estimations	83
Table 4.3	Results of OLS estimations	84
Table 5.1	Sample characteristics	106
Table 5.2	Descriptive statistics and Pearson correlations	107
Table 5.3	Binomial logistic regression estimates full sample (greenfield WOS = 1)	108
Table 5.4	Binomial logistic regression estimates sub-sample JVs (majority greenfield JV = 1)	108
Table 6.1	Different types of clusters	121
Table 6.2	Descriptive statistics and correlation coefficients	127
Table 6.3	Average punctuations by type of subsidiary	127
Table 7.1	Operationalisation of variables	142
Table 7.2	Descriptive statistics and correlations matrix	143
Table 7.3	Descriptive statistics: domestic acquirers versus foreign acquirers	144
Table 7.4	Key variables by economy	145
Table 7.5	Country of origin and performance: the roles of relatedness and ownership	147
Table 7.6	Country of origin and performance: additional robustness checks	149
Table 7.7	Country of origin and performance: acquirers from manufacturing sectors	150
Table 8.1	The sample companies from the Forbes Global 2000 list (2013)	160

xvi   List of Tables

Table 8.2	Corporate reporting channels	163
Table 8.3	Reporting channels used to communicate human rights policies	166
Table 8.4	Human rights reporting intensity scores	167
Table 8.5	Human rights reporting intensity scores—summary statistics	171
Table 9.1	The overview of the CSR studies based on the Hofstede (1980) dimensions	181
Table 9.2	Cultural profiles of Finland and Russia	182
Table 9.3	Case companies' information	185
Table 9.4	The summary of RBPs in case companies	190
Table 10.1	The utilities of digital technologies	201
Table 10.2	Firms in the sample	207
Table 10.3	Data analyzed for case comparison	208

Part I

Risky Business: Multinationals, Governments and Political Risk

In recent years, a number of significant and unprecedented occurrences have happened on the global stage. For example, in the developed world, these can relate to the events relating to the election of Mr Donald Trump as the 45th President of the United States and to the decision of the British public to pursue an independence from the European Union, following the Brexit referendum in 2016. However, in the developing world, these can be linked to the plight of the Rohingya refugees, the actions of the Nicolás Maduro Moros's presidency and the prevailing economic war in Venezuela as well as the controversy surrounding Zimbabwe's recent presidential elections.

All of these events highlight widespread challenges that political actors, institutions and firms face when embarking on international business activities. Therefore, by including three chapters, the aim of the first chapter of this book is to offer a reader a lens to look at those challenges and their possible solutions.

The first chapter (Chap. 1), titled "Legitimacy and Institutional Governance Infrastructure: Understanding Political Risk from a Chinese MNE Perspective" by Xia Han and Xiaohui Liu, seeks to determine how legitimacy affects the international expansion of Chinese multinationals. Using the institutional theory to understand how social acceptance influences perceptions of host-country political risk, the authors draw upon 148 observations to propose that home-country biases affect the legitimacy afforded to Chinese multinationals in host-country environments. They advocate that acceptance from particular host-country stakeholders can act as an alternative mechanism for gaining legitimacy.

Chapter 2, titled "Applying Theory to Understand How Multinational Firms Address Brexit" by Saad Laraqui and Bert J. Jarreau, adopts Dunning's eclectic paradigm, alongside other frameworks, to understand a competitive advantage in order to examine and discuss the implications of the UK referendum on leaving the European Union. According to the authors, the economic disintegration of Brexit presents a challenge for economic rationality; hence, in order to overcome this they propose recommendations designed to minimize the damage and to hasten a recovery.

The final chapter (Chap. 3), titled "Bureaucrats in International Business: A Review of Five Decades of Research on State-Owned MNEs" by Asmund Rygh, provides a holistic review of state-owned multinational firms. By examining 137 studies, the author suggests that despite a common domestic bias ascribed to a business model, state-owned enterprises in emerging economies are internationalizing more and have a greater tolerance to political risk. Nevertheless, despite an increasing interest in these types of firms, this paper propagates the need for more empirical work, particularly with regard to multi-country investigations and in contexts other than China, to develop a much deeper understanding.

1

Legitimacy and Institutional Governance Infrastructure: Understanding Political Risk from a Chinese MNE Perspective

Xia Han and Xiaohui Liu

Introduction

What determines Chinese multinational enterprises' (MNEs) perceived level of political risk in host countries? Research based on developed-country MNEs' experiences has examined the effect of the host-country institutional governance infrastructure on Chinese firms' locational choices, entry strategies, and performance (Ramasamy et al. 2012; Lu et al. 2014). While some studies found that Chinese MNEs have boldly ventured into politically risky contexts (Liu et al. 2016), others reported that these new players have tended to follow their developed-country counterparts by avoiding underdeveloped institutional environments. Given the inconclusive findings of previous research, one may question the extent to which the traditional way of understanding political risk is valid for Chinese MNEs. Yet, little attention has been paid to examining whether the conventional analytical framework focusing on the host-country institutional governance infrastructure can be extended to explain Chinese firms' perception of political hazards in overseas markets.

X. Han
Alliance Manchester Business School, University of Manchester, Manchester, UK
e-mail: xia.han@manchester.ac.uk

X. Liu (✉)
Birmingham Business School, University of Birmingham, Birmingham, UK
e-mail: X.liu.1@bham.ac.uk

© The Author(s) 2019
A. Chidlow et al. (eds.), *The Changing Strategies of International Business*, The Academy of International Business, https://doi.org/10.1007/978-3-030-03931-8_1

More recent research has recognized that other factors, apart from host-country institutional governance infrastructure, also affect the political perils as perceived by Chinese MNEs. For example, Globerman and Shapiro (2009) suggest that affiliation with the home-country government can augment the political obstacles experienced by Chinese firms in the US. Stevens and Newenham-Kahindi (2017) noted the importance of home-country legitimacy with host-country stakeholders in affecting Chinese MNEs' survival in East Africa. As extreme hazards, such as direct expropriation, have faded out, emerging-market MNEs, especially Chinese firms, can be exposed to political challenges that go beyond host-country institutional governance conditions (Bremmer 2014). Given their distinctive home-country characteristics, such as heavy state involvement in business operations and the underdeveloped institutional environment, research has pinpointed the need to understand political risk from a broader perspective. However, extant literature has largely been silent regarding the determinants of Chinese MNEs' perceived level of political risk in global marketplaces.

In this chapter, we draw on the notion of legitimacy from institutional theory to examine (1) whether, and to what extent, the traditional analytical framework focusing on host-country governance conditions can explain the political risk perceived by Chinese firms; and (2) what determines their perceived level of such a risk when venturing abroad. Institutional theory, especially the sociological tradition or neo-institutional theory, has been widely adopted as the theoretical basis in research on emerging markets (Meyer and Peng 2016). A central premise of this perspective concerns the importance of gaining acceptance from institutional constituents in helping organizations to secure their position within an organizational field (DiMaggio and Powell 1983). For firms venturing internationally, they have to receive a 'social license to operate' from the broader sociological context to enhance their chances of survival (Kostova and Zaheer 1999).

While research drawn from the institutional perspective has looked at host-country political and regulatory factors, little attention has been paid to the legitimacy judgements of interested stakeholders, such as employees, customers, and professional associations, in shaping firms' perceived level of political risk. Additionally, a country's institutional governance framework and its underlying societal values can interact in multifaceted ways (Webb et al. 2009). The legitimacy judgement by interested social groups towards MNEs may either reinforce or constrain the effectiveness of explicitly stated rules (Stevens et al. 2015). By underscoring the importance of gaining (or losing) social acceptance, this study sheds new light on the factors that shape Chinese MNEs' perceived level of host-country political risk.

We aim to contribute to a nuanced understanding of political risk in international business literature in two main ways. First, this study departs from existing research that considered whether and how host-country institutional governance factors can influence Chinese firms' overseas expansion (Liu et al. 2016). Instead, we explore whether such a conventional analytical framework can be applied to explain the political hazards perceived by these new players in overseas markets. We complement extant literature by uncovering the effect of home-country legitimacy in affecting the level of political risk perceived by Chinese MNEs operating abroad.

Second, research has posited that gaining legitimacy from host-country social actors can help firms navigate through a risky political environment, in addition to relying on the institutional governance framework (Darendeli and Hill 2016). We delineate the role of interested host-country stakeholders including government, industrial agencies, and the public. By looking at the interaction between their legitimacy judgements towards MNEs and the effectiveness of the host-country institutional governance framework, we advance research by uncovering the interdependence between explicitly stated rules and implicit social norms in explaining Chinese MNEs' perceived level of political risk in overseas markets.

Theoretical Background and Hypotheses

The institutional perspective brings together several lines of research with shared interests in the role of contextual factors in shaping firms' strategies and behaviours (Meyer and Peng 2016). We follow the logic of neo-institutional works by assuming that institutions can provide legitimacy for organizations (DiMaggio and Powell 1983). This line of research has defined institutions as the shared norms and rules that determine the socially acceptable behaviours (Fiaschi et al. 2017). The core idea is that firms that adjust their behaviour to the socially acceptable norms may not guarantee them efficiency, but will grant them the legitimacy needed in a given organizational field (Meyer and Peng 2016).

A country's institutional environment is composed of explicitly stated rules and implicit social norms (Webb et al. 2009). In addition to demonstrating regulatory compliance, MNEs are subject to the legitimacy judgement of interested host-country social stakeholders (Kostova and Zaheer

1999). Their evaluations towards MNEs are constrained by bounded rationality due to imperfect information which may lead them to use 'a number of cognitive shortcuts' (Bitektine 2011, p. 164). By using these cognitive shortcuts, an MNE's legitimacy is likely to be determined by referring to the legitimacy of others that share similar characteristics, such as firms from the same home country, industry, or class (Kostova and Zaheer 1999). As a result, this can generate a spill-over effect where an MNE can either benefit from the legitimacy or be penalized by the illegitimacy of other similar firms (Lange et al. 2011). While there are many cognitive categories, MNEs' home country has been one of the most common criteria used by host-country stakeholders to judge a firm's legitimacy (Stevens and Newenham-Kahindi 2017).

Although previous research has revealed insights into the effect of the home country on MNEs' acceptance by consumers in host countries, little has been said about the political implications with regard to firms' success in overseas markets (Cuervo-Cazurra 2011). Unlike MNEs from advanced economies, the home-country environment within which Chinese firms operate typically suffers from regulatory voids and unsophisticated product designs (Luo and Tung 2007). These disadvantages originating from the home country can generate a negative spill-over effect by imposing a legitimacy deficit on Chinese MNEs, and hence reduce firms' acceptance abroad.

Additionally, a country's explicitly stated rules and underlying societal norms interact in multifaceted ways (Bruton et al. 2010). Political and regulatory reforms can signal what are deemed legitimate practices by influential social groups (Webb et al. 2009). The institutional governance framework, on the other hand, reinforces a society's values and individual behaviours (Bruton et al. 2010). Hence, these two streams of institutional forces should be jointly considered when examining factors that shape MNEs' perceived level of host-country political risk.

Differing from existing research that focuses on host-country institutional governance infrastructure, we examine the role of home-country legitimacy in explaining the political risk perceived by Chinese firms in host countries. The distinctive home-country attributes can influence Chinese MNEs' acceptance in the host country, thus generating political consequences (Madhok and Keyhani 2012). We suggest that Chinese MNEs' home-country legitimacy in the eyes of host-country interested social groups may reduce the importance of the host-country institutional governance infrastructure in shaping firms' perceived political risk.

Hypotheses Development

Direct Effect of Host-Country Institutional Governance Infrastructure

The institutional governance infrastructure of a country infrastructure includes the process by which governments are selected and monitored, governments' competences to formulate and implement policies, and the extent to which citizens respect the institutions that govern economic and social interactions (Globerman and Shapiro 2003). A strong governance infrastructure or framework is paramount in determining a country's attractiveness to foreign direct investment (FDI) (Oh and Oetzel 2011). For Chinese MNEs conducting business abroad, we suggest that they may perceive the host-country political environment as less risky when there is a stronger governance framework for two reasons.

First, on the host-country side, a favourable institutional governance infrastructure is conducive to stimulate FDI (Globerman and Shapiro 2003). An effective governance framework involves a transparent legal system that protects property rights, strong enforcement of court decisions, and creditable policy commitments that promote competition among domestic and foreign companies (Lu et al. 2014). The presence of these conditions can provide institutional support to boost MNEs' operational confidence (Oh and Oetzel 2011). Hence, firms may perceive fewer political perils when a host country has a stronger institutional governance framework. Second, on the home-country side, firms are likely to be granted favourable treatment, such as reduced taxes, when their activities appear consistent with the home-country government's long-term goals (Stevens et al. 2015). Conversely, political obstacles can be imposed on firms. The 'institutional escapism view' has argued that firms respond to the misalignment between their needs and the home-country institutional environment through outward FDI (Luo et al. 2010). The foreign expansion of many Chinese MNEs has been deemed a response to such misalignment (Boisot and Meyer 2008). The burdensome domestic governance environment has made some Chinese firms escape abroad not only in the search of markets, but also more efficient governance conditions (Luo and Tung 2007). Thus, they may perceive the host country as less risky when it features a strong institutional governance infrastructure.

Although some research has reported that Chinese MNEs are prompted to operate in underdeveloped institutional environments (Liu et al. 2016), empirical evidence also suggests that the host-country governance infrastructure matters with respect to these firms' perceived level of political risk. The World Investment and Political Risk Report (2009) noted that emerging-market firms, especially Chinese MNEs, are worried most about breach of contract, war and civil turbulence, and transfer restrictions in host countries. Additionally, the peculiarities of China's domestic governance conditions may provide some arguments for their firms' overseas investment. Firms in China are facing local protectionism and limited protection of property rights. These constraints have made the costs of doing business at the cross-regional level higher than at the cross-national level (Boisot and Meyer 2008).

Hypothesis 1 Chinese MNEs tend to perceive the host-country political environment less risky when there is a stronger host-country institutional governance infrastructure.

The Moderating Role of Legitimacy

Hypothesis 1 highlights the impact of the host-country institutional governance framework on MNEs' perceived level of political risk. There are some boundary conditions which either strengthen or weaken the impact of the institutional governance infrastructure on Chinese MNEs' perceived level of political risk in host countries. Two factors need to be taken into account. First, political and legislative efforts may be made to acknowledge the changing norms and trends in a society (Webb et al. 2009). Second, interested social groups may successfully lobby for shifts in a country's policy framework to reflect their expectations (Ashforth and Gibbs 1990). As a result, a country's institutional governance framework and the legitimacy judgement by key social stakeholders may jointly shape MNEs' survival and prosperity.

As Suchman (1995) suggested, legitimacy represents an overall evaluation by some groups of observers towards organizational activities rather than a consensus of opinions within or across these groups. This implies that gaining (or losing) legitimacy from certain institutional constituents can have a more profound influence than others (Darendeli and Hill 2016). The importance of home-country legitimacy with interested host-country social groups has been recognized as it can interact with the institutional governance infrastructure and jointly influence firms' perceived level of political risk (Stevens and Newenham-Kahindi 2017).

We examine Chinese MNEs' legitimacy with three sets of interested host-country stakeholders. A central set of stakeholders are host-country governments that possess the power to determine the existence of MNEs within their borders (Bitektine 2011). A second group of stakeholders are the host-country industrial agencies that set the entry and operational standards for different industries (García-Canal and Guillén 2008). Another vital group of legitimacy-granting actors is the host-country general public which can influence MNEs' survival through societal values and expectations (Deephouse 1996).

Chinese MNEs' Legitimacy with Host-Country Government

Governments' actions in signalling socially acceptable practices can be as powerful as codified laws (Marquis and Qian 2014). Their legitimization of MNEs may serve as an alternative institutional device that offsets the importance of the institutional governance framework in shaping firms' perceived level of host-country political risk. As firms venturing abroad carry the image of their home country, this may generate a legitimacy spill-over effect and political consequences which can impact MNEs' operations abroad (Fiaschi et al. 2017). The legitimacy judgement of the host-country government towards an MNE can be made by referring to its home country or home-country government (Cuervo-Cazurra 2011). The high degree of legitimacy enjoyed by an MNE's home-country government with the host-country government because of trustworthy and friendly interstate political relations may generate positive spill-over effects (Stevens and Newenham-Kahindi 2017). As a result, firms may receive preferential access to resources which reduce their reliance on the institutional governance framework. In contrast, a perceived lack of legitimacy of an MNE's home-country government can cause them to encounter hostile treatment, despite the presence of rules and laws in the host country.

For Chinese MNEs expanding into foreign markets, the image of their home country or home-country government is not always separable from the firms themselves (Madhok and Keyhani 2012). The greater the legitimacy of the Chinese government with certain host governments, perhaps because of their shared views with regard to foreign policies, the more positive the spill-over effects for Chinese firms. Hence, these firms may be granted access to markets and resources that offset the importance of the host-country governance framework. Conversely, the weak legitimacy of the Chinese government as perceived by some host governments due to, for example, a lack of alignment in international political affairs may expose Chinese firms to more stringent regulations (Bremmer 2014).

Hypothesis 2 The importance of the institutional governance infrastructure in shaping Chinese MNEs' perceived level of host-country political risk will be reduced for those firms gaining a high degree of legitimacy from the host-country government.

Chinese MNEs' Legitimacy with Host-Country Industrial Agencies

In addition to the macro-level governance framework that applies to all foreign investors, firms have to account for industry-related requirements set by host-country industrial agencies. The political science literature has maintained that governments are not unitary actors but consist of many subunits with varying interests (Kistruck et al. 2015). When a country's overall governance framework fails to accommodate their goals, they may signal their own standards of legitimacy (Darendeli and Hill 2016). Thus, despite laws established at national level to regulate all foreign MNEs, considerations over the competitiveness of domestic industries may prompt host-country industrial agencies to set policies targeting different sectors.

While industry-specific requirements may affect every sector of the economy, their impact can be particularly salient for firms in regulated industries including natural resources, telecommunications, and utilities (García-Canal and Guillén 2008). Unlike MNEs in more liberalized sectors that compete on the merit of market demands, those in regulated industries primarily depend on munificent industrial policies (Henisz and Zelner 2001). Hence, industry-related requirements set by the host-country industrial agencies may offset the importance of the country's overall governance framework for firms in regulated sectors.

For Chinese MNEs operating in regulated sectors, the impact of host-country institutional governance infrastructure on the firms' perceived political risk may be limited due to the presence of industry-related restrictions. Given the role of industrial agencies in setting a wide array of requirements, their assessment about the firms' influence on the local economy may reduce the relevance of macro-level governance framework.

Hypothesis 3 The importance of the host-country institutional governance infrastructure in shaping Chinese MNEs' perceived level of host-country political risk will be reduced for those operating in regulated industries.

Chinese MNEs' Legitimacy with Host-Country General Public

The general public, including local communities, consumers, and media, are important institutional constituents in defining and diffusing what is deemed socially acceptable (Stevens et al. 2015). Firms thus need to meet their expectations to gain the 'social license to operate' (Deephouse 1996).

The lack of acceptance by the host-country public may induce political consequences. As governments require legitimacy for themselves from their own constituents, the way that the public reacts to governmental policies targeting a specific group of firms may affect the effectiveness of such regulations (Fiaschi et al. 2017). When the host-country public view an MNE as less legitimate, the government is reluctant to enforce rules in favour of the firm as doing so may trigger public anger and damage the government's own legitimacy. By contrast, when firms enjoy greater legitimacy with the host-country public, the imposition of unfavourable policies against the business may cause the public to withdraw their support for the government (Stevens et al. 2015). Thus, demands exerted by the host-country public may serve as a competing mechanism that reduces the effectiveness of the host-country institutional governance framework.

The underdeveloped home-country institutional environment of Chinese firms can lead them to encounter 'adverse institutional attribution' by the host-country public (Ramachandran and Pant 2010, p. 247). Where China may be judged to have a lower level of economic development, host-country consumers may distrust the quality of Chinese products (Madhok and Keyhani 2012). Moreover, host-country civil societies may be suspicious about Chinese companies because of their weak corporate disclosure (Bremmer 2014). As a result, the host-country public may lobby their government to introduce specific requirements targeting Chinese MNEs despite the presence of the host-country institutional governance framework.

Hypothesis 4 The importance of the institutional governance infrastructure in shaping Chinese MNEs' perceived level of host-country political risk will be reduced for those firms gaining a low degree of legitimacy from the host-country general public.

Sample and Data

The hypotheses were tested using survey data on Chinese enterprises' outward FDI collected by the China Council for the Promotion of International Trade (CCPIT) in 2011. The sample contained firms from 16 provinces and municipalities across China, and hence provided a wide geographical coverage.[1] Given cost and administrative constraints, we approached 2000 firms that were the CCPIT's membership enterprises and also appeared on the Chinese Ministry of Commerce's (MOFCOM) registration list for their outward FDI activities. The respondents were those in charge of firms' overseas subsidiary and international strategies. A total of 365 questionnaires were received, which covered 14 industrial sectors. Responses that were either incomplete or inapplicable were eliminated. This provided us with 183 observations. In addition, investments in the British Virgin Islands and Hong Kong were excluded as these locations often serve the purpose of round-tripping investment (Peng 2012). As a result, the final sample contained 148 observations.

Measurements

Chinese MNEs' Perceived Level of Host-Country Political Risk

The dependent variable is Chinese MNEs' perceived level of host-country political risk. It was operationalized by asking the respondents to evaluate the political environment of their companies' most recently established overseas branch on a 7-point scale (1 = very risky to 7 = very safe) regarding the following items: (i) implementation of rules and laws in the host country, (ii) protection of private property in the host country, (iii) settlement of commercial disputes in the host country, and (iv) control of corruption and bribery in the host country.

Host-Country Institutional Governance Infrastructure

To operationalize host-country institutional governance infrastructure, we follow previous research by adopting the World Governance Indicators (WGI) (Globerman and Shapiro 2003). The WGI covers six dimensions: voice and accountability, political stability, government effectiveness, regulatory quality, rule of law, and control of corruption (Kaufmann et al. 2009). The scores spread between -2.5 and 2.5, with higher scores indicating better governance quality. For our analysis, host countries' WGI scores in 2010 were adopted.

---

[1] The sample firms are located in Beijing, Shanghai, Tianjin, Chongqing, Shandong, Guangdong, Jiangsu, Zhejiang, Fujian, Henan, Hubei, Hunan, Hebei, Heilongjiang, Yunnan and Shaanxi.

Chinese MNEs' Legitimacy with the Host-Country Government

It has been suggested that the legitimacy of an MNE's home country can generate a spill-over effect to influence the political risk faced by its firms abroad (Stevens and Newenham-Kahindi 2017). We measure Chinese MNEs' legitimacy with the host-country government by the perceived strength of interstate political relations. We asked the respondents to evaluate the importance of political relations between China and the host country to their investment on a 7-point scale (1 = very unimportant to 7 = very important).

Chinese MNEs' Legitimacy in Host-Country Regulated Industries

MNEs in regulated industries including natural resources, telecommunications, utilities, petroleum, and financial services may be subject to a higher degree of political intervention than those in less-regulated industries (García-Canal and Guillén 2008). A dummy variable was created to distinguish Chinese firms operating in the above-mentioned regulated industries (1) and otherwise (0).

Chinese MNEs' Legitimacy with the Host-Country General Public

Acquiring acceptance from host-country social stakeholders, including interested groups, consumers, and other members of the civil society, critically affects MNEs' survival abroad (Darendeli and Hill 2016). We measure Chinese MNEs' legitimacy with the host-country public by asking the respondents to evaluate the host-country public reaction to a firm's investment (1 = very low degree of negative reaction to 7 = very high degree of negative reaction).

Control Variables

At the country level, we used the marketization index published by China's National Economic Research Institute to measure variations in regional marketization (Fan et al. 2010). Second, we controlled for Chinese MNEs' home-government support using six items from the survey: (i) financial access, (ii) simplifying the approval of outward FDI projects, (iii) the provision of insurance services, (iv) simplifying the procedures for demonstrating firms have sufficient capital for FDI projects, (v) investment guidelines by industries, and (vi)

14   X. Han and X. Liu

the protection of firms' rights overseas. The respondents were asked to evaluate these items on a 7-point scale (1 = very low support to 7 = very high support).

At the industry level, we account for the scale of industrial competition in a host country using three items from the survey: (i) difficulties in obtaining raw materials, (ii) technology for innovation, and (iii) completion of upstream and downstream industries in the host country.

At the firm level, we capture firm size as the natural logarithm value of total employees, a firm's international experience as the number of its overseas branches, and host-country experience by the number of years that a firm has operated in a host country (Wu and Lin 2010). Moreover, we use a dummy variable to control for a firm's adoption of risk assessment strategies (1 = Yes, 0 = Otherwise) and ownership status (1 = SOE, 0 = Otherwise).

Results

Common Method Bias

As some variables were drawn from the same survey respondents, this may entail a threat of common method bias (CMB) (Podsakoff et al. 2003). In addition to introducing objective measurements, such as the WGI score and China's marketization index, we dealt with this potential issue by performing the Harman single-factor test. The result indicated that the single-factor model demonstrated a poor fit to the data, which only accounted for 36% of the variance. Therefore, CMB is unlikely to be a major concern in this study.

Construct's Reliability and Validity

Descriptive statistics and variable correlations are presented in Table 1.1. Variance inflation factors were well below the acceptable level of 10 (Neter et al. 1996). Thus, it suggests no multicollinearity issue. We assessed the reliability of those multi-item constructs by examining their internal consistency with Cronbach alpha. The internal consistency values for all constructs were above 0.70. We further conducted confirmatory factor analysis (CFA) to examine the convergent and discriminant validities of those multi-item constructs. Our CFA model fits the data well, with all indices meeting their respective criteria (χ^2 (146) = 247.380; $p<0.001$; CMIN/DF = 1.69; CFI = 0.97; NNLI = 0.96; RMSEA = 0.07; SRMR = 0.05). Table 1.2 reports the CFA results, which support convergent validity.

Table 1.1 Correlation matrix

	Mean	SD	1	2	3	4	5	6	7	8	9	10	11	12
1. Chinese MNEs' perceived level of host-country political risk	4.57	1.23												
2. Host-country institutional governance infrastructure	0.44	1.17	0.42**											
3. Chinese MNEs' legitimacy with host-country government	4.12	1.62	0.01	0.02										
4. Chinese MNEs' legitimacy in host-country regulated industries	0.49	0.50	0.21*	0.05	0.12									
5. Chinese MNEs' legitimacy with host-country general public	3.31	1.44	-0.07	-0.12	0.24**	-0.15								
6. Degree of marketization	9.36	1.41	0.10	0.07	0.01	0.16*	-0.06							
7. Ownership	0.26	0.44	-0.08	0.04	-0.04	-0.29	0.01	-0.16						
8. International experience	3.01	5.42	-0.01	-0.10	-0.04	0.11	-0.10	0.05	0.03					
9. Local experience	2.86	2.47	0.01	0.07	0.06	0.05	0.15	-0.12	-0.02	-0.13				
10. Risk assessment	0.70	0.46	0.22**	0.05	-0.09	0.20*	0.00	0.11	-0.18	0.08	0.22**			
11. Firm size	6.29	2.19	0.10	0.11	-0.14	0.22**	0.00	0.16*	0.29**	0.24**	0.04	-0.03		
12. Host-country industry competition	3.21	0.94	0.42**	0.34**	0.13	0.14	0.19*	-0.07	-0.08	-0.26	0.00	0.04	0.03	
13. Home-country government support	4.59	1.09	0.29**	0.10	0.04	0.10	0.16*	0.02	-0.04	0.04	-0.08	0.05	0.13	0.22**

Sample = 148
*$P<0.05$; **$P<0.01$

16   X. Han and X. Liu

Table 1.2 Measurement model and CFA results

Constructs	Operational measures of construct	Factor loadings	t-value
Chinese MNEs' perceived level of host-country political risk			
(Cronbach alpha = 0.940)	Implementation of rules and laws in the host country	0.91	15.18
	Protection of private property in the host country	0.93	15.88
	Settlement of commercial disputes in the host country	0.89	14.68
	Control of corruptions and bribes in the host country	0.85	Fixed
Home-country government support			
(Cronbach alpha = 0.938)	Financial and capital access	0.79	13.28
	Simplifying the approval of outward FDI projects	0.85	15.78
	Provision of insurance products and services	0.81	13.91
	Simplifying the procedures for demonstrating sufficient capital in FDI project	0.83	14.84
	Provision of investment guidelines by industry	0.87	16.79
	Protection of firms' rights in overseas markets	0.93	Fixed
Host-country institutional governance infrastructure			
(Cronbach alpha = 0.975)	Voice and accountability	0.82	16.55
	Political instability	0.85	18.56
	Government effectiveness	0.98	38.46
	Regulatory quality	0.98	37.79
	Rule of law	0.99	45.50
	Control of corruption	0.97	Fixed
Host-country industry competition			
(Cronbach alpha = 0.766)	Difficulty of obtaining raw materials	0.78	6.71
	Difficulty of obtaining technology for innovation	0.72	6.80
	Completion of upstream and downstream industries	0.69	Fixed

In addition, the variance extracted from our constructs is greater than the threshold of 0.50 and larger than the squared correlations between the two constructs (Hair et al. 2006), providing evidence for discriminant validity (Table 1.3).

Hypotheses Tests and Results

The results using the ordinary least squares (OLS) regression are presented in Table 1.4. Model 1 in Table 1.4 contains only the control variables. Model 2 introduces the independent variable, host-country institutional governance infrastructure, and the direct effect of moderating variables. Models 3–6 tested the hypothesized interaction effects.

Table 1.3 Discriminant validity

	Chinese MNEs' perceived level of host-country political risk	Home-country government support	Host-country institutional governance infrastructure	Host-country industry competition
Chinese MNEs' perceived level of host-country political risk	(0.89)			
Home-country government support	0.27	(0.84)		
Host-country institutional governance infrastructure	0.40	0.10	(0.93)	
Host-country industry competition	0.36	0.18	0.30	(0.72)

For the independent variable, host-country institutional governance infrastructure, its effect on a firm's perceived level of host-country political risk is positive and statistically significant in all models ($p<0.01$ in Models 2, 4, 5; $p<0.001$ in Models 3 and 6). Thus, it lends support to Hypothesis 1 that Chinese MNEs tend to perceive the host-country political environment as less risky when there is a stronger host-country institutional governance framework. The direct effects of the moderating variables in Model 2 are statistically insignificant.

With regard to the joint effect of the host-country institutional governance infrastructure, and Chinese MNEs' legitimacy with the host government, the interaction term is negative and statistically significant in Model 3 ($\beta = -0.12$, $p<0.05$) and Model 6 ($\beta = -0.09$, $p<0.05$). This suggests that the importance of the institutional governance infrastructure in shaping Chinese MNEs' perceived level of host-country political risk will be reduced for those firms gaining a high degree of legitimacy from the host-country government. Thus, Hypothesis 2 is supported.

For the interaction between the host-country institutional governance framework and Chinese MNEs' legitimacy in regulated industries, the coefficient of the interaction term in Model 4 is negative but statistically insignificant. It remains the same sign in Model 6 ($\beta = -0.26$; $p<0.10$). Thus, Hypothesis 3 does not receive support.

18 X. Han and X. Liu

Table 1.4 Result of regression analysis

	Model 1	Model 2	Model 3	Model 4	Model 5	Model 6
Main variable						
Host-country institutional governance infrastructure		0.28** (0.08)	0.77*** (0.20)	0.37** (0.11)	0.63** (0.18)	1.14*** (0.25)
Moderators						
Chinese MNEs' legitimacy with host-country government		−0.01 (0.05)	0.02 (0.06)	−0.01 (0.05)	−0.01 (0.05)	0.02 (0.05)
Chinese MNEs' legitimacy in host-country regulated industries		0.17 (0.19)	0.19 (0.19)	0.26 (0.21)	0.22 (0.19)	0.36ǂ (0.21)
Chinese MNEs' legitimacy with host-country general public		−0.09 (0.07)	−0.08 (0.06)	−0.07 (0.06)	−0.05 (0.06)	−0.02 (0.07)
Interactions						
Host-country institutional governance infrastructure * Chinese MNEs' legitimacy with host-country government			−0.12* (0.05)			−0.09* (0.05)
Host-country institutional governance infrastructure * Chinese MNEs' legitimacy in host-country regulated industries					−0.19 (0.15)	−0.26ǂ (0.15)
Host-country institutional governance infrastructure * Chinese MNEs' legitimacy with host-country general public					−0.09* (0.05)	−0.09* (0.05)
Control variables						
Degree of marketization	0.08 (0.07)	0.05 (0.06)	0.06 (0.06)	0.06 (0.06)	0.03 (0.06)	0.06 (0.06)
Ownership	−0.02 (0.22)	0.00 (0.22)	−0.04 (0.22)	−0.01 (0.22)	0.01 (0.22)	−0.04 (0.22)
International experience	0.01 (0.02)	0.01 (0.02)	0.01 (0.02)	0.01 (0.02)	0.01 (0.02)	0.01 (0.02)
Local experience	0.00 (0.04)	0.00 (0.04)	−0.01 (0.04)	0.00 (0.04)	−0.01 (0.04)	−0.01 (0.04)
Risk assessment	0.48* (0.20)	0.43* (0.19)	0.38ǂ (0.19)	0.39ǂ (0.20)	0.48* (0.19)	0.39* (0.19)
Firm size	0.02 (0.05)	0.00 (0.05)	0.01 (0.05)	0.00 (0.05)	0.01 (0.05)	0.01 (0.05)
Host-country industry competition	0.51*** (0.10)	0.41*** (0.11)	0.42*** (0.10)	0.39*** (0.11)	0.39*** (0.11)	0.38*** (0.10)

(*continued*)

Table 1.4 (continued)

	Model 1	Model 2	Model 3	Model 4	Model 5	Model 6
Home-government support	0.20* (0.08)	0.21* (0.08)	0.21* (0.08)	0.21* (0.08)	0.21** (0.08)	0.20* (0.08)
Observations (N)	148	148	148	148	148	148
R-square	0.23	0.30	0.33	0.31	0.32	0.35

†P<0.10; *P<0.05; **P<0.01; ***P<0.001

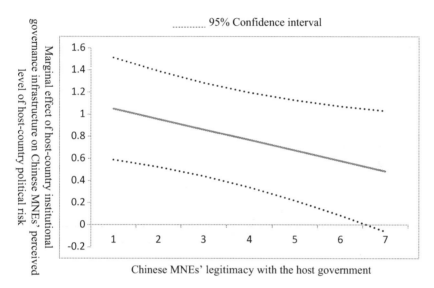

Fig. 1.1 The moderating effect of Chinese MNEs' legitimacy with the host government on the relationship between Chinese MNEs' perceived level of political risk and host-country institutional governance infrastructure

In relation to the interaction effect between the host-country institutional governance infrastructure and Chinese MNEs' legitimacy with the host-country public, their interaction term shows a negative and statistically significant sign in Models 5 and 6 ($\beta = -0.09$; $p<0.05$). Thus, the result is consistent with Hypothesis 4, which posits that Chinese firms' low degree of legitimacy with the host-country public will reduce the importance of the institutional governance framework in shaping firms' perceived level of political risk.

In addition to the results from the regression analysis, we follow Brambor et al. (2006) and further examine the marginal effects of the independent variable at different values of the moderators through plotting graphic displays.

Figure 1.1 presents the marginal effect of the host-country institutional governance infrastructure on Chinese MNEs' perceived level of political risk when firms' legitimacy with the host government becomes stronger. As shown in Fig. 1.1, the marginal effect of the host-country institutional governance framework on Chinese MNEs' perceived political risk diminishes as firms enjoy a higher degree of legitimacy with the host-country government. The downward slope corresponds to Hypothesis 2, suggesting that a high degree of Chinese firms' legitimacy with the host government reduces the importance of the host-country governance framework. Hence, Fig. 1.1 lends further support for Hypothesis 2.

As shown in Fig. 1.2, there is a downward slope for the marginal effect of the host-country governance framework on Chinese MNEs' perceived political risk for firms in less-regulated industries and regulated industries. This suggests that the positive effect of the host-country governance framework on firms' perceived level of political risk tends to be reduced for those in regulated industries. Both the upper and lower bounds of the 95% confidence intervals are located on the same side of the zero line. Thus, the plotting of the marginal effect provides support to Hypothesis 3.

Figure 1.3 depicts the effectiveness of the host-country governance framework becomes negligible when the public see Chinese MNEs' activities more negatively. The plotting is consistent with the OLS regression, which shows that Hypothesis 4 is supported.

Additionally, we conducted robustness checks, and detailed information is available upon request.

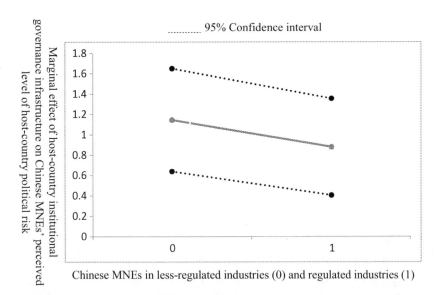

Fig. 1.2 The moderating effect of Chinese MNEs' legitimacy in host-country regulated industries on the relationship between Chinese MNEs' perceived level of political risk and host-country institutional governance infrastructure

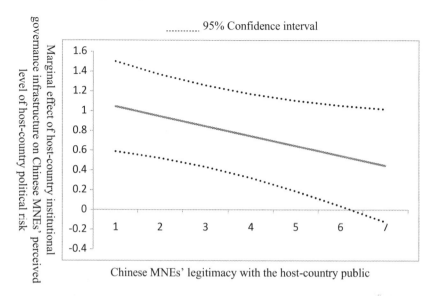

Fig. 1.3 The moderating effect of Chinese MNEs' legitimacy with host-country public on the relationship between Chinese MNEs' perceived level of political risk and host-country institutional governance infrastructure

Discussion

This study examines the impact of host-country institutional governance infrastructure on Chinese MNEs' perceived level of political risk and the extent to which this is subject to firms' legitimacy with interested host-country stakeholders. We obtained several interesting findings. First, our empirical evidence shows that host-country institutional governance frameworks are important in predicting the level of political risk encountered by Chinese companies. Our finding provides contrasting evidence to previous research which argued that Chinese MNEs are proactive players when operating in an underdeveloped institutional context (e.g. Morck et al. 2008). This may be explained by Chinese firms' strong political capability in helping them to manage risky political conditions in overseas markets (Ramasamy et al. 2012).

Second, the condition of bounded rationality prompts host-country stakeholders to use cognitive shortcuts when assessing firms' legitimacy (Stevens and Newenham-Kahindi 2017). Our result indicates that the legitimacy evaluations by a host-country government, industrial agencies, and general public may substitute the role of institutional governance infrastructure in shaping the level of political risk encountered by Chinese firms.

Contributions

This research seeks to make two contributions to the understanding of political risk in international business literature. First, as the image of the home country may travel abroad with firms, it can generate legitimacy spill-over effects (Stevens and Newenham-Kahindi 2017). Chinese MNEs' underdeveloped home-country institutional governance framework can undermine their acceptance and form a source of political challenge when competing abroad. The weak legitimacy of Chinese firms represents a different type of political risk from that experienced by their developed-country counterparts that has not been systematically considered in previous studies. Our research complements the existing literature by suggesting that the level of political risk encountered by MNEs may arise due to their home-countries' lack of acceptance in host countries.

Second, our findings suggest that the legitimacy judgements by interested host-country stakeholders represent alternative legitimating channels in affecting firms' access to resources and the market, hence substituting for the host-country institutional governance framework. We extend current research by uncovering the interdependence between a country's institutional governance infrastructure and the broader sociological context in shaping the level of political risk perceived by MNEs. By looking at the role of home-country legitimacy and its interaction with host-country governance conditions, our research offers a comprehensive account of the determinants of MNEs' perceived level of host-country political risk.

Implications

This study provides implications for managers and policymakers. First, we draw attention to the role of home-country acceptance among host-country influential social groups. Our findings indicate that the weak home-country legitimacy of Chinese MNEs with host-country governments, industrial agencies, and public offsets the role of the host-country institutional governance framework. This implies that firms should develop a better understanding of industry-specific policies and engage in legitimacy-building activities, such as corporate social responsibility programmes, to alleviate the negative legitimacy spill-over effect of their home country.

Second, our findings suggest that the underdeveloped home-country institutional environment can undermine Chinese firms' acceptance in host countries. This implies that MNEs' home-country policymakers should consider enhancing domestic governance conditions to promote Chinese firms' legitimacy in abroad.

Limitations

This study has several limitations which present opportunities for future research. First, our study was based on a sample of Chinese MNEs which did not account for variations with firms from other emerging markets. Future research may test the generalizability of our findings for MNEs from other emerging markets. Second, Chinese MNEs' legitimacy with the host-country government and the public were measured using single survey items. Therefore, more fine-grained measurements of firms' legitimacy deserve careful attention. Finally, our questionnaires were addressed to Chinese MNEs' overseas subsidiaries or those responsible for international strategies. The legitimacy judgements were based on Chinese firms' perceptions of the way they are viewed, rather than directly from host-country stakeholders. This may compromise the objectivity of our measurement. Future research should pay attention to develop measurements which directly reflect host-country stakeholders' legitimacy judgement regarding Chinese companies.

Conclusion

The political risks associated with Chinese MNEs' overseas expansion have been a key topic in international business research. While the traditional analytical framework, which focuses on the host-country governance infrastructure, remains important in explaining the political perils perceived by Chinese firms, their distinctive home-country institutional context implies different challenges. Highlighting the notion of legitimacy under the institution-based view, we examine Chinese MNEs' home-country acceptance in shaping firms' perceived level of host-country political risk. Our findings reveal the relevance of home-country legitimacy in the host country's broader sociological context and suggest the need for a deeper understanding of political risk from Chinese MNEs' perspective.

References

Ashforth, B., & Gibbs, B. (1990). The double-edge of organizational legitimation. *Organization Science, 1*, 177–194.

Bitektine, A. (2011). Toward a theory of social judgments of organizations: The case of legitimacy, reputation, and status. *Academy of Management Review, 36*, 151–179.

Boisot, M., & Meyer, M. (2008). Which way through the open door? Reflections on the internationalization of Chinese firms. *Management and Organization Review, 4*, 349–365.

Brambor, T., Clark, W., & Golder, M. (2006). Understanding interaction models: Improving empirical analyses. *Political Analysis, 14*, 63–82.

Bremmer, I. (2014). The new rules of globalization. *Harvard Business Review, 92*, 103–107.

Bruton, G., Ahlstrom, D., & Li, H.-L. (2010). Institutional theory and entrepreneurship: Where are we now and where do we need to move in the future? *Entrepreneurship Theory and Practice, 34*, 421–440.

Cuervo-Cazurra, A. (2011). Global strategy and global business environment: The direct and indirect influences of the home country on a firm's global strategy. *Global Strategy Journal, 1*, 382–386.

Darendeli, I., & Hill, T. L. (2016). Uncovering the complex relationships between political risk and MNE firm legitimacy: Insights from Libya. *Journal of International Business Studies, 47*, 68–92.

Deephouse, D. (1996). Does isomorphism legitimate? *Academy of Management Journal, 39*, 1024–1039.

DiMaggio, P., & Powell, W. (1983). The iron cage revisited: Collective rationality and institutional isomorphism in organizational fields. *American Sociological Review, 48*, 147–160.

Fan, G., Wang, X., & Zhu, H. (2010). *Marketization index in China: The regional process report*. Beijing: Economic Science Press (in Chinese).

Fiaschi, D., Giuliani, E., & Nieri, F. (2017). Overcoming the liability of origin by doing no-harm: Emerging country firms' social irresponsibility as they go global. *Journal of World Business, 52*, 546–563.

García-Canal, E., & Guillén, M. (2008). Risk and the strategy of foreign location choice in regulated industries. *Strategic Management Journal, 29*, 1097–1115.

Globerman, S., & Shapiro, D. (2003). Governance infrastructure and US foreign direct investment. *Journal of International Business Studies, 34*, 19–39.

Globerman, S., & Shapiro, D. (2009). Economic and strategic considerations surrounding Chinese FDI in the United States. *Asia Pacific Journal of Management, 26*, 163–183.

Hair, J., Black, W., Babin, B., Anderson, R., & Tatham, R. (2006). *Multivariate data analysis*. Upper Saddle River: Pearson Prentice Hall.

Henisz, W., & Zelner, B. (2001). The institutional environment for telecommunications investment. *Journal of Economics & Management Strategy, 10*, 123–147.

Kaufmann, D., Kraay, A., & Mastruzzi, M. (2009). *Governance matters VIII: Aggregate and individual indicators, 1996–2008* (World Bank policy research paper 4978).

Kistruck, G., Morris, S., Webb, J., & Stevens, C. (2015). The importance of client heterogeneity in predicting make-or-buy decisions. *Journal of Operations Management, 33*, 97–110.

Kostova, T., & Zaheer, S. (1999). Organizational legitimacy under conditions of complexity: The case of the multinational enterprise. *Academy of Management Review, 24*, 64–81.

Lange, D., Lee, P., & Dai, Y. (2011). Organizational reputation: A review. *Journal of Management, 37*, 153–184.

Liu, X., Gao, L., Lu, J., & Lioliou, E. (2016). Environmental risks, localization and the overseas subsidiary performance of MNEs from an emerging economy. *Journal of World Business, 51*, 356–368.

Lu, J., Liu, X., Wright, M., & Filatotchev, I. (2014). International experience and FDI location choices of Chinese firms: The moderating effects of home country government support and host country institutions. *Journal of International Business Studies, 45*, 428–449.

Luo, Y., & Tung, R. (2007). International expansion of emerging market enterprises: A springboard perspective. *Journal of International Business Studies, 38*, 481–498.

Luo, Y., Xue, Q., & Han, B. (2010). How emerging market governments promote outward FDI: Experience from China. *Journal of World Business, 45*, 68–79.

Madhok, A., & Keyhani, M. (2012). Acquisitions as entrepreneurship: Asymmetries, opportunities, and the internationalization of multinationals from emerging economies. *Global Strategy Journal, 2*, 26–40.

Marquis, C., & Qian, C. (2014). Corporate social responsibility reporting in China: Symbol or substance? *Organization Science, 25*, 127–148.

Meyer, K., & Peng, M. (2016). Theoretical foundations of emerging economy business research. *Journal of International Business Studies, 47*, 3–22.

Morck, R., Yeung, B., & Zhao, M. (2008). Perspectives on China's outward foreign direct investment. *Journal of International Business Studies, 39*, 337–350.

Neter, J., Kutner, M., Nachtsheim, C., & Wasserman, W. (1996). *Applied linear statistical models*. Chicago: Irwin.

Oh, C. H., & Oetzel, J. (2011). Multinationals' response to major disasters: How does subsidiary investment vary in response to the type of disaster and the quality of country governance? *Strategic Management Journal, 32*, 658–681.

Peng, M. (2012). The global strategy of emerging multinationals from China. *Global Strategy Journal, 2*, 97–107.

Podsakoff, P., MacKenzie, S., Lee, J.-Y., & Podsakoff, N. (2003). Common method biases in behavioral research: A critical review of the literature and recommended remedies. *Journal of Applied Psychology, 88*, 879–903.

Ramachandran, J., & Pant, A. (2010). The liabilities of origin: An emerging economy perspective on the costs of doing business abroad. In L. Tihanyi, P. Torben, & D. Timothy (Eds.), *The past, present and future of international business and management* (pp. 231–265). Bingley: Emerald Group Publishing Limited.

Ramasamy, B., Yeung, M., & Laforet, S. (2012). China's outward foreign direct investment: Location choice and firm ownership. *Journal of World Business, 47*, 17–25.

Stevens, C., & Newenham-Kahindi, A. (2017). Legitimacy spillovers and political risk: The case of FDI in the East African community. *Global Strategy Journal, 7*, 10–35.

Stevens, C., Xie, E., & Peng, M. (2015). Toward a legitimacy-based view of political risk: The case of Google and Yahoo in China. *Strategic Management Journal, 37*, 945–963.

Suchman, M. (1995). Managing legitimacy: Strategic and institutional approaches. *Academy of Management Review, 20*, 571–610.

Webb, J., Tihanyi, L., Ireland, D., & Sirmon, D. (2009). You say illegal, I say legitimate: Entrepreneurship in the informal economy. *Academy of Management Review, 34*, 492–510.

World Governance Indicators: China. (2011). http://info.worldbank.org/governance/wgi/index.aspx#reports. Accessed 28 Nov 2016.

Wu, W.-Y., & Lin, C.-Y. (2010). Experience, environment, and subsidiary performance in high-tech MNEs. *Journal of Business Research, 63*, 1301–1309.

2

Applying Theory to Understand How Multinational Firms Address Brexit

Saad Laraqui and Bert J. Jarreau

Introduction

Britain's highly successful aerospace and financial services industries face an uncertain future due to Brexit. If a transitional arrangement is not worked out by March 2019 between Britain and the 27 EU member states to preserve the status quo for a few years while a new trade deal is finalized, British businesses in these industries would immediately face a range of tariff and non-tariff barriers.

Anything that interferes with Europe's highly connected aerospace industry will hurt British companies and their suppliers. For example, consider Airbus, Rolls-Royce, and BAE Systems.

The wings of Airbus civil aircraft, the most technologically intensive part of the plane, are all made and designed in Britain. Airbus UK, which employs 10,000 people, built about 1000 wings for Airbus in 2016. This business depends on the smooth transfer of products and skilled staff to and from Airbus factories in France and Germany. If Britain is outside the EU's customs union and single market, the supply chain may no longer be sustainable.

S. Laraqui • B. J. Jarreau (✉)
University of Maryland University College Europe, Kaiserslautern, Germany
e-mail: Saad.laraqui@faculty.umuc.edu; Bert.jarreau@faculty.umuc.edu

© The Author(s) 2019
A. Chidlow et al. (eds.), *The Changing Strategies of International Business*, The Academy of International Business, https://doi.org/10.1007/978-3-030-03931-8_2

Fabrice Brégier, Airbus president and chief operating officer, warned that a "hard Brexit" could mean shifting wing production elsewhere (Symonds 2017).

Airbus is one of largest customers of Rolls-Royce, the world's second-largest aero-engine manufacturer located in London. Rolls-Royce has 23,000 workers in the UK and a total of 55,000 worldwide. Tariffs could reduce the advantage it enjoys against its main rival, America's GE. Also, leaving the European Aviation Safety Agency, which regulates the industry, would cause enormous problems to Rolls-Royce and its suppliers in Britain. Rolls-Royce wants to continue being able to move parts and staff freely between the UK and the EU. Like Airbus, Warren East, CEO of Rolls-Royce, has warned about the perils of a "hard Brexit" (Johnston 2017; Symonds 2017).

BAE Systems, Britain's largest manufacturing firm and the third-largest arms company in the world, is better insulated from Brexit because it does relatively little business with Europe compared with America, where it derives 36 percent of its sales. However, Brexit could mean BAE being cut out of future European defense programs. BAE Systems is part of a consortium of British and French companies working on an advanced drone, but the project is dependent on the French and British governments' commitment, which is not guaranteed. Since the election of Emmanuel Macron as France's president, France and Germany have announced a project to build a European fighter (Symonds 2017).

Similar to the aerospace industry, the financial services industry in nervous about Brexit. The financial services industry has billions invested in London, where international banks employ close to 150,000 staff (Barber 2017).

HSBC pledged to move 1000 jobs to Paris, where it owns a French subsidiary and a banking license (Jenkins 2017). Other international banks doing business in London are looking to relocate operations to Paris' great rivals, Frankfurt and Dublin. Goldman Sachs is among several banks to choose Frankfurt, while Citigroup and Bank of America picked Dublin for investment banking and markets operations (Barber 2017).

An Ernst and Young study of public statements by financial services companies found that of the 222 groups monitored, 19 had spoken of a move to Dublin, compared with 18 that have mentioned Frankfurt. Luxembourg came in the third place, with 11 mentions (Jenkins 2017).

To help provide understanding to these concerns, this chapter examines international business (IB) theories to help inform multinational enterprise (MNE) investment decisions.

Firm-Specific Assets, Competitive Advantages, Dynamic Capabilities and Ownership–Location–Internalization (OLI) Eclectic Paradigm of MNE Activity

FSAs, Competitive Advantages, and Dynamic Capabilities

Firm-specific assets (FSAs) refer to any tangible or intangible resource available exclusively to the firm, either because they are owned by the firm or are made available by third parties for the firm's use (Narula et al. 2017). The resource-based theory of the firm, which builds on the seminal contributions of Penrose (1959), postulates that resources that are valuable, rare, and difficult to imitate are the source of the competitive advantages of firms (Barney 2001; Conner 1991; Peng 2001; Wernerfelt 1995). Competitive advantage results from the ownership of FSAs that are efficiently combined in a value-creating strategy, which currently or potentially competing firms cannot implement simultaneously (Narula et al. 2017). A competitive advantage is sustainable when other firms do not manage to duplicate the benefits of this strategy (Barney 1991). The firm's ability not just to possess, but to grow or acquire more assets of this kind, affords it a sustainable competitive advantage over other firms, and this accumulation process is also reflected in the literature on dynamic capabilities (Dunning and Lundan 2010).

The literature on dynamic capabilities has examined how firms identify and develop new opportunities, how they coordinate the assets required to exploit such opportunities, and how, in the course of doing so, they develop new business models and governance forms (Teece and Pisano 1994; Teece et al. 1997). The dynamic capabilities framework has drawn from several different schools of thought, including transaction cost economics, the behavioral theory of the firm, and evolutionary economics, with the aim of offering an integrative and managerially relevant paradigm that recognizes the challenges related to value appropriation as well as dynamic value creation (Teece 2007; Augier and Teece 2007; Di Stefano et al. 2010).

Dynamic capabilities are second- or higher order capabilities that extend beyond the capabilities required for the firm to carry out its existing value-adding activities. Dynamic capabilities involve the ability of the firm to create new products or services and to restructure its activities to achieve a better fit with the competitive environment (Winter 2003).

OLI Eclectic Paradigm of MNE Activity

The eclectic or OLI paradigm asserts that to engage in cross-border investment, a firm must possess unique and sustainable ownership-specific advantages such as firms of other nationalities. Such advantages consist of asset-specific advantages (O_A), particularly those related to property rights and other intangible assets, and those advantages (O_T) that arise from the ability of a firm to coordinate multiple and geographically dispersed value-added activities and to capture the gains of risk diversification (Dunning 1988a). It seeks to offer a general framework for determining the extent and pattern of both foreign-owned production undertaken by a country's own enterprises and that of domestic production owned or controlled by foreign enterprises (Dunning and Lundan 2008b).

Ownership-Specific Advantages (O)

Firms develop their ownership advantages based on the mobile and immobile assets of the countries in which they operate (Dunning 1979; Hu 1992, 1993; Nachum 1999; Porter 1990).

Ownership-specific advantages (O) refer to the competitive advantages of the enterprises seeking to engage in foreign direct investment (FDI). The greater the competitive advantages of the investing firms, the more they are likely to engage in their foreign production (Dunning 2000).

Many IB scholars have relied on a three-way classification of FSAs (Cantwell and Narula 2001; Dunning 1988b; Dunning and Lundan 2008b; Dunning and Rugman 1985; Narula et al. 2017). The first class is associated with proprietary tangible and intangible assets (asset-type FSA: O_A FSA) such as technologies, intellectual property, systems, and know-how.

The second class is associated with institutional assets (institutional type FSA: O_I FSA). O_I FSA comprise the incentive structure of a particular firm, which comprise internally generated and externally imposed incentives, regulations, and norms. Examples include contracts, covenants, codes, and trust-based relations (Dunning and Lundan 2008b). Institutional advantages (O_I) cover the range of formal and informal institutions that govern the value-added processes within firms (Dunning and Lundan 2008a, b). Such advantages are partly endogenous and partly exogenous to the firm. The exogenous element results from the degree to which the informal (and formal) institutions in the firm's home country, or in important host countries, have impacted the way in which incentives are set within the firm. The endogenous influence is the result of entrepreneurial or managerial activity, which manifests itself in a particular kind of corporate culture, which may also be encapsulated in the firm's core values or a mission statement (Dunning and Lundan 2010).

The third class has to do with organizational capabilities to efficiently control, coordinate, and organize intra-firm activities to generate economic rents from O_A FSA (transaction-type FSA: O_T FSA) (Narula et al. 2017). O_T FSA is largely concerned with managerial expertise of efficiently running a complex organization by creating and coordinating efficient internal hierarchies and markets within the MNE (Dunning and Lundan 2008b; Narula 2014). From the theoretical perspective of the knowledge-based view (e.g., Grant 1996; Kogut and Zander 1992), the MNE's capability to efficiently transfer O_A FSAs between geographically dispersed locations constitutes a substantial portion of O_T FSA of the MNE (Narula et al. 2017).

In addition, O_T FSA is associated with the geographical dispersion of operations, as it mirrors "the capacity of MNE hierarchies vis-à-vis external markets to capture the transactional benefits (or lessen the transactional costs) arising from the common governance of a network of O_A FSAs located in different countries" (Dunning 1988b, p. 2). O_T FSAs are regarded as more home country specific than O_A FSAs because their development is usually dependent on institutions and relational assets with local actors usually obtained through accumulation of relevant experience (Narula 2002, 2012; Nelson and Winter 1982).

An important aspect of the O advantages of MNEs is that while some of them may be monopolistic in nature, others stem from its dynamic capabilities, that is, the ability to coordinate transactions and to reconfigure assets across borders. As a consequence, dynamic capabilities are relevant to assessing the welfare impact of MNEs on the home and host countries (Dunning and Lundan 2010).

O_A, O_I, and O_T FSAs are complementary and crucial for rent generation (Narula et al. 2017).

Location-Specific Advantages (L)

The spatial distribution of location-bound resources, capabilities, and institutions (L) is assumed to be uneven and, hence, will confer a competitive advantage on the countries or regions possessing them. The O_I advantages are interrelated with all other elements of the paradigm, since they influence both what form (I) and where (L) the MNE will choose to exploit, or add to, its O advantages (Dunning and Lundan 2010).

Location-specific advantages (L) refer to the alternative countries or regions for undertaking the value-adding activities of MNEs. The more the immobile, natural or created resources, which firms need to use jointly with their own competitive advantages, favor a presence in a foreign location, the more the firms will choose to augment or exploit their O-specific advantages by engaging in FDI (Dunning 2000).

For the financial services industry, London has location-specific advantages such as infrastructure, the rule of law, and its time zone to serve Asia (Barber 2017). Although Paris is Europe's only global city on a par with London, it has earned a reputation as a hostile tax location with onerous labor laws. By contrast, Frankfurt is home to the European Central Bank as well as the financial center for Europe's biggest economy. Dublin is an established low-tax banking center (Jenkins 2017).

Internalization-Specific Advantages (I)

FDI will take place when the enterprise perceives it to be in its best interest to add value to its O advantages rather than to sell them, or their right of use, to independent foreign firms. The market internalization (I) advantages reflect either the greater organizational efficiency or superior incentive structures of hierarchies, or the ability of (large) firms to exercise monopoly power over the assets under their governance (Dunning and Lundan 2010). Internalization-specific advantages (I) refer to how firms organize the creation and exploitation of their core competencies. The greater the net benefits of internalizing cross-border intermediate product markets, the more likely a firm will prefer to engage in foreign production itself rather than license the right to do so (Dunning 2000).

The eclectic paradigm has evolved throughout the life of Professor John Dunning and it developed in the following five stages as described in Dunning and Lundan (Dunning and Lundan 2008a, b):

Mark I—Focused on why firms invest overseas rather than through arms-length mechanisms such as trade and licensing, and what the determinants of the amount and composition of international production are.

Mark II—Brought within the O, L, and I the development and application of the eclectic paradigm to macro/country-level/development issues, applications to different industries, and incorporating and clearly defining the role of geography.

Mark III—Brought within the fold of the eclectic paradigm the understanding and application of alliance capitalism.

Mark IV—Provided a strategy dimension as it relates to the eclectic paradigm.

Mark V—Incorporated institutional economics within the eclectic paradigm.

Relational Assets

Professor John Dunning (2002, 2003, 2004), over almost half a century ago, stood as one of the most significant in providing a theoretical framework to analyze the nature, significance, and governance of relational assets to examine their relevance in explaining the growth, structure, and form of MNE-related activity. Professor Dunning argued that social capital plays a critically important role in business strategy and performance, where social capital consists of resources that are embedded in networks of relationships. He focused on the concept of relational assets, which he viewed as a dimension of social capital. The core idea is that relational assets comprise an actor's ability to form and govern beneficial relationships with other actors, including other firms and individuals within a firm. Firms and individuals use their relational assets to gain access to other actors' assets and to coordinate the use of their partners' assets with the focal actor's own resources. Relational assets emphasize attitudinal attributes such as values, honesty, trust, cultural sensitivity, and reciprocity. They range from firm-level measures such as alliance experience and reputations to country-level measures such as corruption and civic engagement. The basic idea is that the ability to leverage resources that other actors control arises from the ability to engender trust in one's own judgment and intentions.

Professor Dunning placed relational assets in the context of his OLI eclectic paradigm of MNE activity (Dunning 2002, 2003, 2004). Relational assets provide ownership advantages through superiority in coordinating the use of functional assets; locational advantages through superiority in business infrastructures; and internalization advantages by providing linkages to many other assets. He suggested that MNEs tend to have more relational assets than domestic firms, owing to a greater number and intensity of linkages. Professor Dunning proposed that a firm's ability to create and use relational assets will lead to an increase in MNE-related business activity. He suggested that international business theory needs to give greater attention to relational assets as key sources of firm advantage; business managers need to develop greater skills in creating relational assets; policy makers need to improve social capital and relational assets within their environments; and supra-national agencies need to foster international respect for the underpinnings of relational assets, such as trust and reciprocity.

Relational assets are a combination of O_A FSAs, O_I FSAs, and O_T FSAs. Using the OLI eclectic paradigm of MNE activity (Dunning 1980), and especially relational assets, help explain how MNEs such as Airbus, Rolls-Royce, BAE Systems, HSBC, Goldman Sachs, Citigroup, and Bank of America go about assessing their investment decisions regarding Brexit.

Relationship-Specific Competitive Advantages

Social Capital

Social capital refers to the competitive advantage that is created based on the way an individual is connected to others (Arena and Uhl-Bien 2016). Professor Dunning argued that social capital plays a critically important role in business strategy and performance, where social capital consists of resources that are embedded in networks of relationships. He focused on the concept of relational assets, which he viewed as a dimension of social capital. The core idea is that relational assets comprise an actor's ability to form and govern beneficial relationships with other actors, including other firms and individuals within a firm. Firms and individuals use their relational assets to gain access to other actors' assets and to coordinate the use of their partners' assets with the focal actor's own resources. Relational assets emphasize attitudinal attributes such as values, honesty, trust, cultural sensitivity, and reciprocity. They range from firm-level measures such as alliance experience and reputations to country-level measures such as corruption and civic engagement. The basic idea is that the ability to leverage resources that other actors control arises from the ability to engender trust in one's own judgment and intentions (Dunning 1980, 2002, 2003, 2004).

Competitive Advantage Theoretical Frameworks

Both the resource-based view and the relational view serve as theoretical frameworks to explain firms' competitive advantages (Mesquita et al. 2008). In traditional perspectives on competitive advantage, such as the resource-based view (Barney 1991; Dierickx and Cool 1989; Penrose 1959; Wernerfelt 1984), where the firm is seen as a pool of resources, including vital intangible resources, which can create competitive advantage and superior profits, scholars have envisioned firms as independent entities. Consequently, these perspectives have provided only a partial account of firm performance in view of the accumulated evidence of the proliferation and significance of interfirm alliances (Lavie 2006).

Relational view of competitive advantage scholars explain that competitive advantages arise not from the firm but from interfirm sources of advantage (Dyer and Singh 1998; Gomes-Casseres 1984; Lavie 2006; Smith et al. 1995). The relational view assumes that the sources of competitive advantage may span firm boundaries, just as interdisciplinary and cross-functional strengths lead to a competitive advantage within the firm. It is assumed that interfirm networks may be more efficient arrangements for achieving a resource-based advantage than single firms (Dyer and Nobeoka 2000). In addition, the relational view focuses on networks as units of analysis, where advantages that are difficult to replicate by rivals are created through investments in special assets among firms, exchanging knowledge, complementary resources, and building effective governance mechanisms (Mizuki 2014).

In his seminal work, Lavie (2006) reformulated the resource-based view for an interconnected firm by suggesting that a firm's competitive advantage comes from three main sources: first, the firm's internal resources generate "internal rent"; second, "appropriated relational rent" results from deliberately recombining, exchanging, and co-developing idiosyncratic shared resources between the firm and its partners; and, third, a firm may also receive unintended benefits owing to both shared and non-shared resources of partners due to an "inbound spillover" effect.

Asset augmentation of the firm primarily originates from the recombination of complementary assets both within the firm's existing asset portfolio and those of other economic actors, and that recombinant firm-specific assets (RFSAs) are an essential element for doing so (Hennart 2009; Narula et al. 2017; Verbeke 2013). The MNE's capability to tap into multiple locations and create value by recombining a variety of knowledge assets dispersed across the MNE network has been widely recognized as a prime source of competitive advantage (Doz et al. 2001; Meyer et al. 2011; Rugman and Verbeke 2001; Teece 2014; Verbeke 2013).

Whether or not a firm will be able to recombine assets efficiently will depend on the firm's absorptive capacity (Cohen and Levinthal 1990). The higher a firm's absorptive capacity, the higher the likelihood that a firm will be able to exploit RFSAs efficiently (Narula et al. 2017).

Because the MNE network integrates not only internally generated competences but also externally based location-specific assets (Kogut and Zander 1992; Narula 2014; Verbeke 2013), network recombination is primarily relevant to mature MNEs that have substantial operations (i.e., subsidiaries) across many different locations (Narula et al. 2017).

Social Capital Theory

Social capital theory (Putnam 1995) explores the benefits and costs derived from social ties and relationships. One of the most widely cited frameworks for examining social capital is the conceptual model proposed by Nahapiet and Ghoshal (1998), which focused on the relationships between social capital and the level of access to parties for the purpose of combining and exchanging intellectual capital. Intellectual capital refers to the knowledge and knowing capability of a social collectivity, such as an organization, intellectual community, or professional practice (Nahapiet and Ghoshal 1998).

Corporate social capital concerns social structures such as networks and ties and their associated norms and values as they affect the firm and its performance. A firm's internal social capital is embedded in the relationships between the organization's members—for example, relationships based on reciprocity and norms of teamwork, and openness and willingness to exchange information help individuals to access resources within an organization and to develop their own knowledge and skills. A firm's external social capital is embedded in relationships beyond the boundaries of the firm, for example, relationships with customers, suppliers, and external organizations such as universities, banks, venture capitalists, and governmental bodies make possible achieving ends that would otherwise not be attainable and at lower costs (Andrew and Klaus 2009).

Andrew and Klaus (2009) integrated the role of corporate social capital in the resource-based view of the firm. They argued that social capital figures prominently among such intangible resources and showed that an explicit inclusion of the role of social capital further strengthens the analytical powers of the resource-based view in relation to the relative merits of firms and markets as organizational forms, the rationale of interfirm networks as an alternative to spot-market exchanges and coordination by a single centralized authority, and the role of social capital as a governance mechanism in such interfirm networks.

Discussion of a Dynamic Framework

The authors propose an analytical framework for examining and evaluating the main relationships between MNEs operating in the UK and their respective governments. This dynamic representation, presented in Fig. 2.1, draws

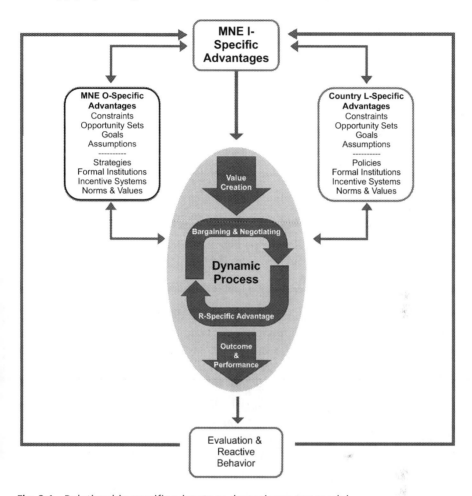

Fig. 2.1 Relationship-specific advantage dynamic process model

on some ideas first set out by Lecraw and Morrison (1991) and later by Dunning and Lundan (2008a, b), but extends their analysis by incorporating the relationship-specific advantage (Dunning 2002, 2003, 2004) as an enabler in transforming a static model into a dynamic model. The framework is essentially grounded on the interaction between the O advantages of firms and the L advantages of countries and how these, in turn, affect the I advantage of MNEs and their organization of cross-border, value-added activities. The revisited configuration of the OLI contains eight components, or stages, which may precede some course of action, or set of actions, taken by governments through an embedded relationship-specific advantage.

The schema is essentially *dynamic* in its approach. It assumes that, at a given moment of time, and within a particular global economic environment:

1. MNEs possess a set of O-specific advantages and constraints and, according to their goals, and their opportunity sets and organizational structures, will pursue certain strategies to advance those goals.
2. Likewise, nation-states possess a set of L-specific advantages and constraints which, according to their goals and opportunity sets, will lead them to take certain actions.
3. Such actions between the O and the L—as directed toward MNEs—refer to how firms organize the creation and exploitation of their core competencies. The greater the net benefits of internalizing cross-border intermediate product markets, the more likely a firm will prefer to engage in foreign production itself rather than license the right to do so (Dunning 2000).

The particularity of this Mark I configuration of the OLI is that the I remains an outcome of the interaction between the O and the L but the I is also an initial phase of an iterative process. This initial phase can also be an application of the eclectic paradigm to macro/country-level/development issues, applications to different industries, and incorporating and clearly defining the role of geography as described on Mark II of the OLI paradigm.

The main feature of this dynamic framework is the rotating effect between bargaining/negotiating and R-specific advantage. This is an element that provides an impetus similar to an engine. This impetus is drawn from Mark III of the eclectic paradigm with an application of alliance capitalism as well as from Mark IV with a strategy dimension as it relates to the eclectic paradigm.

The UK economic architecture of the UK economy will necessarily go through a transformative phase to absorb the shock of Brexit, then regain a level of competitiveness of the pre-Brexit vote. Based on key determinants of competitiveness, our assumption is that Brexit may have impacted negatively the three tenets as they relate to the UK, its industries, and firms—namely, ownership-specific advantage, location-specific advantage, and internalization-specific advantage.

These ownership-specific, location-specific and internalization-specific advantages can shed light on how Brexit can be rationalized, and a road map can be unfolded leading to a recovery strategy. All five marks of the eclectic paradigm can lead us out of a deadlock where traditional economic models or frameworks cannot provide a rational explanation of the new direction taken by the UK to engage in a reversal of its economic integration with the EU.

While it can be theorized that all three UK tenets of the eclectic paradigm (O, L, and I) may have suffered from Brexit as an economic shock, it can be assumed that in the long run the O-, L-, and I-specific advantages will recover. How it is going to happen in the realm of the eclectic paradigm is worth exploring to shed light on how the UK should redistribute its resources and reshape its policies. As suggested by Dunning (2001), the eclectic paradigm allows for differences in the strategic response of firms to any given configuration of OLI variables.

The following is discussed in Dunning (2001) and is still relevant to our dynamic framework:

> At a given moment of time, the extent and pattern of MNE activity represents a point on a set of trajectories towards (or, for that matter, away from) their internationalization path. That trajectory itself is set by the continuous and iterative interaction between the OLI configuration over successive time periods and the strategy of firms in response to these configurations that, in turn, will influence the OLI configuration in a subsequent moment of time. Let OLI_{t0} be the OLI configuration in time $t0$, OLI_{t1} the OLI configuration in time $t1$, S_{t-n} the past (i.e., pre $t0$) strategies of firms still being worked out, and $\Delta S_{t0 \to t1}$ any change in the strategic response of firms to that configuration between time $t0$ and $t1$. Then, ceteris paribus:

$$OLI_{t1} = f\left(OLI_{t0} S_{t-n} \Delta S_{t0 \to ti}\right) \qquad (2.1)$$

> If we extend the analysis to a second time period $t2$, then:

$$OLI_{t2} = f\left(OLI_{t1} S_{t-n} \Delta S_{t1 \to t2}\right) \qquad (2.2)$$

This analysis further suggests that S_{t-n} and $S_{t0 \to t2}$ determine the path of the movement from OLI_{t0} to OLI_{t2}.

The strategic response is, of course, just one of the many *endogenous* variables which might affect the OLI configuration of firms (mainly by its impact on O and I advantages). Others include: technological and/or organizational innovations; changes in the composition of senior management; increases in labor productivity; new marketing techniques; mergers and acquisitions; and so on. No less significant are *exogenous* changes, such as changes in: population; raw material prices; exchange rates; national government policies; actions taken by international agencies; and so on. If we take all endogenous variables other than strategy to be *EN,* and all exogenous variables to be *EX,* and we assume that changes in *EN* and *EX* do not affect the firms' strategies, then we can rewrite Eq. (2.1) as:

$$OLI_{t1} = f\left(OLI_{t0}S_{t-n}\Delta_{St0\to t0}\Delta_{ENti\to}t1\ \Delta_{EXt0\to t1}\right) \qquad (2.3)$$

Equation (2.2) can be similarly reconstructed, and it is easy to incorporate any change in strategy which embraces the response to Δ_{EN} and Δ_{EX} if it occurs before $_{t1}$ is reached by adding * to $\Delta S_{t0\to t1}$ in the equation.

All O-specific advantages—asset-type O_A, transactional-type O_T, and institutional-type O_I will experience a reorganization at the firm level that will necessitate the UK firms to deploy new types of relations with the rest of the world outside the EU. The authors believe that a relationship-specific advantage will be at play in the recovery of the O_A and O_T at the firm level as well as a new O_I resulting from an evolution of the institutional apparatus of the UK at the country level.

The UK's L-specific advantage is probably the most impacted tenet of the eclectic paradigm as the UK negotiates a soft Brexit. The UK needs to provide an internally coherent paradigm that integrates effectively transaction costs economics (TCE) and resource-based view (RBV) components to make its location attractive outside of market-seeking FDI.

The UK's I-specific advantage recovery will result from a strategic blending of Coasean and Penrosean thinking. The UK firms will need to figure out a new alignment of its assets. The R-specific advantage may be at play in positioning UK firms' interest with other nations.

The UK seems to be inclined to pursue a new path leading them to favor bilateral agreements and shy away from multilateral cooperative agreements. Those motives are mostly political and contrast with traditional motives of the activities in the IB literature.

According to John Dunning, the following are the basic motives for economic integration (Dunning and Lundan 2008b; Dunning and Robson 1987):

* To increase efficiency or resource usage and to increase the economic and strategic (including political) strength of region and member countries.
* To overcome structural market distortions (e.g. tariff barriers, subsidies) and to encourage competition.

Applying Theory to Understand How Multinational Firms Address... 41

- To reduce imperfections in foreign exchange, capital, and labor markets.
- To facilitate the possibility of product and process specialization of firms within the region and promote trade in intermediate products.
- To facilitate the conduct of optimal policies and to secure gains from policy coordination in circumstances of structural and policy interdependence.
- To develop economic and strategic strength by the adoption of a common policy toward non-member countries.
- To increase market size and improve the technological capability of member countries.

Based on the above key motives of economic integration, most economists find it difficult to rationalize or justify the decision of the UK to reconfigure their regional integration stand. When it comes to the cost and benefit of economic integration, it is generally accepted that the cost of economic integration is upfront, while its benefits are downward. Reversing the process of economic integration raises questions about balancing its cost and benefit and how it is going to impact inward and outward FDI in the UK as well as the competitiveness of its industries.

Is the cost of reversing economic integration mostly downward? Is its benefit mostly upfront? The authors propose to study this phenomenon in a follow-on study. At the same time, they will assess the relationship-specific advantages of MNE activities in the UK by analyzing the inward and outward FDI and key economic indicators.

The key challenge facing the UK is to maintain its competitiveness at the country level and of its main industries while not losing all the benefits generated by many decades of transformation of its economic fabric in the context of EU integration.

As a follow-on to this chapter, the authors will investigate and shed light on how the UK may or may not continue realizing the objectives underlined by the above motives for economic integration. Maneuvering backward from a UK economy integrated into the EU market is going to impact the allocation of resources and force UK MNEs to reconsider how their activities are distributed around the world. Using the OLI paradigm and bringing its fourth leg, the relationship-specific advantage, into play, the authors will assess the viability and potential of the UK to enter into a new role or position in the world economy.

Most countries around the world are engaged in one form or the other in economic integration. The integration of major blocs is a prerequisite for a full integration of the world market. The past few decades have demonstrated this phenomenon and have shown an acceleration of a long-term trend toward greater economic interdependence not only between countries but also between economic blocs. This acceleration was noticeably revealed in the 1990s by the economic and political shakeups that took place in Central and Eastern Europe, the achievement of the internal market of the EU, and the beginning of the North American Free Trade Agreement (NAFTA) between the US, Canada, and Mexico. However, today with the Brexit vote and President Trump's "America First" movement, the global economy has entered a new era undermining economic integration.

As a follow-on to this chapter, the authors will analyze at the firm level whether corporate integration will become necessary for UK firms to compete:

* Efficiency-seeking FDI will strengthen the O-specific advantages of firms; and
* Strategic-asset-seeking FDI will strengthen the I-specific advantages by providing firms with increased agility.

At the industry level, where an industry is as competitive as its supply chain's weakest link, the authors will analyze if the UK's highest performing industries will gain O- and I-specific advantages.

And last at the country level, the authors will analyze if the L-specific advantages of the UK will deteriorate and if the UK's R-specific advantage through increased bilateral economic agreements will mitigate a weakening L-specific advantage of the UK.

The authors wish to gather feedback on the validity of their hypothesis as well as how to select some key determinants and factors to comprehend and measure the phenomenon of reversing economic integration in the UK.

Policy Recommendations

Brexit will have a major impact on FDI in the UK and creates major challenges for the UK to attract FDI, especially in the actual period where the negotiation is taking place, which generates additional economic and political uncertainty.

Our underlying premise is that FDI in the UK is inevitably going to decline throughout the revitalization of all three tenets of the eclectic paradigm. However, O-specific advantage remains a prerequisite for the recovery of the UK economy before it can lead to a significant positive change in the L-specific advantage, as well as the I-specific advantage. Greenfield investments will be particularly hit hard, while existing foreign investors in the UK and new foreign investors via mergers and acquisitions (M&A) and non-equity form of investment will become more important components in the mix of FDI coming into the UK.

As the UK will strengthen its O-specific advantages, the UK location will need to become more attractive. As such, the UK needs to consider reconfiguring its new investor strategy to focus on the highest potential sectors and markets, put more resources into supporting existing foreign investors, and consider expanding their mandate to encompass M&A and strategic alliances as key pillars of UK FDI strategy.

Given the regional UK diversity, L-specific advantage should take into consideration centralized and local governments in the UK to maintain or increase investment promotion activities, expanding services for existing investors, which is critical to retaining investment and jobs in the UK and ultimately influencing a new I-specific advantage.

Conclusion

Like a thriller, a lot of suspense is keeping the business community waiting for a verdict that has a potential to impact the competitiveness of major industries all over Europe and beyond. The UK aerospace and financial services industries are both examples of what is awaiting to soon unravel and trigger a redistribution of resources through inward and outward FDI.

The wings of Airbus civil aircraft may end up being trimmed and thousands of UK jobs displaced or shredded. Some of the most technologically intense supply chains may no longer be sustainable as their weakest link may be worsened by an unfavorable Brexit outcome. Similarly, the future of the European fighter may be jeopardized.

However, we may hope that the rivalry among Paris, Frankfurt, and Dublin may lead to a stronger EU that is less bureaucratic and more agile.

The UK's ability to form and govern beneficial relationships with other actors, including other non-EU firms and individuals within a firm, may provide the UK economy an opportunity to strengthen its competitiveness at the global level. UK MNEs will be recombining, exchanging, and co-developing idiosyncratic shared resources between its own firms and its new foreign partners leading UK firm's internal resources generate greater "internal rent" (Narula et al. 2017).

The performance of UK firms is at stake and it remains to be seen if the firms' external social capital will free UK firms from the EU bureaucracy of its institutions and ultimately lead UK MNEs to higher level of competitiveness.

UK firms' O_A and O_I are fully engaged in a spin that is accelerating as the uncertainty between a hard and soft Brexit still hangs above the UK economy. The UK government needs to slow down this "spin" and start working toward providing the strongest O_I to its own MNEs as well as facilitating the reconfiguration of its industry's supply chains' I-specific advantages. The question will remain how much UK R-advantages (Dunning 2002, 2003, 2004) will bring back the UK economy to its golden age.

References

Andrew, M. C., & Klaus, N. (2009). Social capital and the resource-based view of the firm. *International Studies of Management & Organization, 39*(2), 7–32. https://doi.org/10.2753/IMO0020-8825390201.

Arena, M. J., & Uhl-Bien, M. (2016). Complexity leadership theory: Shifting from human capital to social capital. *People & Strategy, 39*(2), 22–27.

Augier, M., & Teece, D. J. (2007). Dynamic capabilities and multinational enterprise: Penrosean insights and omissions. *Management International Review, 47*(2), 175–192.

Barber, L. (2017, December 20). Brexit and the city: London's financial industry grapples with the biggest demerger in its history. *The World in 2018*. Retrieved from https://www.economist.com/theworldin

Barney, J. (1991). Firm resources and sustained competitive advantage. *Journal of Management, 17*(1), 99–120. https://doi.org/10.1177/014920639101700108.

Barney, J. B. (2001). Is the resource-based "view" a useful perspective for strategic management research? Yes. *Academy of Management Review, 26*(1), 41–56.

Cantwell, J., & Narula, R. (2001). The eclectic paradigm in the global economy. *International Journal of the Economics of Business, 8*, 155–172. https://doi.org/10.1080/13571510110051504.

Cohen, W. M., & Levinthal, D. A. (1990). Absorptive capacity: A new perspective on learning and innovation. *Administrative Science Quarterly, 35*, 128–152. https://doi.org/10.2307/2393553.

Conner, K. R. (1991). A historical comparison of resource-based theory and five schools of thought within industrial organization economics. *Journal of Management, 17*(1), 121–154.

Di Stefano, G., Peteraf, M., & Verona, G. (2010). Dynamic capabilities deconstructed: A bibliographic investigation into the origins, development, and future directions of the research domain. *Industrial and Corporate Change, 19*(4), 1187–1204.

Dierickx, I., & Cool, K. (1989). Asset stock accumulation and sustainability of competitive advantage. *Management Science, 35*(12), 554–571. https://doi.org/10.1287/mnsc.35.12.1514.

Doz, Y., Santos, J., & Williamson, P. J. (2001). *From global to metanational: How companies win in the knowledge economy.* Boston: Harvard Business Press.

Dunning, J. H. (1979). Explaining changing patterns of international production: In defense of the eclectic theory. *Oxford Bulletin of Economics and Statistics, 41*(4), 34–48.

Dunning, J. H. (1980). Toward an eclectic theory of international production: Some empirical tests. *Journal of International Business Studies, 11*(1), 9–31. https://doi.org/10.1057/palgrave.jibs.8490593.

Dunning, J. H. (1988a). *Explaining international production.* London: Unwin Hyman.

Dunning, J. H. (1988b). The eclectic paradigm of international production: A restatement and some possible extensions. *Journal of International Business Studies, 19*, 1–31. https://doi.org/10.4337/9781843767053.

Dunning, J. H. (2000). The eclectic paradigm as an envelope for economic and business theories of MNE activity. *International Business Review, 9*, 163–190. https://doi.org/10.1016/S0969-5931(99)00035-9.

Dunning, J. H. (2001). The eclectic (OLI) paradigm of international production: Past, present and future. *International Journal of the Economics of Business, 8*(2), 173–190. https://doi.org/10.1080/13571510110051441.

Dunning, J. H. (2002). Relational assets, networks and international business activity. In F. J. Contractor & P. E. Lorange (Eds.), *Cooperative strategies and alliances* (pp. 569–594). Oxford: Pergamon Press.

Dunning, J. H. (2003). Relational assets, networks and international business activity. In J. H. Dunning & G. Boyd (Eds.), *Alliance capitalism and corporate management: Entrepreneurial cooperation in knowledge based economies* (pp. 1–23). Northampton: Edward Elgar Publishing.

Dunning, J. H. (2004). Relational assets: The new competitive advantages of MNEs and countries. In J. H. Dunning & R. Narula (Eds.), *Multinationals and industrial competitiveness: A new agenda* (pp. 201–239). Northampton: Edward Elgar Publishing.

Dunning, J. H., & Lundan, S. M. (2008a). Institutions and the OLI paradigm of the multinational enterprise. *Asia Pacific Journal of Management, 25*(4), 573–593.

Dunning, J. H., & Lundan, S. M. (2008b). *Multinational enterprises and the global economy* (2nd ed.). Cheltenham: Edward Elgar.

Dunning, J. H., & Lundan, S. M. (2010). The institutional origins of dynamic capabilities in multinational enterprises. *Industrial and Corporate Change, 19*(4), 1225–1246. https://doi.org/10.1093/icc/dtq029.

Dunning, J. H., & Robson, P. (1987). Multinational corporate integration and regional economic integration. *Journal of Common Market Studies, 26*(2), 103–125. https://doi.org/10.1111/j.1468-5965.1987.tb00308.x.

Dunning, J. H., & Rugman, A. M. (1985). The influence of Hymer's dissertation on the theory of foreign direct investment. *The American Economic Review, 75*(2), 228–232.

Dyer, J. H., & Nobeoka, K. (2000). Creating and managing a high-performance knowledge-sharing network: The Toyota case. *Strategic Management Journal, 21*(3), 345–367. https://doi.org/10.1002/(SICI)1097-0266(200003)21:3%3C345::AID-SMJ96%3E3.0.CO;2-N.

Dyer, J. H., & Singh, H. (1998). The relational view: Cooperative strategy and sources of interorganizational competitive advantage. *Academy of Management Review, 23*(4), 660–680. https://doi.org/10.5465/AMR.1998.1255632.

Gomes-Casseres, B. (1984). Group versus group: How alliance networks compete. *Harvard Business Review, 62*(4), 4–11.

Grant, R. M. (1996). Toward a knowledge-based theory of the firm. *Strategic Management Journal, 17*, 109–122. https://doi.org/10.1002/smj.4250171110.

Hennart, J. F. (2009). Down with MNE-centric theories! Market entry and expansion as the bundling of MNE and local assets. *Journal of International Business Studies, 40*(9), 1432–1454. https://doi.org/10.1057/jibs.2009.42.

Hu, Y. S. (1992). Global or stateless corporations are national firms with international operations. *California Management Review, 34*, 107–126.

Hu, Y. S. (1993). *Exploding the globalization myth: Competitive advantage and corporate nationality, A recovery strategy for Europe.* London: Federal Trust.

Jenkins, P. (2017, July 12). 1Are banks in the UK en marche to Paris? *Financial Times.* https://www.ft.com/content/d79c035a-66f2-11e7-8526-7b38dcaef614

Johnston, C. (2017, June 20). Rolls-Royce boss warns against a 'hard Brexit.' *BBC News.* http://www.bbc.com/news/business-40332913

Kogut, B., & Zander, U. (1992). Knowledge of the firm, combinative capabilities, and the replication of technology. *Organization Science, 3*(3), 383–397. https://doi.org/10.1287/orsc.3.3.383.

Lavie, D. (2006). The competitive advantage of interconnected firms: An extension of the resource-based view. *Academy of Management Review, 31*(3), 638–658. https://doi.org/10.5465/AMR.2006.21318922.

Lecraw, D. J., & Morrison, A. J. (1991). Transnational corporations-host country relations: A framework for analysis. *South Carolina Essays in International Business*, No. 9.

Mesquita, L., Anand, J., & Brush, T. (2008). Comparing the resource-based and relational views: Knowledge transfer and spillover in vertical alliances. *Strategic Management Journal, 29*(9), 913–941. https://doi.org/10.1002/smj.699.

Meyer, K. E., Mudambi, R., & Narula, R. (2011). Multinational enterprises and local contexts: The opportunities and challenges of multiple embeddedness. *Journal of Management Studies, 48*, 235–252. https://doi.org/10.1111/j.1467-6486.2010.00968.x.

Mizuki, K. (2014). Relational view: Four prerequisites of competitive advantage. *Annals of Business Administrative Science, 13*(2), 77–90. https://doi.org/10.7880/abas.13.77.

Nachum, L. (1999). *The origins of the international competitiveness of firms: The impact of location and ownership in professional service industries*. Aldershot/Brookfield: Edward Elgar.

Nahapiet, J., & Ghoshal, S. (1998). Social capital, intellectual capital, and the organizational advantage. *Academy of Management Review, 23*(2), 242–266. https://doi.org/10.5465/AMR.1998.533225.

Narula, R. (2002). Innovation systems and 'inertia' in R&D location: Norwegian firms and the role of systemic lockin. *Research Policy, 31*(5), 795–816. https://doi.org/10.1016/S0048-7333(01)00148-2.

Narula, R. (2012). Do we need different frameworks to explain infant MNEs from developing countries? *Global Strategy Journal, 2*(3), 188–204. https://doi.org/10.1111/j.2042-5805.2012.01035.x.

Narula, R. (2014). Exploring the paradox of competence-creating subsidiaries: Balancing bandwidth and dispersion in MNEs. *Long Range Planning, 47*, 4–15. https://doi.org/10.1016/j.lrp.2013.10.006.

Narula, R., Leel. J., & Hillemann, J. (2017, December). *Asset recombination as the driver of sustainable competitive advantage: An entrepreneurship/capabilities-based perspective*. Paper session presented at the 43rd European International Business Academy Conference, Milan.

Nelson, R., & Winter, S. (1982). *An evolutionary theory of economic change*. Cambridge, MA: Harvard University Press.

Peng, M. W. (2001). The resource-based view and international business. *Journal of Management, 27*(6), 803–829.

Penrose, E. (1959). *The theory of the growth of the firm*. Oxford: Oxford University Press.

Porter, M. (1990). *The competitive advantage of nations*. London/Basingstoke: Macmillan.

Putnam, R. D. (1995). Bowling alone: America's declining social capital. *Journal of Democracy, 6*(1), 65–78. https://doi.org/10.1353/jod.1995.0002.

Rugman, A. M., & Verbeke, A. (2001). Subsidiary-specific advantages in multinational enterprises. *Strategic Management Journal, 22*, 237–250. https://doi.org/10.1002/smj.153.

Smith, K. G., Carroll, S. J., & Ashford, S. J. (1995). Intra- and interorganizational cooperation: Toward a research agenda. *Academy of Management Journal, 38*(1), 7–23. https://doi.org/10.2307/256726.

Symonds, M. (2017). Up in the air. In *The world in 2018* (Vol. 101, 32nd ed.). Hartford: The Economist Newspaper Limited.

Teece, D. J. (2007). Explicating dynamic capabilities: The nature and microfoundations of (sustainable) enterprise performance. *Strategic Management Journal, 28*(13), 1319–1350.

Teece, D. J. (2014). A dynamic capabilities-based entrepreneurial theory of the multinational enterprise. *Journal of International Business Studies, 45*, 8–37. https://doi.org/10.1057/jibs.2013.54.

Teece, D. J., & Pisano, G. (1994). The dynamic capabilities of firms: An introduction. *Industrial and Corporate Change, 3*(3), 537–556.

Teece, D. J., Pisano, G., & Shuen, A. (1997). Dynamic capabilities and strategic management. *Strategic Management Journal, 18*(7), 509–533.

Verbeke, A. (2013). *International business strategy* (2nd ed.). New York: Cambridge University Press.

Wernerfelt, B. (1984). A resource-based view of the firm. *Strategic Management Journal, 5*(2), 171–180. https://doi.org/10.1002/smj.4250050207.

Wernerfelt, B. (1995). The resource-based view of the firm: Ten years after. *Strategic Management Journal, 16*, 171–174.

Winter, S. G. (2003). Understanding dynamic capabilities. *Strategic Management Journal, 24*(10), 991–995.

3

Bureaucrats in International Business: A Review of Five Decades of Research on State-Owned MNEs

Asmund Rygh

Introduction

The World Bank's (1995) report *Bureaucrats in Business* demonstrated the enduring role of state ownership despite the previous decade's extensive privatisation efforts. Two decades later, state-owned enterprises (SOEs) are in focus due to their international expansion. United Nations Conference on Trade and Development (UNCTAD) (2017) identify almost 1500 state-owned multinational enterprises (SOMNEs) that have 86,000 foreign affiliates and originate in a wide range of developed and emerging markets and operate across many industries. Substantial research and policy-maker interest has followed (Cuervo-Cazurra et al. 2014; Shapiro and Globerman 2012).

Although SOMNEs may seem a novel issue, already Dresang and Sharkansky (1965) studied SOEs jointly owned by several governments in the East African Community. In the 1970s, US business scholar Lamont raised concerns regarding European SOMNEs (Lamont 1973, 1979). A milestone in the literature was Mazzolini's extensive studies of European SOEs (Mazzolini 1979a, b, 1980a, b, c, d). Moderate research interest in SOMNEs continued into the 1980s (e.g., Aharoni 1986; Laux 1983, 1984; Vernon 1979; Negandhi et al. 1986; Monsen and Walters 1983; Anastassopoulos et al. 1987), including some attention to emerging market SOMNEs (Kumar 1981). Then, however, while the end of the Cold War and

---

A. Rygh (✉)
Alliance Manchester Business School, University of Manchester, Manchester, UK
e-mail: asmund.rygh@manchester.ac.uk

© The Author(s) 2019
A. Chidlow et al. (eds.), *The Changing Strategies of International Business*, The Academy of International Business, https://doi.org/10.1007/978-3-030-03931-8_3

massive privatisations spurred great research interest in privatisation and state ownership (see Megginson and Netter 2001), interest in SOMNEs all but disappeared, with few exceptions (Wettenhall 1992, 1993), some related to internationalisation in (de)regulated industries (García-Canal and Guillén 2008; Colli et al. 2014; Alonso et al. 2013). Only recently have SOMNEs again become a research topic in their own right, explained in large part by SOMNEs from emerging markets, in particular China. This literature has expanded rapidly (e.g., Knutsen et al. 2011; Cui and Jiang 2012; Shapiro and Globerman 2012; Estrin et al. 2016) with notable special issues and books (see Cuervo-Cazurra et al. 2014; Xie and Redding 2018; Cuervo-Cazurra 2018). Although most recent studies focus on China (Martin and Li 2015), there are also some studies in other contexts, including multi-country studies (Götz and Jankowska 2016).

This chapter is the so far most comprehensive (albeit not exhaustive) review of literature on SOMNEs. We do not restrict the review to a particular set of journals or particular keyword search results (as in a typical systematic review), and an important aim has been to also include less accessible but key contributions on SOMNEs in books, book chapters, and reports by reputable international organisations. However, we limit the review to published studies in English and omit a discussion of sovereign wealth funds, previous socialist MNEs (Gwiazda 1985), and state-influenced enterprises without state equity.

The overview in Fig. 3.1 highlights the notable literature in the late 1970s and 1980s, while also illustrating the strong recent growth as the last 15 years alone produced about two-thirds of the reviewed studies. Figure. 3.1 also indicates the importance of "grey literature" (books, chapters, and reports) on SOMNEs.

The 134 studies reviewed demonstrate effects of state ownership on key international business strategies such as foreign market entry modes and location decisions. Yet, specific results are mixed and context seems to play a key role. We also find surprisingly little evidence on SOMNEs' international performance and on home and host-country effects of SOMNE activities.

The next section briefly reviews key characteristics of SOEs and their motives and resources for internationalisation mentioned in the literature. The following four sections discuss, respectively, literature on the effects of state ownership on foreign market entry, on host-country location choice, on international performance, and on home and host countries. The chapter ends with some brief concluding remarks.

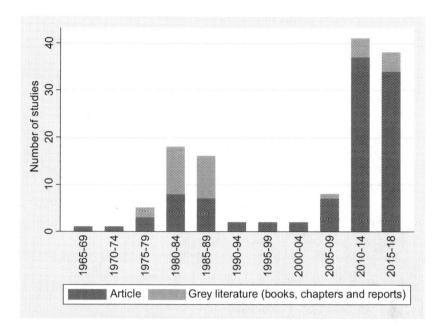

Fig. 3.1 Reviewed studies over time

Characteristics of SOMNEs

Economic theory suggests state ownership can address market failures such as natural monopoly, externalities, or public goods (see e.g., Cuervo-Cazurra et al. 2014). Other goals cited in the SOE literature include redistribution, industrial policy (Negandhi et al. 1986), controlling "strategic" sectors of the economy such as energy, besides motivations such as ideology or nationalism (Cuervo-Cazurra et al. 2014). This mix of economic and non-economic goals (Negandhi and Ganguly 1986; Negandhi et al. 1986; He et al. 2016a) may also affect SOE internationalisation. Many studies argue that internationalisation is less likely for SOEs (Mazzolini 1979b; Rapp 1986; Estrin et al. 2016). Based on case studies of European SOEs, Mazzolini (1979b) noted that when SOEs pursue domestic social goals, international activities are usually less relevant. For this reason, SOEs may pay less attention to international opportunities and be less able to exploit them. Politicians seeking re-election may also prefer domestic projects that visibly benefit voters (Boyd 1986; Strange 2018), while unions tend to be stronger in SOEs and often oppose international expansion (Monsen and Walters 1983). However, these arguments may need modification when studying autocratic SOMNE home countries where politicians are more autonomous in their decisions (Strange 2018; Clegg et al. 2018).

On the other hand, SOEs may internationalise to pursue industrial policy goals such as securing natural resource access (Noreng 1981; Franko 1975; Mazzolini 1979b; Khandwalla 1986; Kaynak 1989; Bass and Chakrabarty 2014) or upgrading and diversifying the domestic economy (Rudy et al. 2016; Karolyi and Liao 2017). Furthermore, SOMNEs pursue foreign policy goals. SOMNE managers interviewed by Mazzolini (1979a) considered SOE foreign direct investment (FDI) an unobtrusive way to establish links between countries. Examples of cross-border cooperation through SOEs are numerous (Katz and Kosacoff 1983; Mascarenhas 1989; Vernon 1979). For Chinese FDI (dominated by SOEs until recently), studies demonstrate links to diplomacy and foreign policy (Kaplinsky and Morris 2009; Wang 2002). Some SOMNEs are jointly owned by two or more governments (Anastassopoulos et al. 1987) allowing countries to pool resources (Dresang and Sharkansky 1965), achieve economies of scale (Kumar 1981), and address cross-border market failures (Rygh 2018). To achieve such goals, governments may support SOE internationalisation in various ways (Hennart et al. 2017; Landoni 2018).

While SOMNEs theoretically can address market failures at home or even market failures in other countries' territories (Cuervo-Cazurra et al. 2014), one could imagine contracting with private MNEs to provide such services. Rygh (2018) reviews theoretical arguments on conditions under which state ownership may be optimal, based on agency theory (risk aversion and financial constraints) and incomplete contracting (non-contractible quality and credible commitments). Rygh (2018) finds corresponding arguments may also apply to international operations, although the incomplete contracts rationale becomes more complex when SOEs operate in other governments' jurisdictions. The notion that state ownership may imply less risk aversion and a longer time horizon is found also in other studies (Hveem et al. 2012; Vernon 1979; Knutsen et al. 2011; Musacchio and Lazzarini 2018).

However, SOE internationalisation is not always directed by the home government (Mazzolini 1979b; Anastassopoulos et al. 1987). Studies based on agency and public choice theory identify particular governance issues in SOMNEs related to multilayered and complex governance involving politicians and SOE managers who may pursue private interests (Aharoni 1982; Musacchio and Lazzarini 2018; Knutsen et al. 2011; Morck et al. 2008). Internationalisation can even be a strategy for SOEs to gain more autonomy (Aharoni 1981; Choudhury and Khanna 2014). Conversely, SOE internationalisation may result from the SOE becoming more autonomous (Hafsi and Koenig 1988; Hafsi and Thomas 1988). Often, partial private ownership has supported SOMNE internationalisation (Hennart et al. 2017; Musacchio and Lazzarini 2018). The relationship may also be dynamic, with successful

SOMNEs experiencing renewed intervention by the home government (Rodrigues and Dieleman 2018).

Finally, absent government non-economic objectives, SOE internationalisation may depend on firm-specific or industry-specific factors similarly as for private firms (Florio 2013; Anastassopoulos et al. 1987; Collins 1986; Alonso et al. 2013). Indeed, home governments could have financial motivations for SOMNEs. Jones and Wortzel (1982) argue that foreign exchange earned by SOEs allows governments to reduce taxes or increase welfare spending at home. Kostecki (1981) argues state trading companies can be used as part of strategic trade policy, pointing out that using state trading monopolies may be more politically acceptable at home than direct tariffs (Negandhi and Ganguly 1986).

Studies also consider the particular resources (as compared to private MNEs) that SOMNEs may build on for their internationalisation. This may include financial resources such as explicit or implicit subsidies and softer budget constraints from the home government (Nielsen 1981; Morck et al. 2008; Buckley et al. 2007; Kowalski et al. 2013) or political resources in the form of home government political and diplomatic support (Kumar 1981; Mazzolini 1979b; Knutsen et al. 2011; Duanmu 2014). On the other hand, following conventional arguments on inefficiencies of state ownership, SOEs may lack technical and managerial resources to undertake internationalisation (Rugman and Li 2007). Therefore, Li and Oh (2016, 780) and Gao et al. (2015) call state ownership a "double edged resource for firms' international investments."

As discussed above, SOMNEs internationalise with widely different motivations and resources. Indeed, SOMNEs are likely as different as governments, and the following review of studies on SOMNEs' international strategies suggests that contextual factors play a key role, as proposed by Aharoni (2018).

Foreign Market Entry

A key international business research topic is the choice of mode for operating in foreign markets (i.e., exports vs FDI, wholly owned subsidiary vs joint venture, and greenfield investment vs acquisition). The discussion of SOE's motivations suggested that SOEs, when they do internationalise, may often prefer the mode of exports to FDI. The domestic bias of European SOEs demonstrated in Mazzolini's (1979b) case studies is confirmed by recent statistical studies (Majocchi and Strange 2012; Benito et al. 2011; Hobdari et al. 2011). Several early studies also noted a lower propensity among resource sector SOEs to integrate vertically across borders (Rodrik 1982; Vernon and Levy 1982; Radetzki 1989).

However, this is not always true for more recent studies on emerging markets. Wang et al. (2012a) find state ownership increases FDI volume by Chinese firms. Hong et al. (2014) also find state ownership promotes Chinese FDI, an effect moderated by various firm level and industry factors. Hu and Cui (2014) find no effect for Chinese firms. Xia et al. (2013) argue that SOEs, given stronger (political) resources in their home market, are less prone than privately owned enterprises (POEs) to respond to inward FDI by conducting outward FDI, finding empirical support for this. Huang et al. (2017) develop an argument based on resource dependence theory that manufacturing firms' internationalisation will be hindered by state ownership. Their empirical analysis using Chinese firms confirms this effect. He et al. (2016b) find a curvilinear relationship with the highest level of international diversification at intermediate levels of state ownership, reflecting contradicting effects between goal conflicts and SOE resource support. Moreover, this curvilinear relationship is positively moderated by institutional ownership among the private co-owners.

Few studies of emerging market SOMNEs exist beyond China (Martin and Li 2015). Kalotay and Sulstarova (2010) find state ownership increases Russian outward FDI. Lien et al. (2005) find state ownership promotes Taiwanese outward FDI, except for FDI to China. Cahen (2015) finds, based on a case study of Brazilian Petrobras, that SOEs do not hesitate to enter international markets. Using a multi-country sample, Estrin et al. (2016) find state ownership deters outward FDI, but this effect becomes less important when the home-country institutional environment improves and there is less scope for politicians to keep SOE assets domestic for rent-seeking. In contrast, Clegg et al. (2018) find that SOMNEs from autocratic countries are more likely to make foreign acquisitions, suggesting acquisitions may be different. Wang et al. (2012b) find a higher government affiliation level implies a more positive effect on outward FDI. However, Huang et al. (2017) find the opposite result. Liang et al. (2014) find political connections promote Chinese firms' degree of globalisation (DOG) before institutional reform, while state ownership control has a positive effect on DOG after reform.

Further FDI choices relate to the establishment mode (acquisition vs greenfield) and the level of ownership (wholly owned subsidary vs joint venture). Mazzolini (1979b, 1980d) found SOEs tended to carry out greenfield investments rather than make acquisitions when going abroad. Interviewed SOE managers stated that at home SOEs were expected to contribute to new economic activity and employment (i.e., through greenfields), and this practice was brought abroad. SOEs' propensity to choose greenfields was also mentioned by UNCTAD (2013). Again, however, more recently this result seems to reverse for some emerging market countries like China, whose SOMNEs prefer acquisitions (Meyer et al. 2014).

Studying the choice between full ownership or joint venture, Cui and Jiang (2012) argue a higher level of state ownership increases the resource dependence of the firm on its home state, and also negatively influences the firm's host-country image. The latter implies that SOMNEs seek to conform to host-country institutional pressures to choose joint ownership. Using Chinese FDI data, the authors find support for their hypotheses. Also Lee et al. (2014) find state ownership to be associated with lower equity levels, ascribing this, however, to the Chinese state's reluctance to commit SOE assets abroad.

Meyer et al. (2014) study jointly the decisions of greenfield versus acquisition and the degree of control in the investment object. They argue foreign SOEs face special institutional pressures in host countries and choose lower control levels in acquisitions in order to appear more attentive to local interests. These effects are stronger in more liberal economies (where SOEs are argued to be perceived as less legitimate) and in high-technology economies (where host-country national security concerns are argued to be greater). While state ownership could lead to a greater "liability of foreignness" (Gaur et al. 2011), opposition to SOMNEs also depends on factors such as the similarity between countries (Shi et al. 2016).

Li et al. (2014) theoretically disaggregate the effect of state ownership in the Chinese context, arguing that centrally owned SOEs are used as political instruments, while locally owned SOEs focus on economic efficiency. Due to this, the latter type of SOEs is more able and willing than centrally owned SOES to accommodate host-country interests through joint ownership and greenfields.

Considering deal characteristics, Bass and Chakrabarty (2014) find that petroleum SOMNEs tend to target more long-term exploration resources. Del Bo et al. (2017) find that M&As involving SOEs are characterised by a greater amount of assets involved, higher solvency ratios, broader experience of deals, and closer proximity to the targets of the acquirers.

Finally, studies explore how state ownership moderates the effects of important entry mode determinants. Pan et al. (2014) argue SOEs' higher risk tolerance and the additional support SOEs receive from their home government make SOEs less concerned about potential transaction costs. Pan et al. (2014) find state ownership negatively moderates the relationship between host-country risk and ownership control in the subsidiary. Li and Xie (2013)

56   A. Rygh

find SOEs are less affected by variables related to information asymmetry in cross-border acquisitions such as target technology level, unrelatedness of industry, and cultural distance, consistent with a lesser focus on minimising transaction costs.

Location Decisions

As noted above, SOE investment may be linked to natural resource seeking, industrial policy, and foreign policy. Buckley et al. (2007) studied host-country factors attracting Chinese SOE FDI. While they did not find Chinese FDI was asset-seeking, an interesting finding was that Chinese FDI seems undeterred by host-country political risk. Explicitly comparing Chinese SOEs with POEs, Ramasamy et al. (2012) find POEs are market seekers, while SOEs' FDI goes to natural resource rich and politically risky environments. Amighini et al. (2013) find Chinese private MNEs are attracted by large markets and strategic assets, while being averse to economic and political risks. In contrast, SOEs invest more in natural resource sectors and are less concerned about host-country political and economic conditions. Lin and Farrell (2013) and Duanmu (2012) also find a higher SOE political risk tolerance. The lesser risk aversion of SOEs is confirmed for Spanish MNEs in regulated industries by García-Canal and Guillén (2008) in terms of policy and macroeconomic risk, and for Norwegian MNEs by Knutsen et al. (2011) for political risk and corruption risk, indicating this risk tolerance effect is not unique to Chinese SOMNEs.

The notion that state ownership protects against political risk is found already in early studies (Mazzolini 1979b; Kumar 1981; Anastassopoulos et al. 1987). Buckley et al. (2007) noted that Chinese SOE FDI may benefit from political connections between home and host countries. Later studies make related arguments (Cui and Jiang 2012; Knutsen et al. 2011; Duanmu 2014). Duanmu (2014) finds the effect of state ownership in reducing Chinese MNEs' aversion to political risk depends on the political relationships between the countries, and on the degree of economic dependence of the host country on China. Jandhyala and Weiner (2014) find evidence that state ownership reduces the role of international investment agreements (IIAs) in protecting cross-border investments, due to stronger political support as well as potentially less protection from IIAs. Finally, Clegg et al. (2018) find that SOMNEs from autocratic countries are more likely to carry out M&As in other autocratic countries.

However, alternative explanations exist for SOMNEs' political risk tolerance. Buckley et al. (2007) also note Chinese SOEs may simply lack risk management capabilities, while Knutsen et al. (2011) point to potential moral hazard problems, whereby SOE managers expect the home government to come to their rescue if they get into trouble. Alternatively, in line with Vernon (1979), Knutsen et al. (2011) speculate the government owner, being highly diversified, might have higher general risk tolerance than private owners. Also Eliassen and Grøgaard (2007) suggest SOEs could have a greater risk tolerance based on their discussion of the internationalisation of telecommunications firms. Finally, García-Canal and Guillén (2008) argue managers of partially SOMNEs will display the highest propensity to take risks, since they do not have the protected positions of fully SOMNE managers, while also needing to cater to private shareholders.

Focusing on Chinese cross-border M&As, Yang and Deng (2015) find M&As are more numerous in host countries with large market size, abundant natural resources and strategic assets, high economic freedom, and low government effectiveness, while state ownership in the investing Chinese MNEs strengthens these effects. Karolyi and Liao (2017) find government-related acquirers more likely come from autocratic countries and countries with large foreign currency reserves, and tend to target natural resource-rich countries and opportunities for diversification of the home economy.

Sometimes, SOE location choices seem contrary to home government interests. Substantial Chinese FDI goes to tax havens (Buckley et al. 2008). Although one would expect tax planning to be less prevalent in SOEs (Shapiro and Globerman 2012), some studies found evidence of SOMNE tax planning (Laux 1984; Mazzolini 1979b). Ding (2000) argues that members of the Chinese elite use SOE FDI for "informal privatisation" of public assets. Other examples of apparently lacking home government control of SOE international location include British Petroleum's (BP) disregard of the British boycott of Rhodesia (Wettenhall 1992, 1993).

Finally, Young et al. (1996) suggest Chinese SOMNEs "leapfrog" stages by going directly to developed country markets, and that a longer-term perspective leads to acquisitions as the preferred mode. Wei et al. (2015) find the internationalisation of Chinese SOEs does not conform to the Uppsala model in terms of the role of psychic distance, and that the government speeds up the internationalisation of SOEs.

International Performance

Despite the focus on economic performance differences in the general SOE literature (Megginson and Netter 2001), besides anecdotal evidence (Aharoni

2013; Musacchio and Lazzarini 2018), very little systematic evidence exists on SOMNE performance. Some early studies claimed SOEs generally had poor international performance (Kumar 1981; Kaynak 1989). However, Miroudot and Ragoussis (2013) find no differences between SOE and POE foreign affiliates in terms of productivity or export performance, although SOE affiliates tend to have more employees, higher labour costs, and a higher capital stock. Guo and Clougherty (2015) claim Chinese SOEs are less able than POEs to realise synergy and competitiveness gains from cross-border acquisitions. Guo et al. (2016) argue Chinese SOMNEs overpay more in acquisitions than private MNEs. Bernard and Weiner (1996) find no evidence that petroleum SOEs perform less well on export pricing.

Using market-based measures of performance, Chen and Young (2010) and Ning et al. (2014) find international investors react negatively to SOMNE cross-border M&As, expecting principal-principal conflicts relating to the potentially different goals of state and private owners. Du et al. (2015) and Du and Boateng (2015) find the opposite for investor reactions on Chinese stock exchanges, while Tao et al. (2017) confirm the negative result also in China. Using a global sample, Karolyi and Liao (2017) indicate less positive market reactions for targets to SOMNE acquisitions are influenced by selection bias: Controlling for target characteristics, they find SOMNE acquisitions to instead have better performance.

Zhang et al. (2011) find state ownership in Chinese MNEs hinders completion of foreign acquisitions, which is ascribed to opposition in host countries. However, Li et al. (2017) find that state ownership does not affect the completion rate of M&As, although deals take longer to complete.

Xiao et al. (2013) find incorporated firms (including state-owned ones), privately owned firms, and foreign owned firms to benefit more from internationalisation than (unincorporated) state-owned firms and collective enterprises. The authors also find centralised state ownership to positively moderate the internationalisation-performance relationship. Benito et al. (2016) study Norwegian publicly listed enterprises, finding some evidence that SOEs benefit more from internationalisation than do POEs.

Home and Host-Country Effects

Despite current concerns in many host countries about SOMNEs, related to "unfair competition" and "national security" concerns, and leading to high-profile cases such as CNOOC and Dubai Ports' failed acquisition attempts in the US (Shapiro and Globerman 2012; Reddy et al. 2016), and concerns about SOMNEs' effects on international trade (Kowalski et al. 2013), very little systematic evidence exists on their host-country effects. Interestingly, current debates resemble those in the US in the 1970s. Lamont (1979) proposed, among other things, to create US SOEs in resource industries, while Monsen and Walters (1983) suggested a review unit for foreign SOE investments. Various host-country responses to SOMNEs were also discussed by Aharoni and Seidler (1986). Interestingly, Prasad (1986) found American business leaders were little concerned about competition from foreign SOMNEs. Aharoni (1980) reminded that many private firms also receive substantial support from their governments. Also, costs associated with various government objectives (Anastassopoulos et al. 1987) imposed on an SOE may be equivalent to a tax (Kowalski et al. 2013) counteracting any subsidies they receive.

Strikingly, little is known even about home-country effects of SOMNEs, despite potential theoretical benefits (Rygh 2018) and the apparent willingness of home governments to support SOMNEs. A single study of this question found that SOE social objectives may be weakened in favour of profit objectives when SOEs go abroad (Clifton et al. 2016).

Concluding Remarks

This review covering five decades has demonstrated that state ownership often has effects on international strategies. However, such effects seem to depend on contextual and historical factors such as the home country's economic development level and institutions (see also Aharoni 2018; Colli et al. 2014). A domestic bias and preference for greenfields of European SOMNEs contrast with the key role of state ownership and a preference for acquisitions by emerging market MNEs, in particular from China. However, even for China there seem to be indications of change as private MNEs play an increasingly important role in the home economy. Improved SOMNE governance and greater focus on financial outcomes may play a role (Musacchio and Lazzarini 2018), although similar arguments were made regarding European SOMNEs already by Lamont (1979). Also, little is known about SOMNE international performance or home and host-country effects.

Future reviews could explore in more detail these results and their implications. The much stronger linkages to core international business theories in recent literature, despite early theory-driven studies such as Collins (1986), are another interesting aspect. Finally, although comprehensive, our review is not exhaustive. Future reviews could consider further SOMNE research topics including transparency (Cannizzaro and Weiner 2018), responsible investments (Vasudeva 2013), local responsiveness (Wei and Nguyen 2017), and role in global value chains (Horner 2017). New studies continuously emerge in this vibrant research area and an updated review will soon be needed.

Acknowledgements We thank Gabriel R.G. Benito, Jeremy Clegg, Birgitte Grøgaard, Philipp Strobl, Hinrich Voss, and participants at BI Norwegian Business School seminars, the 2014 SMS Conference, the 2016 EIBA Conference, and the 2018 AIB-UK&I Conference for helpful comments.

References

Aharoni, Y. (1980). The state owned Enterprise as a competitor in international markets. *Columbia Journal of World Business, 15*(1), 14–22.

Aharoni, Y. (1981). Managerial discretion. In Y. Aharoni & R. Vernon (Eds.), *State-owned enterprise in the Western economies* (pp. 184–193). London: Croom Helm.

Aharoni, Y. (1982). State-owned enterprise: An agent without a principal. In L. Jones (Ed.), *Public enterprise in less-developed countries* (pp. 67–76). Cambridge: Cambridge University Press.

Aharoni, Y. (1986). *The evolution and management of state owned enterprises.* Cambridge, MA: Ballinger.

Aharoni, Y. (2013). The road to relevance. *Advances in International Management, 26*, 127–169.

Aharoni, Y. (2018). The evolution of state-owned multinational enterprise theory. In A. Cuervo-Cazurra (Ed.), *State-owned multinationals: Governments in global business.* (pp. 9–44). Cham, Switzerland: Springer International Publishing.

Aharoni, Y., & Seidler, L. K. (1986). Foreign subsidiaries of state-owned enterprises: Host country responses. In A. R. Negandhi, H. Thomas, & K. L. K. Rao (Eds.), *Multinational corporations and state-owned enterprises: A new challenge in international business* (pp. 151–162). London: JAI Press.

Alonso, J. M., Clifton, J., Díaz-Fuentes, D., Fernández-Gutiérrez, M., & Revuelta, J. (2013). The race for international markets: Were privatized telecommunications incumbents more successful than their public counterparts? *International Review of Applied Economics, 27*(2), 215–236.

Amighini, A. A., Sanfilippo, M., & Rabellotti, R. (2013). Do Chinese state-owned and private enterprises differ in their internationalization strategies? *China Economic Review, 27*, 312–325.

Anastassopoulos, J.-P., Blanc, G., & Dussauge, P. (1987). *State-owned multinationals.* New York: Wiley.

Bass, A. E., & Chakrabarty, S. (2014). Resource security: Competition for global resources, strategic intent, and governments as owners. *Journal of International Business Studies, 45*(8), 961–979.

Benito, G. R. G., Lunnan, R., & Tomassen, S. (2011). Distant encounters of the third kind: Multinational companies locating divisional headquarters abroad. *Journal of Management Studies, 48*(2), 373–394.

Benito, G. R. G., Rygh, A., & Lunnan, R. (2016). The benefits of internationalization for state owned enterprises. *Global Strategy Journal, 6*(4), 269–288.

Bernard, J.-T., & Weiner, R. J. (1996). Export pricing in state-owned and private MNEs: Evidence from the international petroleum market. *International Journal of Industrial Organization, 14*(5), 647–668.

Boyd, C. W. (1986). The comparative efficiency of state owned enterprises. In A. R. Negandhi, H. Thomas, & K. L. K. Rao (Eds.), *Multinational corporations and state-owned enterprises: A new challenge in international business* (pp. 179–194). London: JAI Press.

Buckley, P. J., Jeremy Clegg, L., Cross, A. R., Liu, X., Voss, H., & Zheng, P. (2007). The determinants of Chinese outward foreign direct investment. *Journal of International Business Studies, 38*(4), 499–518.

Buckley, P. J., Cross, A. R., Tan, H., Xin, L., & Voss, H. (2008). Historic and emergent trends in Chinese outward direct investment. *Management International Review, 48*(6), 715–748.

Cahen, F. R. (2015). Internationalization of state-owned enterprises through foreign direct investment. *Revista de Administração de Empresas, 55*(6), 645–659.

Cannizzaro, A. P., & Weiner, R. J. (2018). State ownership and transparency in foreign direct investment. *Journal of International Business Studies, 49*(2), 172–195.

Chen, Y. Y., & Young, M. N. (2010). Cross-border mergers and acquisitions by Chinese listed companies: A principal–principal perspective. *Asia Pacific Journal of Management, 27*(3), 523–539.

Choudhury, P., & Khanna, T. (2014). Toward resource independence-why state-owned entities become multinationals: An empirical study of India's public R&D laboratories. *Journal of International Business Studies, 45*(8), 943–960.

Clegg, L. J., Voss, H., & Tardios, J. A. (2018). The autocratic advantage: Internationalization of state-owned multinationals. *Journal of World Business.* https://doi.org/10.1016/j.jwb.2018.03.009.

Clifton, J., Fuentes, D. D., & Warner, M. (2016). The loss of public values when public shareholders go abroad. *Utilities Policy, 40*, 134–143.

Colli, A., Mariotti, S., & Piscitello, L. (2014). Governments as strategists in designing global players: The case of European utilities. *Journal of European Public Policy, 21*(4), 487–508.

Collins, P. (1986). Multinational state-owned enterprises and the eclectic theory. In A. R. Negandhi, H. Thomas, & K. L. K. Rao (Eds.), *Multinational corporations and state-owned enterprises: A new challenge in international business* (pp. 43–58). London: JAI Press.

Cuervo-Cazurra, A. (2018). State-owned multinationals: An introduction. In A. Cuervo-Cazurra (Ed.), *State-owned multinationals: Governments in global business* (pp. 1–6). Cham, Switzerland: Springer International Publishing.

Cuervo-Cazurra, A., Inkpen, A., Musacchio, A., & Ramaswamy, K. (2014). Governments as owners: State-owned multinational companies. *Journal of International Business Studies, 45*(8), 919–942.

Cui, L., & Jiang, F. (2012). State ownership effect on firms' FDI ownership decisions under institutional pressure: A study of Chinese outward-investing firms. *Journal of International Business Studies, 43*(3), 264–284.

Del Bo, C. D., Ferraris, M., & Florio, M. (2017). Governments in the market for corporate control: Evidence from M&A deals involving state-owned enterprises. *Journal of Comparative Economics, 45*(1), 89–109.

Ding, X. L. (2000). Informal privatization through internationalization: The rise of Nomenklatura capitalism in China's offshore businesses. *British Journal of Political Science, 30*(1), 121–146.

Dresang, D. L., & Sharkansky, I. (1965). Public corporations in single-country and regional settings: Kenya and the East African community. *Integration, 19*(4), 303–328.

Du, M., & Boateng, A. (2015). State ownership, institutional effects and value creation in cross-border mergers & acquisitions by Chinese firms. *International Business Review, 24*(3), 430–442.

Du, M., Boateng, A., & Newton, D. (2015). The impact of state ownership, formal institutions and resource seeking on acquirers' returns of Chinese M&A. *Review of Quantitative Finance and Accounting, 47*(1), 159–178.

Duanmu, J.-L. (2012). Firm heterogeneity and location choice of Chinese multinational enterprises (MNEs). *Journal of World Business, 47*(1), 64–72.

Duanmu, J.-L. (2014). State-owned MNCs and host country expropriation risk: The role of home state soft power and economic gunboat diplomacy. *Journal of International Business Studies, 45*(8), 1044–1060.

Eliassen, K. A., & Grøgaard, B. (2007). Internationalisation. In J. From & K. A. Eliassen (Eds.), *The privatisation of European telecommunications* (pp. 241–255). Burlington: Ashgate Publishing.

Estrin, S., Meyer, K. E., Nielsen, B. B., & Nielsen, S. (2016). Home country institutions and the internationalization of state owned enterprises: A cross-country analysis. *Journal of World Business, 51*(2), 294–307.

Florio, M. (2013). Rethinking on public Enterprise: Editorial introduction and some personal remarks on the research agenda. *International Review of Applied Economics, 27*(2), 135–149.

Franko, L. G. (1975). Patterns in the multinational spread of continental European enterprise. *Journal of International Business Studies, 6*(2), 41–53.

Gao, L., Liu, X., & Lioliou, E. (2015). A double-edged sword: The impact of institutions and political relations on the international market expansion of Chinese state-owned enterprises. *Journal of Chinese Economic and Business Studies, 13*(2), 105–125.

García-Canal, E., & Guillén, M. F. (2008). Risk and the strategy of foreign location choice in regulated industries. *Strategic Management Journal, 29*(10), 1097–1115.

Gaur, A. S., Kumar, V., & Sarathy, R. (2011). Liability of foreignness and internationalization of emerging market firms. *Advances in International Management, 24*, 211–233.

Götz, M., & Jankowska, B. (2016). Internationalization by State-Owned Enterprises (SOEs) and Sovereign Wealth Funds (SWFs) after the 2008 crisis. Looking for generalizations. *International Journal of Management and Economics, 50*(1), 63–81.

Guo, W., & Clougherty, J. A. (2015). The effectiveness of the state in Chinese outward foreign direct investment: The "go global" policy and state-owned enterprises. *Advances in International Management, 28*, 141–159.

Guo, W., Clougherty, J. A., & Duso, T. (2016). Why are Chinese MNEs not financially competitive in cross-border acquisitions? The role of state ownership. *Long Range Planning, 49*, 614–631.

Gwiazda, A. (1985). Eastern block international enterprises: Still in Statu Nascendi. *Management International Review, 25*(3), 57–64.

Hafsi, T., & Koenig, C. (1988). The state-SOE relationship – Some patterns. *Journal of Management Studies, 25*(3), 235–249.

Hafsi, T., & Thomas, H. (1988). Understanding the international competitive behavior of state-owned enterprises. *International Studies of Management & Organization, 18*(2), 60–82.

He, X., Eden, L., & Hitt, M. A. (2016a). The renaissance of state-owned multinationals. *Thunderbird International Business Review, 58*(2), 117–129.

He, X., Eden, L., & Hitt, M. A. (2016b). Shared governance: Institutional investors as a counterbalance to the state in state owned multinationals. *Journal of International Management, 22*(2), 115–130.

Hennart, J.-F., Sheng, H. H., & Marcos Carrera, J. (2017). Openness, international champions, and the internationalization of Multilatinas. *Journal of World Business, 52*(4), 518–532.

Hobdari, B., Gregoric, A., & Sinani, E. (2011). The role of firm ownership on internationalization: Evidence from two transition economies. *Journal of Management & Governance, 15*(3), 393–413.

Hong, J., Wang, C., & Kafouros, M. (2014). The role of the state in explaining the internationalization of emerging market enterprises. *British Journal of Management, 26*, 45–62.

Horner, R. (2017). Beyond facilitator? State roles in global value chains and global production networks. *Geography Compass, 11*(2), 1–13.

Hu, H. W., & Cui, L. (2014). Outward foreign direct investment of publicly listed firms from China: A corporate governance perspective. *International Business Review, 23*(4), 750–760.

Huang, Y., Xie, E., Li, Y., & Reddy, K. S. (2017). Does state ownership facilitate outward FDI of Chinese SOEs? Institutional development, market competition, and the logic of interdependence between governments and SOEs. *International Business Review, 26*(1), 176–188.

Hveem, H., Knutsen, C. H., & Rygh, A. (2012). State ownership, political risk and foreign direct investment. In K. Eliassen (Ed.), *Business and politics in a new global order* (pp. 89–110). Oslo: Gyldendal Norsk Forlag AS.

Jandhyala, S., & Weiner, R. J. (2014). Institutions Sans Frontières: International agreements and foreign investment. *Journal of International Business Studies, 45*(6), 649–669.

Jones, L., & Wortzel, L. (1982). Public enterprise and manufactured exports in less-developed countries: Institutional and market factors determining comparative advantage. In L. Jones (Ed.), *Public enterprise in less developed countries* (pp. 217–242). Cambridge: Cambridge University Press.

Kalotay, K., & Sulstarova, A. (2010). Modelling Russian outward FDI. *Journal of International Management, 16*(2), 131–142.

Kaplinsky, R., & Morris, M. (2009). Chinese FDI in Sub-Saharan Africa: Engaging with large dragons. *European Journal of Development Research, 21*(4), 551–569.

Karolyi, G. A., & Liao, R. C. (2017). State capitalism's global reach: Evidence from foreign acquisitions by state-owned companies. *Journal of Corporate Finance, 42*, 367–391.

Katz, J., & Kosacoff, B. (1983). Multinationals from Argentina. In S. Lall (Ed.), *The new multinationals: The spread of third world enterprises* (pp. 137–219). New York: Wiley.

Kaynak, E. (1989). Managing firms across borders: Operating organisations' behaviour and strategy formulation in public enterprises. *International Journal of Public Sector Management, 2*(2), 28–42.

Khandwalla, P. N. (1986). Performance determinants of public enterprises: Significance and implications for multinationalization. In A. R. Negandhi, H. Thomas, & K. L. K. Rao (Eds.), *Multinational corporations and state-owned enterprises: A new challenge in international business* (pp. 195–220). London: JAI Press.

Knutsen, C. H., Rygh, A., & Hveem, H. (2011). Does state ownership matter? Institutions' effect on foreign direct investment revisited. *Business and Politics, 13*(1), art. 2.

Kostecki, M. (1981). State trading. In Y. Aharoni & R. Vernon (Eds.), *State-owned enterprise in the Western economies* (pp. 170–183). London: Croom Helm.

Kowalski, P., Büge, M., Sztajerowska, M., & Egeland, M. 2013. *State-owned enterprises* (OECD Trade Policy Paper no. 147). Paris: OECD Publishing.

Kumar, K. (1981). Multinationalization of third-world public sector enterprises. In K. Kumar & M. G. MacLeod (Eds.), *Multinationals from developing countries* (pp. 187–201). Lexington: D.C. Heath, Lexington Books.

Lamont, D. F. (1973). Joining forces with foreign state enterprises. *Harvard Business Review, 51*(4), 68–79.

Lamont, D. F. (1979). *Foreign state enterprises: A threat to American business.* New York: Basic Books.

Landoni, M. (2018). Corporatization and internationalization of state-owned enterprises: The role of institutional intermediaries. *International Journal of Public Sector Management, 31*(2), 221–240.

Laux, J. K. (1983). Expanding the state: The international relations of state-owned enterprises in Canada. *Polity, 15*(3), 329–350.

Laux, J. K. (1984). Public enterprises and Canadian foreign economic policy. *Publius: The Journal of Federalism, 14*(4), 61–80.

Lee, Y., Hemmert, M., & Kim, J. (2014). What drives the international ownership strategies of Chinese firms? The role of distance and home-country institutional factors in outward acquisitions. *Asian Business & Management, 13*(3), 197–225.

Li, J., & Oh, C. H. (2016). Research on emerging-market multinational enterprises: Extending Alan Rugman's critical contributions. *International Business Review, 25*(3), 776–784.

Li, J., & Xie, Z. (2013). Examining the cross-border acquisition strategy of Chinese companies: The moderating roles of state ownership and institutional transition. *Journal of Leadership & Organizational Studies, 20*(4), 436–447.

Li, M. H., Cui, L., & Lu, J. (2014). Varieties in state capitalism: Outward FDI strategies of central and local state-owned enterprises from emerging economy countries. *Journal of International Business Studies, 45*(8), 980–1004.

Li, J., Xia, J., & Lin, Z. (2017). Cross-border acquisitions by state-owned firms: How do legitimacy concerns affect the completion and duration of their acquisitions? *Strategic Management Journal, 38*(9), 1915–1934.

Liang, H., Ren, B., & Sun, S. L. (2014). An anatomy of state control in the globalization of state-owned enterprises. *Journal of International Business Studies, 46*, 223–240.

Lien, Y.-C., Piesse, J., Strange, R., & Filatotchev, I. (2005). The role of corporate governance in FDI decisions: Evidence from Taiwan. *International Business Review, 14*(6), 739–763.

Lin, X., & Farrell, C. (2013). The internationalization strategies of Chinese state and private sector Enterprises in Africa. *Journal of African Business, 14*(2), 85–95.

Majocchi, A., & Strange, R. (2012). International diversification. *Management International Review, 52*, 1–22.

Martin, X., & Li, C. (2015). What do we know about state-owned emerging-economy firms, and how? Evaluating literature about inward and outward multinational activities. *Advances in International Management, 28*, 403–439.

Mascarenhas, B. (1989). Domains of state-owned, privately held, and publicly traded firms in international competition. *Administrative Science Quarterly, 34*(4), 582–597.

Mazzolini, R. (1979a). European government-controlled enterprises: Explaining international strategic and policy decisions. *Journal of International Business Studies, 10*(3), 16–27.

Mazzolini, R. (1979b). *Government controlled enterprises: International strategic and policy decisions.* Chichester/New York: Wiley.

Mazzolini, R. (1980a). European government-controlled enterprises: An organizational politics view. *Journal of International Business Studies, 11*, 48–58.

Mazzolini, R. (1980b). Government controlled enterprises-What's the difference? *Columbia Journal of World Business, 15*(2), 28–39.

Mazzolini, R. (1980c). Government policies and government controlled enterprises. *Columbia Journal of World Business, 15*(3), 47–54.

Mazzolini, R. (1980d). The international strategy of state-owned firms: An organizational process and politics perspective. *Strategic Management Journal, 1*(2), 101–118.

Megginson, W. L., & Netter, J. M. (2001). From state to market: A survey of empirical studies on privatization. *Journal of Economic Literature, 39*(2), 321–389.

Meyer, K. E., Ding, Y., Li, J., & Zhang, H. (2014). Overcoming distrust: How state-owned enterprises adapt their foreign entries to institutional pressures abroad. *Journal of International Business Studies, 45*(8), 1005–1028.

Miroudot, S., & Ragoussis, A. (2013). New actors in the international investment scenario: Objectives, performance and advantages of affiliates of state-owned enterprises and sovereign wealth funds. In R. Echandi & P. Sauvé (Eds.), *Prospects in international investment law and policy* (pp. 51–72). Cambridge: World Trade Forum.

Monsen, R. J., & Walters, K. D. (1983). *Nationalized companies: A threat to American business.* New York: McGraw-Hill.

Morck, R., Yeung, B., & Zhao, M. (2008). Perspectives on China's outward foreign direct investment. *Journal of International Business Studies, 39*(3), 337–350.

Musacchio, A., & Lazzarini, S. G. (2018). State-owned enterprises as multinationals: Theory and research directions. In A. Cuervo-Cazurra (Ed.), *State-owned multinationals: Governments in global business* (pp. 255–276). Cham, Switzerland: Springer International Publishing.

Negandhi, A. R., & Ganguly, S. (1986). Comparing private and public enterprises in an international context: Some hypotheses. In A. R. Negandhi, H. Thomas, & K. L. K. Rao (Eds.), *Multinational corporations and state-owned enterprises: A new challenge in international business* (pp. 13–42). London: JAI Press.

Negandhi, A. R., Thomas, H., & Emmons, W. (1986). State-owned enterprises: A new challenge. In A. R. Negandhi, H. Thomas, & K. L. K. Rao (Eds.), *Multinational corporations and state-owned enterprises: A new challenge in international business* (pp. 1–9). London: JAI Press.

Nielsen, R. P. (1981). Competitive advantages of state owned and controlled businesses. *Management International Review, 21*(3), 56–66.

Ning, L., Kuo, J.-M., Strange, R., & Wang, B. (2014). International investors' reactions to cross-border acquisitions by emerging market multinationals. *International Business Review, 23*, 811–823.

Noreng, Ø. (1981). State-owned oil companies: Western Europe. In R. Vernon & Y. Aharoni (Eds.), *State-owned enterprise in the Western economies* (pp. 133–144). New York: St. Martin's Press.

Pan, Y., Teng, L., Supapol, A. B., Lu, X., Huang, D., & Wang, Z. (2014). Firms' FDI ownership: The influence of government ownership and legislative connections. *Journal of International Business Studies, 45*(8), 919–942.

Prasad, S. B. (1986). American executives' perception of foreign state enterprises. *Journal of International Business Studies, 17*(2), 145–152.

Radetzki, M. (1989). The role of state owned enterprises in the international metal mining industry. *Resources Policy, 15*(1), 45–57.

Ramasamy, B., Yeung, M., & Laforet, S. (2012). China's outward foreign direct investment: Location choice and firm ownership. *Journal of World Business, 47*, 17–25.

Rapp, L. (1986). *Public Multinational Enterprises and Strategic Decision-Making* (ILO Multinational Enterprises Programme Working Paper no. 34). Geneva: International Labour Organisation.

Reddy, K. S., Xie, E., & Huang, Y. (2016). Cross-border acquisitions by state-owned and private enterprises: A perspective from emerging economies. *Journal of Policy Modeling, 38*, 1147–1170.

Rodrigues, S. B., & Dieleman, M. (2018). The internationalization paradox: Untangling dependence in multinational state hybrids. *Journal of World Business, 53*(1), 39–51.

Rodrik, D. (1982). Changing patterns of ownership and integration in the international Bauxite-Aluminium industry. In L. Jones (Ed.), *Public enterprise in less developed countries* (pp. 189–215). Cambridge: Cambridge University Press.

Rudy, B. C., Miller, S. R., & Wang, D. (2016). Revisiting FDI strategies and the flow of firm-specific advantages: A focus on state-owned enterprises. *Global Strategy Journal, 6*(1), 69–78.

Rugman, A. M., & Li, J. (2007). Will China's multinationals succeed globally or regionally? *European Management Journal, 25*(5), 333–343.

Rygh, A. (2018). Welfare effects of state owned multinational enterprises: A view from agency and incomplete contracts theory. *International Journal of Public Sector Management, 31*(2), 207–220.

Shapiro, D. M., & Globerman, S. (2012). The international activities and effects of state-owned enterprises. In K. Sauvant, L. Sachs, & W. S. Jongbloed (Eds.), *Sovereign investment: Concerns and policy reactions* (pp. 98–141). New York: Oxford University Press.

Shi, W., Hoskisson, R. E., & Zhang, Y. A. (2016). A geopolitical perspective into the opposition to globalizing state-owned enterprises in target states. *Global Strategy Journal, 6*(1), 13–30.

Strange, R. (2018). Corporate ownership and the theory of the multinational enterprise. *International Business Review.* https://doi.org/10.1016/j.ibusrev. 2018.05.004.

Tao, F., Liu, X., Gao, L., & Xia, E. (2017). Do cross-border mergers and acquisitions increase short-term market performance? The case of Chinese firms. *International Business Review, 26*(1), 189–202.

UNCTAD. (2013). *World investment report 2013*. Geneva: UNCTAD.

UNCTAD. (2017). *World investment report 2017*. Geneva: UNCTAD.

Vasudeva, G. (2013). Weaving together the normative and regulative roles of government: How the Norwegian sovereign wealth fund's responsible conduct is shaping firms' cross-border investments. *Organization Science, 24*(6), 1662–1682.

Vernon, R. (1979). The international aspects of state-owned enterprises. *Journal of International Business Studies, 10*(3), 7–15.

Vernon, R., & Levy, B. (1982). State-owned enterprises in the world economy: The case of iron ore. In L. Jones (Ed.), *Public enterprise in less developed countries* (pp. 169–188). Cambridge: Cambridge University Press.

Wang, M. Y. (2002). The motivations behind China's government-initiated industrial investments overseas. *Pacific Affairs, 75*(2), 187–206.

Wang, C., Hong, J., Kafouros, M., & Boateng, A. (2012a). What drives outward FDI of Chinese firms? Testing the explanatory power of three theoretical frameworks. *International Business Review, 21*(3), 425–438.

Wang, C., Hong, J., Kafouros, M., & Wright, M. (2012b). Exploring the role of government involvement in outward FDI from emerging economies. *Journal of International Business Studies, 43*, 655–676.

Wei, Z., & Nguyen, Q. T. K. (2017). Subsidiary strategy of emerging market multinationals: A home country institutional perspective. *International Business Review, 26*(5), 1009–1021.

Wei, T., Clegg, J., & Ma, L. (2015). The conscious and unconscious facilitating role of the Chinese government in shaping the internationalization of Chinese MNCs. *International Business Review, 24*(2), 331–343.

Wettenhall, R. (1992). The globalisation of public enterprise: Some Australian evidence. *Australian Journal of Public Administration, 51*(2), 184–197.

Wettenhall, R. (1993). The globalization of public enterprises. *International Review of Administrative Sciences, 59*(3), 387–408.

World Bank. (1995). *Bureaucrats in business: The economics and politics of government ownership*. Washington, DC: World Bank.

Xia, J., Ma, X., Lu, J. W., & Yiu, D. W. (2013). Outward foreign direct investment by emerging market firms: A resource dependence logic. *Strategic Management Journal, 35*, 1343–1363.

Xiao, S. S., Jeong, I., Moon, J. J., Chung, C. C., & Chung, J. (2013). Internationalization and performance of firms in China: Moderating effects of governance structure and the degree of centralized control. *Journal of International Management, 19*(2), 118–137.

Xie, E., & Redding, K. S. (2018). State-owned enterprises in the contemporary global business scenario: Introduction. *International Journal of Public Sector Management, 31*(2), 98–112.

Yang, M., & Deng, P. (2015). Cross-border M&As by Chinese companies in advanced countries: Antecedents and implications. *Thunderbird International Business Review, 59*(3), 263–280.

Young, S., Huang, C.-H., & McDermott, M. (1996). Internationalization and competitive catch-up processes: Case study evidence on Chinese multinational enterprises. *Management International Review, 36*, 295–314.

Zhang, J., Zhou, C., & Ebbers, H. (2011). Completion of Chinese overseas acquisitions: Institutional perspectives and evidence. *International Business Review, 20*(2), 226–238.

Part II

Paths to Performance and Current Perspectives on Emerging Markets

Much of the received wisdom in international business is based upon studies focusing on developed economies. However, emerging economies have also become increasingly important. As such, it is necessary for both researchers and practitioners to understand the internal and external dynamics of doing business within these markets.

Although emerging markets are economically, politically and institutionally different they possess the potential for high rewards for companies regardless of their size. After all, such markets offer a significant pool of a growing global demand as well as an availability of highly skilled and cost-competitive labour force.

Such advantages drive the growing need to understand the factors that influence firm's behaviour as well as performance in and from emerging markets within the international business context. Therefore, by including five chapters, the aim of the second chapter is to provide a reader with an insight into the paths to performance and current perspectives on emerging markets.

The first chapter (Chap. 4) titled "Contextual Transfer Barriers, Social Interaction, and Innovation Transfer Performance" by Olivia H. Kang and Pao T. Kao provides a meaningful discussion into the topic of transfer barriers that exist in organizations. Using a mixed method approach from 25 Swedish multinational companies and their R&D centres in China, the authors show that knowledge shared within multinational companies is impacted by contextual barriers and that social interactions between sending and receiving such knowledge play a vital role in helping to overcome contextual barriers.

Chapter 5, titled "Equity Ownership Strategy in Greenfield Investments: Influences of Host Country Infrastructure and MNE Resources in Emerging Markets", by Ahmad Arslan, Jorma Larimo and Desislava Dikova, provides an interesting discussion concerning equity ownership strategies in 922 greenfield investments by Nordic multinational companies in emerging markets. Using resource dependence theory as their theoretical underpinning and a secondary data, the authors demonstrate that host country investment experience moderates the effect of physical infrastructure on equity ownership strategy.

Chapter 6, titled "The Value of Local Externalities in Country-of-Origin Clusters: Evidence from China" by Berrbizne Urzelai and Francisco Puig, highlights the perceptions of the role that country-of-origin clusters play in a sample of 24 managers from European small and medium enterprises' subsidiaries located in China and suggests that the higher value of the externalities is perceived in the dimensions of networking and legitimacy as well as when the subsidiary pursues simultaneously efficiency and markets in their investments.

Chapter 7, titled "Acquirer's Country of Origin and Target Firm's Performance", by Jinlong Gu, Yong Yang and Roger Strange, addresses ambiguity in the literation pertaining to foreign acquisitions and target firm performance by examining the relationship between the type of acquisition and performance between foreign and domestic acquisitions from 45 economies between 2004 and 2013. Theoretically anchored on internalization theory, this work suggests that the acquisition type does impact target firm performance and that firms acquired by foreign organizations perform better than those acquired by domestic organizations.

The final chapter (Chap. 8), titled "Human Rights Reporting of BRIC and Non-BRIC MNEs: An Exploratory Comparative Analysis" by Stefan Zagelmeyer, examines the issue of international business and human rights through the lens of non-financial, corporate reporting practices in order to better understand the similarities and divergences of human rights reporting across countries and between multinational enterprises from BRIC and non-BRIC countries. Using a secondary data and drawing on a randomly selected multinational companies, the author finds that human rights reporting will dissipate when multinational companies within emerging economies mature.

4

Contextual Transfer Barriers, Social Interaction, and Innovation Transfer Performance

Olivia H. Kang and Pao T. Kao

Introduction

When multinational corporations (MNCs) intend to share knowledge and transfer innovation to their overseas subsidiaries as well as partners (e.g., suppliers and customers), there are often barriers to hinder their efforts. There are direct barriers, such as lack of willingness to send or receive (Katz and Allen 1982; Michailova and Husted 2003), as well as insufficient capability to transfer or absorb new knowledge (Allen 1977; Cohen and Levinthal 1990; Szulanski 1996). Typically, these barriers exist in sending organizations, receiving organizations, or both, and can prohibit the knowledge sharing process.[1]

There are also barriers presented in the context where knowledge sharing processes are taken place (Ambos et al. 2006; Gupta and Govindarajan 1994; Simonin 1999; Szulanski 1996). For instance, there can be strong difference in cultural and institutional settings in senders and receiver's respective countries (Ado et al. 2016; Busse et al. 2016; Ho et al. 2017; Lin et al. 2008). Additionally, the technological standards adopted by senders and receivers

---

[1] We use senders and receivers in this chapter to simply refer to the two organizations involved in the transfer. We are aware that the use of sender-receiver could bring out an assumption that there is a specific communication channel involved (Noorderhaven and Harzing 2009), and we do not held this assumption in this study.

O. H. Kang • P. T. Kao (✉)
Department of Business Studies, Uppsala University, Uppsala, Sweden
e-mail: Olivia.Kang@fek.uu.se; Pao.Kao@fek.uu.se

© The Author(s) 2019
A. Chidlow et al. (eds.), *The Changing Strategies of International Business*, The Academy of International Business, https://doi.org/10.1007/978-3-030-03931-8_4

can also be varied in different parts of the world (Dyer and Hatch 2006). Lastly, the markets where senders and receivers are located can also be in different stage of development and condition (Buckley et al. 2003; Busse et al. 2016). These contextual barriers exist in the surrounding environment, rather than in the organization per se. As such, despite being aware of these contextual barriers and their potential influence on the process of knowledge sharing (Busse et al. 2016), it is rather difficult for MNCs to alter or change them directly.

While past studies have tended to focus on the transfer barriers that exist in the organizations, the influences of contextual barriers on knowledge sharing process have received relatively limited attention. Particularly for the transfer within an organization, scholars tend to look for factors internally hindering the transfer process such as sender's motivation and involvement (Björkman et al. 2004; Ciabuschi et al. 2011; Gupta and Govindarajan 2000); receiver's motivation and capability (Gupta and Govindarajan 2000; Lane et al. 2001), as well as receiver's autonomy (Ciabuschi et al. 2012; Noorderhaven and Harzing 2009; Szulanski 1996). The contextual barriers are rather overlooked, as literature generally assumes external obstacles do not matter much particularly when knowledge is shared within MNCs (Szulanski 1996). Yet, studies have shown that, in a mature stage of a joint venture, contextual barriers still play a relative important role affecting knowledge sharing process. Hence, there is a lack of understanding and gap in literature on MNCs handling contextual barriers during the process of sharing knowledge and innovation transfer.

In this study, we want to fill this gap by investigating contextual barriers' influence on MNCs innovation transfer process. More specifically, we aim to answer following questions: How MNCs address contextual barriers through social interactions? And what effects these social interactions have on innovation transfer performance? Social interactions, that is, interpersonal connection building and social network developing, are proved to be an effective tool for knowledge sharing and innovation transfer within MNCs (Maurer et al. 2011; Noorderhaven and Harzing 2009; Vahlne and Johanson 2017).

Social interactions describe a range of activities held between senders and receivers, for instance, face-to-face meeting, temporary task team, and workshop and conference. Participating individuals establish and develop social relations during these occasions, and create social capital (Adler and Kwon 2002). With social capital, a collaborative and a supportive environment can be sustained and enable MNCs to address contextual barriers and facilitate knowledge sharing and innovation transfer (Inkpen and Tsang 2005; Kostova and Roth 2003).

Therefore, we adopt a sequential mixed-method research design integrating survey and interview data to understand the impact of social interactions on the contextual barriers and transfer performance. Our findings show that, in contrast to conventional wisdom, knowledge sharing within MNCs will be impacted by contextual barriers. Social interactions between sending and receiving units play a vital role for MNCs to overcome contextual barriers. Yet, there is a price to pay in terms of the efficiency of the transfer, as social interaction may take time to organize and can be costly. Hence, our study contributes to the continue discussions of knowledge sharing within MNCs, and shed light on the double-edge role of social interaction in innovation transfer.

The chapter is organized as follows: the next section reviews the literature on social interactions and contextual transfer barriers. The method section covers a mixed-method research design, operationalization of variables, and data collection. This is followed by analysis, result, and discussion. Lastly, a concluding remark, implications for management, and topics for future research is presented.

Literature Review and Conceptual Framework

Contextual Transfer Barrier and Transfer Performance

Literature has long been argued that MNCs enjoy a competitive advantage on sharing knowledge within the boundary of the firm relatively uncomplicated and easy manner (Kogut and Zander 1993; Zander and Kogut 1995). Innovation invented in the headquarters or subsidiaries can be transferred to other part of the corporation across the international border (Bartlett and Ghoshal 1989; Gupta and Govindarajan 2000). Although the view on MNCs has gradually shifted from a centrally and hierarchically constructed organization (Buckley and Casson 1976; Dunning 1980) to a dispersed network with units embedded in various environments (Ghoshal and Bartlett 1990; Forsgren et al. 2006), the ability to facilitate and coordinate knowledge flow remain to be a core advantage of MNCs, and an important research topic for management scholars (Ambos et al. 2006; Björkman et al. 2004; Ciabuschi et al. 2011, 2012).

Knowledge sharing is not easy even if it is within MNCs, and it has been widely discussed in the International Business literature (see a review by Hutzschenreuter and Matt 2017). While most of the researches focus on factors resided in either or both sending and receiving units, we find very little attention paid to the contextual barriers affecting the process and performance of knowledge sharing in MNCs. It might be the case that MNCs are assumed to be an entity with strong shared organizational culture, and therefore the transfer made within should not be interfered much by the factors outside the organizations (Ambos et al. 2006; Szulanski 1996).

However, MNCs and their subsidiaries are embedded in home and host countries with significant difference in institutional environment (Eden and Miller 2004; Xu and Shenkar 2002). The institutional distance has a clear impact on the success of transferring routines within MNCs (Kostova and Roth 2002; Zaheer 1995). In fact, subsidiaries of MNCs in respective host countries are influenced by distinctive socialization process based on local and national context (Kostova et al. 2008; Phillips and Tracey 2009). These differences can pose contextual barriers and challenges to the knowledge sharing process (Forsgren 1997).

Contextual barriers are defined as factors that exist in the environment which hinder the flow of knowledge between sending and receiving units (Ambos et al. 2006; Busse et al. 2016; Gupta and Govindarajan 1994; Simonin 1999). Contextual barriers are difficult to change, as they exist in the external environment of the organizations. Culture differences are found to be a major obstruction to the communication, which can make knowledge sharing challenging (Busse et al. 2016; Lin et al. 2008). Individual involved in knowledge sharing may misread cues and cause misunderstandings because of their ignorance of the counterpart's culture (Busse et al. 2016). Different institutions can have great variety of organization routine and management control system. Knowledge or innovation may need to be translated or interpreted so that it can be understood from a receiving unit's point of view (Gupta and Govindarajan 1994; Ho et al. 2017).

Additionally, technological standards adopted by sending and receiving units can also be varied in different parts of the world. Although modification may not be difficult, it will still take extra effort to do so (Dyer and Hatch 2006). Lastly, the market condition where sending and receiving units are located may also be distinctive. It will be problematic for sending unit to impose certain innovations that simply is susceptible to market conditions (Buckley et al. 2003; Busse et al. 2016). We propose these following hypotheses:

Hypothesis 1a Contextual barriers are negatively related with the efficiency of innovation transfer

Hypothesis 1b Contextual barriers are negatively related with the effectiveness of innovation transfer

Social Interaction and Social Capital

Past studies show that social interactions facilitate knowledge sharing within MNCs (Björkman et al. 2004; Noorderhaven and Harzing 2009). Hansen (1999) and Amesse and Cohendet (2001) show that direct contacts between individuals are vital in achieving an effective knowledge sharing process. Particularly for knowledge that is tacit and abstract in nature, social interactions are necessary for the process of sharing (Dhanaraj et al. 2004; Lawson et al. 2008; Noorderhaven and Harzing 2009). Since tacit knowledge tends to be context specific (Polanyi 1967), it makes even more subjective to the influence of contextual barriers during the transfer process.

MNCs can encourage social interactions between sending and receiving units to help information flow, knowledge sharing, and overcome contextual barriers. Two-way information exchanges in the social interactions can increase the transparency of the information in the sharing process (Lawson et al. 2008), and avoid transmission losses (Noorderhaven and Harzing 2009). Besides, non-verbal and visual cues can be carried out in social interactions, which will enrich communication and enable individuals to develop rapport between each other (Gupta and Govindarajan 2000; Dhanaraj et al. 2004; Kraut et al. 2002). Through the activities in these social interactions, individuals can connect and develop ties that allow information to pass through (Granovetter 1973, 1983).

Gupta and Govindarajan (2000) found that a subsidiary can build a linkage to the rest of MNCs through social interactions, thus facilitating knowledge flow. Björkman et al. (2004) also shows that interaction between managers within MNC units lead to knowledge sharing. Social interactions in MNCs can take place in the form of team meetings, cross-functional teams, joint workshops, and temporary or permanent task forces (Bresman et al. 1999; Gupta and Govindarajan 1994; Noorderhaven and Harzing 2009). Contacts and relationship can be built through interactions on the individual level, which allow the development of trust, share norms, as well as common identification (Inkpen and Tsang 2005; Mäkelä et al. 2007).

We suggest these social ties between individuals create sufficient social capital to help overcome the contextual barriers existed in the knowledge sharing process. Social capital is defined as an aggregated resource "embedded within, available through, and derived from the network of relationship possessed by an individual or social units" (Nahapiet and Ghoshal 1998, p. 243). Social capital in this broader definition accommodates both the private and public good perspective (Adler and Kwon 2002; Inkpen and Tsang 2005; Kostova and Roth 2003), and the resources (e.g., knowledge) is included in its notion. As social ties develop, the resources become more available to the member of these connected relationship (Oh et al. 2004).

Ongoing social interactions enable the accumulation of social capital, which facilitate the continuing flow of information and knowledge sharing (Gooderham et al. 2011; Inkpen and Tsang 2005; Kostova and Roth 2003; Nahapiet and Ghoshal 1998). Through social capital, individuals are bridged and connected despite the presence of contextual barriers (Oh et al. 2004). New information and knowledge can be easier to share and adapt within cooperative environment (Noorderhaven and Harzing 2009; Lynskey 1999). However, Maurer et al. (2011) caution for striving quantify of ties to create stronger social capital, and suggest it is the strength of ties facilitate the transfer tacit and complex knowledge. Hence, we postulate the following hypotheses:

Hypothesis 2a Social interaction mediates the relationship between contextual barriers and the efficiency of innovation transfer.

Hypothesis 2b Social interaction mediates the relationship between contextual barriers and the effectiveness of innovation transfer.

Methodology

We adopted a sequential mixed-method research design to first examine the relationship between variables and then provide rich information to support our findings. By the term "sequential," we mean there are two phases of data collection and analyses (Creswell 2014). Doing so, we give priority to the quantitative data collected and analyzed in the first phase, and use qualitative data to provide support and contextualize our findings (Birkinshaw et al. 2010; Bresman et al. 1999).

Quantitative Survey Data Collection

In the first phase, survey was conducted to collect quantitative data. This survey was part of a broader research project focusing on MNCs' technology development and transfer. While the overall questionnaire was developed to collect data on both aspects, we carefully selected questions that specifically related to the theoretical concepts in this study. These questions are anchored in the literature and asked informants to respond in a seven-point Likert scale. The standardized questionnaire was pretested through pilot interviews to revise ambiguous questions.

The survey was administrated through face-to-face interviews with project and R&D managers and engineers involved in the innovation transfer process. More often than not several respondents were present at the interview, having been responsible for different aspects of the innovation development and transfer. The respondents were encouraged to elaborate on their answers, while at the same time carefully selecting the most appropriate answer in the questionnaire. Each survey took about two to four hours to complete. The research method employed for the data collection offers the advantage of providing high-quality data, by reducing the missing data for individual questions to a minimum and ensuring that the objectives of the questions are met (cf. Fowler 1993). To have more than one respondent in these surveys also enable us to avoid respondent bias due to memory loses, as the answers from other respondents can be used for the purpose of validation and triangulation.

Data was collected from 25 participating MNCs in different manufacturing industries, for example, paper and pulp, machinery and equipment, electrical machinery, and motor vehicles. The final sample contains a total of 173 observations of transferring a new technology, relating to 87 different innovations. These technology transfer projects were all completed but not more than ten years at the time of our interview. All these MNCs are located in advance economies, and these technology transfer projects are predominately taken place in Europe (77.7 percent), Asia (18.8 percent), and North America (3.5 percent).

Qualitative Interview Data Collection

In the second phase of the research, we collected qualitative data to build up an illustrating case to assist our understanding of the use of social interaction in technology transfer projects. Qualitative data was collected through face-to-face semi-structured interviews and onsite observations (Cassell and Symon 2004). These interviews and onsite observations provide first-hand description by the informants on how social interactions are purposely adopted by the focal firm in transferring technology to customers (King 2004; Kvale 1996). Each interview lasted about one to one-and-half hour, and the observations took place during a meeting between the focal firm and their customer. Our interviews were designed to probe further what social interac-

80 O. H. Kang and P. T. Kao

tions were utilized, how and where they took place, and the potential influence over the transfer process (Yeung 1995; Yin 2009). The insights obtained from the qualitative data provided a context that is not available to quantitative studies, which enable us to approach the research phenomenon with a reflective and holistic view (Silverman 2010).

We chose to focus on the technology transferred between a Swedish iron powder manufacture (HG), their R&D center in China (C-R&D), and their customers (DX) in automobile part and component manufacturing. Iron powder is widely used in the automobile industry to manufacture parts and components. HG is one of the world's leading suppliers of iron powder, and owns factories producing iron powder in Sweden and the United States. We approached HG and requested interviews with managers in headquarter in Sweden, regional headquarters and R&D center in China. We also gain access to one of their tech workshops with customers DX held in Shanghai to shadow and observe their interactions. In total, five interviews and one onsite observation were conducted.

Operationalization of Variables

The independent variable, *Contextual Barriers*, refers to factors that will potentially create difficulties in the transfer process between sending and receiving units. Following Busse et al. (2016), we include three items, that is, difference in market condition, technology standard, and culture.

The dependent variable, *Transfer Performance*, measures both efficiency by looking at the cost and the speed of the transfer (Teece 1977; Hansen et al. 2005; Pérez-Nordtvedt et al. 2008), and effectiveness on the implementation and adaptation of the transfer (Zander and Kogut 1995; Szulanski 1996; Pérez-Nordtvedt et al. 2008).

The moderating variable, *Social Interaction*, is measured by the extensiveness of the communication between individuals in sending and receiving units. This variable is indicated by the use of face-to-face meetings (Bresman et al. 1999), the use of temporary trainings (Barner-Rasmussen and Björkman 2005), the use of cross unit teams and project groups (Ghoshal et al. 1994), as well as the use of conferences and workshops.

Lastly, we control for four variables that may have an impact on the dependent variable. *Age of Relationship* looks at the duration of the relationship between sending and receiving units. *Level of Previous Relationship* takes into account the intensiveness of the relationship between sending and receiving units. One may expect when relationship between parties is in a more matured stage and more intensive, there may be existing routines developed to facilitate the transfer (Nelson and Winter 1982; Szulanski 1996). In addition, stronger trust and attachment can also be formed when both parties worked together in the past (Gulati 1995; Inkpen and Beamish 1997). Additionally, we control for *Relevance of Technology*, as there may be stronger incentives from either sending or receiving units to achieve a better transfer performance when they perceive the technology is more valuable, or important to the organization (Schulz 2003). Moreover, *Knowledge Tacitness* is adopted to control the level of transferability, since tacit knowledge is associated with great transfer challenges. Tacit knowledge is less codified, which can cause difficulties for sending units to share and for receiving unit to adapt (Kogut and Zander 1993; Zander and Kogut 1995; Szulanski 1996).

The Appendix lists the variables and their indicators used in the questionnaire, measured in a seven-point Likert scale except for the age of relationship. All variables showed high inter-item reliability with Cronbach's alpha above the recommended threshold value of 0.70 (Hair et al. 2006), except for the *Transfer Efficiency* variable (Cronbach's alpha 0.67). However, when there are a small number of items in the scale (fewer than ten), the mean inter-item correlation (MIC) value can be used to further support the reliability of the items. Optimal MIC values range from 0.2 to 0.4 (recommended by Briggs and Cheek 1986). The MIC value for the *Transfer Efficiency* variable was 0.39 which is within the rage of optimal MIC values. We further take Herman's factor analysis to examine the extent of common method bias (Podsakoff and Organ 1986). The result shows five factors with eigenvalues greater than 1.0, and together they accounted for 65.7 percent of the total variance explained with first two factors are loaded 17.7 and 15.2 percent, respectively. This indicates that common method bias is not a significant problem.

Analysis and Findings

Quantitative Analysis

We first adopt Fishbein's (1963) equation for basic multi-attribute measurement model before analyzing the data in OLS regression. Descriptive statistics and the correlation matrix of the variables can be seen in Table 4.1. Some significant correlations exist between variables; however, a rule of thumb is above 0.7 (cf. Hair et al. 2006) and none of the correlations were high enough to indicate potential multicollinearity. To check for further multicollinearity

Table 4.1 Descriptive statistics and correlations

Variable	Mean	SD	1	2	3	4	5	6	7	8
1 Transfer efficiency	3.79	1.29	–	0.62**	-0.34	-0.27**	0.06	-0.11	-0.07	-0.07
2 Transfer effectiveness	5.03	1.49	0.62**	–	-0.41	-0.11	0.14	0.08	0.04	-0.18*
3 Contextual transfer barrier	2.36	1.36	-0.33**	-0.40**	–	0.09	-0.22**	-0.16*	0.06	0.08
4 Social interaction	3.89	1.53	-0.27**	-0.11	0.09	–	0.04	0.12	-0.02	-0.01
5 Age of relationship	17.96	17.07	0.06	0.14	-0.22**	0.04	–	0.43**	-0.13	0.03
6 Previous relationship	4.74	1.57	-0.11	0.08	-0.16*	0.12	0.43**	–	0.09	-0.16*
7 Relevance of innovation	5.15	1.31	-0.07	0.04	0.07	-0.02	-0.13	0.09	–	0.18*
8 Tacit knowledge	2.50	1.55	-0.07	-0.18	0.08	-0.01	-0.03	-0.16*	0.18*	–

$N = 173$

$**P < 0.01$; $*P < 0.05$

All two-tailed tests

in moderating variables, the variance inflation factor (VIF-values) were calculated. A common cut-off threshold for VIF-value is 10 (cf. Hair et al. 2006, p. 230), none were greater than 1.43 thus multicollinearity does not appear to pose any severe problems.

Moreover, Kolmogorov-Smirnov test was carried out to check for normal distribution. The result shows that all variables but the dependent variable *contextual barriers* have significance value greater than 0.06 (less than 0.05 will indicate a tendency of non-normality). To further examine the actual degree of departure from normality, a normal probability plot was carried out, and all the variables were normally distributed (Hair et al. 2006). Lastly, heteroscedasticity and non-linearity diagnosis were made by plotting the studentized residual against the predicted dependent variable. There seems to be no heteroscedasticity and non-linearity problem.

The first regression analyses using the *transfer efficiency* as a dependent variable (see Table 4.2) showed that there was no significant effect on the *transfer efficiency* by the control variables (model 1: F-value 1.75 and adjusted R^2 0.02). Model 2 (F-value 4.03 at $p < 0.01$ and adjusted R^2 0.12) showed that the *contextual transfer barrier* has a negative effect on the *transfer efficiency*. As well as *social interaction* showing a negative effect on the *transfer efficiency* (model 3: F-value 2.65 at $p < 0.05$ and adjusted R^2 0.08). In model 4 (F-value 3.74 at $p < 0.001$ and adjusted R^2 0.15), the

Table 4.2 Results of OLS estimations[a]

Independent variables	Dependent variable: transfer efficiency			
	Model 1	Model 2	Model 3	Model 4
Age of relationship	0.19(1.91)[†]	0.10(0.93)	0.11(1.05)	0.05(0.45)
Previous relationship	−0.22(−2.16)*	−0.16(−1.60)	−0.09(−0.82)	−0.91(−0.85)
Relevance of innovation	−0.02(−0.21)	0.08(0.89)	0.06(0.60)	0.09(0.93)
Tacit knowledge	−0.12(−1.22)	−1.80(−1.89)[†]	−0.21(−2.13)*	−0.19(−2.01)*
Contextual transfer barrier	–	−0.33(−3.55)***	–	−0.33(−3.43)***
Social interaction	–	–	−0.24(−2.49)**	−0.19(−1.97)[†]
Barrier * Social interaction	–	–		0.05(0.56)
R^2	0.06	0.16	0.11	0.20
Adjusted R^2	0.02	0.12	0.08	0.15
F-value	1.75	4.03**	2.65*	3.74***

***$P < 0.001$; **$P < 0.01$; *$P < 0.05$; †$P < 0.10$
All two-tailed tests
[a]Standardized coefficients with *t*-values in parentheses

84   O. H. Kang and P. T. Kao

Table 4.3 Results of OLS estimations[a]

Independent variables	Dependent variable: transfer effectiveness			
	Model 1	Model 2	Model 3	Model 4
Age of relationship	0.16(1.76)[†]	0.64(0.72)	0.13(1.39)	0.05(0.61)
Previous relationship	−0.04(−0.47)	−0.02(−0.23)	0.01(0.10)	−0.04(−0.56)
Relevance of innovation	0.13(1.51)	0.17(2.08)[*]	0.16(1.88)[†]	0.28(3.85)[***]
Tacit knowledge	−0.21(−2.43)[*]	−0.22(−2.76)[**]	−0.25(−2.87)[**]	−0.30(−4.15)[***]
Contextual transfer barrier	–	−0.41(−5.23)[***]	–	0.12(1.64)[†]
Social interaction	–	–	−0.09(−1.05)	−0.56(−7.64)[***]
Barrier * Social interaction	–	–	–	0.20(2.64)[**]
R^2	0.06	0.24	0.08	0.39
Adjusted R^2	0.03	0.21	0.05	0.36
F-value	2.17[†]	8.30[***]	2.47[*]	12.01[***]

[***]$P < 0.001$; [**]$P < 0.01$; [*]$P < 0.05$; [†]$P < 0.10$
All two-tailed tests
[a]Standardized coefficients with t-values in parentheses

interaction effect showing the usage of social interaction to overcome contextual transfer barriers showed no significance. The results indicate that contextual transfer barriers deter transfer efficiency and the social interaction also does not lead to efficient transfer. This is due to the fact that social interaction is costly and time consuming. Accordingly, hypothesis 1a is supported. However, the moderating effect of social interaction on contextual transfer barrier showed no significance; therefore hypothesis 2a is not supported.

In the regression analyses with *transfer effectiveness* as the dependent variable (see Table 4.3), the control variables explained very little of the variance (model 1: F-value 2.17 at $p < 0.10$ and adjusted R^2 0.03). In model 2 (F-value 8.30 at $p < 0.001$ and adjusted R^2 0.21), contextual transfer barrier showed negative effect on transfer effectiveness. Thus, hypothesis 1b is supported. However, social interaction showed no significance on transfer effectiveness (model 3: F-value 2.47 at $p < 0.05$ and adjusted R^2 0.05). In line with the prediction for hypothesis 2b, model 4 (F-value 12.01 at $p < 0.001$ and adjusted R^2 0.36) showed that social interaction used to overcome contextual transfer barriers will have a positive effect on the transfer effectiveness indicating that social interaction is an effective tool when considering the transfer effectiveness. Consequently, hypothesis 2b is supported.

Qualitative Analysis

We analyzed qualitative data in order to construct an illustration case to understand how social interaction helps companies to ease the contextual barriers hindering the innovation transfer. We coded the interviews based on the key constructs, and presented in Fig. 4.1.

HG is a world leading iron powder producer based in Sweden. It entered China and formed a wholly own sales subsidiary in the late 1990s. As Chinese automotive industry was taking off after China's accession to WTO in 2001, HG realized that China has become an important market for automobile globally, and established an R&D centered in Shanghai (C-R&D) in 2005. While some of the customers from HG are foreign-owned, most of them are purely local and they need assistance applying iron powder in producing auto parts and components.

HG's C-R&D is designed to assist customers with know-how on applying iron powder to accommodate the demand from automakers to localize the auto supply chain. C-R&D is equipped with a metallography lab similar to its other R&D facilities in Sweden and the United States. The aim of C-R&D is mainly to support and educate local customers through organizing powder metallurgy school, specific training programs, and workshops. Approximately 180 people attend these training courses annually. Even though automotive industry is not a small community in China, HG is well known.

In addition, C-R&D center worked with customers during product development stage, which could extend over a period of three to four years in

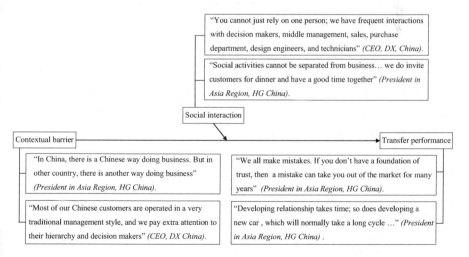

Fig. 4.1 Results of qualitative data

automotive industry. During this period, HG, C-R&D, and customer like DX, and possibly end customer (e.g., automaker) interacted frequently. These interactions contain both business and social components, and people from multiple fields, such as R&D, production, sales and commercial side, and management all work in parallel. For HG, it is important to broader contacts with customers so that not all the relationship is dependent on one person.

Both HG and DX consider that business culture in China, technical requirement, and market demand are quite different from elsewhere. These differences can hinder the communications between various actors, and affect the process of sharing knowledge and transferring technology. Social interactions can help to ease these differences, but it will take time and effort for a company to prove trusting relationship to the customer.

Discussion

The findings from our quantitative and qualitative data seem to point out a consistent theme—contextual barriers indeed influence the performance of transfer in terms of efficiency (cost and speed) and effectiveness (implementation and adaptation). While social interaction can help MNCs overcome the presence of the contextual barriers and improve the effectiveness of transfer, it does not address the issue of transfer efficiency. These results show support to most of our hypotheses (H1a, H1b, H2b), and we believe the rejection to H2a is not entirely surprising.

As social capital will take time and resource to accumulate, multiple social interactions may be needed. Social interactions like team meetings, workshops, and temporary or permanent task forces can be costly, and they may need to be repeated again and again to achieve a certain effect (Maurer et al. 2011). In other words, social interactions will not be a quick fix if it is going to be done properly to create social capital (Oh et al. 2004). The interview data of our focal case firm, HG, also shows the same pattern. Social interactions should be taken as a long-term strategic solution with the aim to establish mutual exchange relationship between parties.

Contextual barriers are shown to have an impact on both transfer performance and they deserve more attention from management scholars. MNCs do not exist in a vacuum, and they are very much subject to the institutional norm and culture tradition of the countries where units are located (Kostova et al. 2008). Despite the knowledge based view suggesting the reason for MNCs' existence is because their capability to share knowledge across borders efficiently (Kogut and Zander 1993), MNCs cannot escape the influence from the external environment on their internal actions (Forsgren 1997).

Our findings also suggest that a balanced view is needed when it comes to quality of transfer, and transfer cost and speed. Like in most of the management issues, it might be very tricky to strive for high-quality result on the one hand, and fast speed and low cost on the other hand. Therefore, how to achieve a balance is a strategic challenge. An occasion to prioritize quality over cost and speed could be when the knowledge in question is novel and unique, and then it may worthwhile for MNCs to make sure the transfer is done properly.

Concluding Remark, Future Research and Application to Managers

Contextual barriers play an important role in influencing knowledge sharing and innovation transfer within MNCs and as well as between partners. Our findings support past studies that social interactions between sending and receiving units help achieve transfer effectiveness when contextual barriers are presented, but has no effect on transfer efficiency. Our studies contribute to the ongoing discussion on the facilitating effect of social interactions in knowledge sharing process (Gupta and Govindarajan 2000; Björkman et al. 2004; Maurer et al. 2011; Noorderhaven and Harzing 2009).

For managers in control of knowledge sharing process, our studies suggest that social interactions are valuable to assimilating knowledge particularly when sending and receiving units are located in very different countries. Yet, these social interactions are costly endeavor. Therefore, the question arises "Is the knowledge being transferred worth its cost?" Hence, the identification of those novel and unique knowledge or technology becomes part of the strategic decision to transfer implementation.

Future studies may want to examine and identify appropriate type of social interactions in relating to contextual barriers, as well as characteristic of knowledge and technology. There may be a combination of social interactions, contextual barriers, and type of knowledge that can maximize both transfer effectiveness and efficiency. Additionally, with digital communication technology being advanced significantly, face-to-face interactions do not necessarily have to take place in person. Would a virtual task team constitute the social interactions needed to accumulate social capital? Future research can explore the alternatives for social interactions and how they can assist in knowledge sharing process.

Appendix: Dependent, Independent, Moderation, and Control Variables

Dependent variables	Operationalization (indicator)	Question(s) in the questionnaire	Cronbach's alpha
Transfer efficiency	Cost of this particular Speed of this particular transfer	The actual cost of technology transfer was higher than expected (reverse coded) The speed of technology transfer was faster than expected	0.67 MIC-0.39
Transfer effectiveness	Quality of adaptation in this particular transfer	This receiver adopted the technology very quickly This receiver adopted the technology easily	0.73
Independent variable	Operationalization (indicator)	Question(s) in the questionnaire	Cronbach's alpha
Contextual transfer barriers	Factors existed in sender's and receiver's environment that may influence this particular transfer	Market condition differences in sender's and receiver's countries make transfer problematic Technological standard condition differences in sender's and receiver's countries make transfer problematic Cultural and institutional differences in sender's and receiver's countries make transfer problematic	0.74
Moderation variable	Operationalization (indicator)	Question(s) in the questionnaire	Cronbach's alpha
Social interaction	Extensiveness of the communication between individuals from sending and receiving units in this particular transfer	Face-to-face meetings Temporary trainings Cross unit teams and project groups Conferences and workshops	0.71
Control variables	Operationalization (indicator)	Question(s) in the questionnaire	Cronbach's alpha

Dependent variables	Operationalization (indicator)	Question(s) in the questionnaire	Cronbach's alpha
Age of relationship		The age of relationship between your unit and the unit receiving this particular transfer	
Level of previous relationship		To what extent have you previously cooperated together with this particular receiving unit?	0.72
		To what extent have you previously shared knowledge with this particular receiving unit?	
		To what extent existing routines of sharing knowledge with this particular receiving unit drove the transfer?	
Relevance of technology		The technology is important to your unit	0.77
		The technology is important to the division	
		The technology is important to the whole company	
Tacit knowledge		The technology is easily codified	0.71
		The technology is rather explicit	

References

Adler, P. S., & Kwon, S.-W. (2002). Social capital: Prospects for a new concept. *The Academy of Management Review, 27*(1), 17–40.

Ado, A., Su, Z., & Wanjiru, R. (2016). Learning and knowledge transfer in Africa-China JVs: Interplay between informalities, culture, and social capital. *Journal of International Management, 23*(2), 166–179.

Allen, T. J. (1977). *Managing the flow of technology: Technology transfer and the dissemination of technological information within the R & D organization (Book).*

Research Supported by the National Science Foundation. Cambridge, MA: MIT Press, 329p.

Ambos, T. C., Ambos, B., & Schlegelmilch, B. B. (2006). Learning from foreign subsidiaries: An empirical investigation of headquarters' benefits from reverse knowledge transfers. *International Business Review, 15*(3), 294–312.

Amesse, F., & Cohendet, P. (2001). Technology transfer revisited from the perspective of the knowledge-based economy. *Research Policy, 30*(9), 1459–1478.

Barner-Rasmussen, W., & Björkman, I. (2005). Surmounting interunit barriers factors associated with interunit communication intensity in the multinational corporation. *International Studies of Management & Organization, 35*(1), 28–46.

Bartlett, C. A., & Ghoshal, S. (1989). *Managing across borders: The transnational solution*. London: Hutchinson Business.

Birkinshaw, J., Bresman, H., & Nobel, R. (2010). Knowledge transfer in international acquisitions: A retrospective. *Journal of International Business Studies, 41*(1), 21–26.

Björkman, I., Barner-Rasmussen, W., & Li, L. (2004). Managing knowledge transfer in MNCs: The impact of headquarters control mechanisms. *Journal of International Business Studies, 35*(5), 443–455.

Bresman, H., Birkinshaw, J., & Nobel, R. (1999). Knowledge transfer in international acquisitions. *Journal of International Business Studies, 30*(3), 439–462.

Briggs, S. R., & Cheek, J. M. (1986). The role of factor analysis in the development and evaluation of personality scales. *Journal of Personality, 54*(1), 106–148.

Buckley, P. J., & Casson, M. (1976). *The future of the multinational enterprise*. New York: Macmillan.

Buckley, P. J., Clegg, J., & Tan, H. (2003). The art of knowledge transfer: Secondary and reverse transfer in China's telecommunications manufacturing industry. *MIR: Management International Review, 43*(2), 67–93.

Busse, C., Schleper, M. C., Niu, M., & Wagner, S. M. (2016). Supplier development for sustainability: Contextual barriers in global supply chains. *International Journal of Physical Distribution & Logistics Management, 46*(5), 442–468.

Cassell, C., & Symon, G. (2004). *Essential guide to qualitative methods in organizational research*. London: Sage.

Ciabuschi, F., Dellestrand, H., & Kappen, P. (2011). Exploring the effects of vertical and lateral mechanisms in international knowledge transfer projects. *Management International Review, 51*(2), 129–155.

Ciabuschi, F., Dellestrand, H., & Kappen, P. (2012). The good, the bad, and the ugly: Technology transfer competence, rent-seeking, and bargaining power. *Journal of World Business, 47*(4), 664–674.

Cohen, W. M., & Levinthal, D. A. (1990). Absorptive capacity: A new perspective on learning and innovation. *Administrative Science Quarterly, 35*(1), 128–152.

Creswell, J. W. (2014). *Research design: Qualitative, quantitative, and mixed methods approaches* (4th ed.). Los Angeles/London/New Delhi/Singapore/Washington, DC: SAGE.

Dhanaraj, C., Lyles, M. A., Steensma, H. K., & Tihanyi, L. (2004). Managing tacit and explicit knowledge transfer in IJVs: The role of relational embeddedness and the impact on performance. *Journal of International Business Studies, 35*(5), 428–442. https://doi.org/10.1057/palgrave.jibs.8400098.

Dunning, J. H. (1980). Toward an eclectic theory of international production: Some empirical tests. *Journal of International Business Studies, 11*(1), 9–31.

Dyer, J. H., & Hatch, N. W. (2006). Relation-specific capabilities and barriers to knowledge transfers: Creating advantage through network relationships. *Strategic Management Journal, 27*(8), 701–719.

Eden, L., & Miller, S. R. (2004). Distance matters: Liability of foreignness, institutional distance and ownership strategy. In *Advances in international management* (Vol. 16, pp. 187–221). Bingley: Emerald.

Fishbein, M. (1963). An investigation of the relationships between beliefs about an object and the attitude toward that object. *Human Relations, 16*(3), 233–239.

Forsgren, M. (1997). The advantage paradox of the multinational corporation. In I. Bjorkman & M. Forsgren (Eds.), *The nature of the international firm: Nordic contributions to international business research* (1st ed., pp. 69–85). Copenhagen: Handelshojskolens Forlag.

Forsgren, M., Holm, U., & Johanson, J. (2006). *Managing the embedded multinational: A business network view.* Cheltenham: Edward Elgar Publishing.

Fowler, F. J. (1993). *Survey research methods* (2nd ed.). Newbury Park: Sage.

Ghoshal, S., & Bartlett, C. A. (1990). The multinational corporation as an interorganizational network. *The Academy of Management Review, 15*(4), 603–625.

Ghoshal, S., Korine, H., & Szulanski, G. (1994). Interunit communication in multinational corporations. *Management Science, 40*(1), 96–110.

Gooderham, P., Minbaeva, D. B., & Pedersen, T. (2011). Governance mechanisms for the promotion of social capital for knowledge transfer in multinational corporations. *Journal of Management Studies, 48*(1), 123–150.

Granovetter, M. (1973). The strength of weak ties. *The American Journal of Sociology, 78*(6), 1360–1380.

Granovetter, M. (1983). The strength of weak ties: A network theory revisited. *Sociological Theory, 1*, 201–233.

Gulati, R. (1995). Social structure and alliance formation patterns: A longitudinal analysis. *Administrative Science Quarterly, 40*(4), 619–652.

Gupta, A. K., & Govindarajan, V. (1994). Organizing for knowledge flows within MNCs. *International Business Review, 3*(4), 443–457.

Gupta, A. K., & Govindarajan, V. (2000). Knowledge flows within multinational corporations. *Strategic Management Journal, 21*(4), 473–496.

Hair, J. F., Black, W. C., Babin, B. J., Anderson, R. E., & Tatham, R. L. (2006). *Multivariate data analysis* (6th ed.). Upper Saddle River: Pearson Prentice Hall.

Hansen, M. T. (1999). The search-transfer problem: The role of weak ties in sharing knowledge across organization subunits. *Administrative Science Quarterly, 44*(1), 82–111.

Hansen, M. T., Mors, M. L., & Løvås, B. (2005). Knowledge sharing in organizations: Multiple networks, multiple phases. *Academy of Management Journal, 48*(5), 776–793.

Ho, M. H.-W., Ghauri, P. N., & Larimo, J. A. (2017, July). Institutional distance and knowledge acquisition in international buyer-supplier relationships: The moderating role of trust. *Asia Pacific Journal of Management.*

Hutzschenreuter, T., & Matt, T. (2017). MNE internationalization patterns, the roles of knowledge stocks, and the portfolio of MNE subsidiaries. *Journal of International Business Studies, 48*(9), 1131–1150.

Inkpen, A. C., & Beamish, P. W. (1997). Knowledge, bargaining power, and the instability of international joint ventures. *The Academy of Management Review, 22*(1), 177–202.

Inkpen, A. C., & Tsang, E. W. K. (2005). Social capital, networks, and knowledge transfer. *Academy of Management Review, 30*(1), 146–165.

Katz, R., & Allen, T. J. (1982). Investigating the not invented here (NIH) syndrome: A look at the performance, tenure, and communication patterns of 50 R & D project groups. *R&D Management, 12*(1), 7–20.

King, N. (2004). Using interviews in qualitative research. In C. Cassell & G. Symon (Eds.), *Essential guide to qualitative methods in organizational research* (pp. 11–22). London: Sage.

Kogut, B., & Zander, U. (1993). Knowledge of the firm and the evolutionary theory of the multinational corporation. *Journal of International Business Studies, 24*(4), 625–645.

Kostova, T., & Roth, K. (2002). Adoption of an organizational practice by subsidiaries of multinational corporations: Institutional and relational effects. *The Academy of Management Journal, 45*(1), 215–233.

Kostova, T., & Roth, K. (2003). Social capital in multinational corporations and a micro-macro model of its formation. *Academy of Management Review, 28*(2), 297–317.

Kostova, T., Roth, K., & Dacin, M. T. (2008). Institutional theory in the study of multinational corporations: A critique and new directions. *Academy of Management Review, 33*(4), 994–1006.

Kvale, S. (1996). *Interviews: An introduction to qualitative research interviewing.* Thousand Oaks: Sage.

Lane, P. J., Salk, J. E., & Lyles, M. A. (2001). Absorptive capacity, learning, and performance in international joint ventures. *Strategic Management Journal, 22*(12), 1139–1161.

Lawson, B., Tyler, B., & Cousins, P. (2008). Antecedents and consequences of social capital on buyer performance improvement. *Journal of Operations Management, 26*(3), 446–460.

Lin, C., Tan, B., & Chang, S. (2008). An exploratory model of knowledge flow barriers within healthcare organizations. *Information & Management, 45*(5), 331–339.

Lynskey, M. J. (1999). The transfer of resources and competencies for developing technological capabilities-the case of Fujitsu-ICL. *Technology Analysis & Strategic Management, 11*(3), 317–336.

Mäkelä, K., Kalla, H. K., & Piekkari, R. (2007). Interpersonal similarity as a driver of knowledge sharing within multinational corporations. *International Business Review, 16*(1), 1–22.

Maurer, I., Bartsch, V., & Ebers, M. (2011). The value of intra-organizational social capital: How it fosters knowledge transfer, innovation performance, and growth. *Organization Studies, 32*(2), 157–185.

Michailova, S., & Husted, K. (2003). Knowledge-sharing hostility in Russian firms. *California Management Review, 45*(3), 59–77.

Nahapiet, J., & Ghoshal, S. (1998). Social capital, intellectual capital, and the organizational advantage. *The Academy of Management Review, 23*(2), 242–266.

Nelson, R., & Winter, S. (1982). *An evolutionary theory of technical change*. Cambridge, MA: Harvard.

Noorderhaven, N., & Harzing, A.-W. (2009). Knowledge-sharing and social interaction within MNEs. *Journal of International Business Studies, 40*(5), 719–741.

Oh, H., Chung, M.-H., & Labianca, G. (2004). Group social capital and group effectiveness: The role of informal socializing ties. *The Academy of Management Journal, 47*(6), 860–875.

Pérez-Nordtvedt, L., Kedia, B. L., Datta, D. K., & Rasheed, A. A. (2008). Effectiveness and efficiency of cross-border knowledge transfer: An empirical examination. *Journal of Management Studies, 45*(4), 714–744.

Phillips, N., & Tracey, P. (2009). Institutional theory and the MNC. *The Academy of Management Review, 34*(1), 169–171.

Podsakoff, P. M., & Organ, D. W. (1986). Self-reports in organizational research: Problems and prospects. *Journal of Management, 12*(4), 531–544.

Polanyi, M. (1967). *The tacit dimension* (Vol. 4). London: Routledge.

Schulz, M. (2003). Pathways of relevance: Exploring inflows of knowledge into subunits of multinational corporations. *Organization Science, 14*(4), 440–459.

Silverman, D. (2010). *Doing qualitative research: A practical handbook*. London: Sage.

Simonin, B. L. (1999). Ambiguity and the process of knowledge transfer in strategic alliances. *Strategic Management Journal, 20*(7), 595–623.

Szulanski, G. (1996). Exploring internal stickiness: Impediments to the transfer of best practice within the firm. *Strategic Management Journal, 17*(S2), 27–43.

Teece, D. J. (1977). Technology transfer by multinational firms: The resource cost of transferring technological know-how. *The Economic Journal, 87*(346), 242–261.

Vahlne, J.-E., & Johanson, J. (2017). From internationalization to evolution: The Uppsala model at 40 years. *Journal of International Business Studies, 48*(9), 1087–1102.

Xu, D., & Shenkar, O. (2002). Institutional distance and the multinational Enterprise. *The Academy of Management Review, 27*(4), 608–618.

Yeung, H. W. (1995). Qualitative personal interviews in international business research: Some lessons from a study of Hong Kong transnational corporations. *International Business Review, 4*(3), 313–339.

Yin, R. K. (2009). *Case study research: Design and methods, Applied social research methods* (Vol. 5, 4th ed.). Los Angeles: Sage.

Zaheer, S. (1995). Overcoming the liability of foreignness. *Academy of Management Journal, 38*(2), 341–363.

Zander, U., & Kogut, B. (1995). Knowledge and the speed of the transfer and imitation of organizational capabilities: An empirical test. *Organization Science, 6*(1), 76–92.

5

Equity Ownership Strategy in Greenfield Investments: Influences of Host Country Infrastructure and MNE Resources in Emerging Markets

Ahmad Arslan, Jorma Larimo, and Desislava Dikova

Introduction

Foreign direct investment (FDI) establishment mode strategy is typically viewed as the multinational enterprises' (MNE) choice whether to acquire an existing local enterprise (acquisition) or to establish a start-up from scratch (greenfield investment) (Dikova and Van Witteloostuijn 2007; Slangen and Hennart 2008; Slangen 2011; Arslan et al. 2015). Cross-border mergers and acquisitions (M&As), as a specific entry strategy have received increasing attention of IB researchers (see, e.g. Chen 2008; Contractor et al. 2014; Arslan and Dikova 2015; Ahammad et al. 2017; Dikova et al. 2017). Despite their popularity, M&As are not always among the strategic options of MNEs especially when investing in emerging markets (EMs), where suitable acquisition targets often lack. Under such circumstances, MNEs must choose to

---

A. Arslan (✉)
Department of Marketing, Management & International Business, Oulu Business School, University of Oulu, Oulu, Finland
e-mail: Ahmad.arslan@oulu.fi

J. Larimo
School of Marketing & Communications, University of Vaasa, Vaasa, Finland
e-mail: Jorma.larimo@uva.fi

D. Dikova
Institute for International Business, Vienna University of Economics & Business Administration, WU-Wien, Vienna, Austria
e-mail: Desislava.dikova@wu.ac.at

© The Author(s) 2019
A. Chidlow et al. (eds.), *The Changing Strategies of International Business*, The Academy of International Business, https://doi.org/10.1007/978-3-030-03931-8_5

establish presence in EMs through greenfield investment. In fact, greenfield investments account for the majority of global FDI flows, that is, 63% (UNCTAD 2015).

Earlier research has established that greenfields can offer specific investment advantages. For example, it is relatively easier to transfer MNE practices to greenfield subsidiaries compared to acquired ones, thereby, making their integration into MNE's global strategy relatively smooth (Meyer and Su 2015; Ayden et al. 2017). Greenfield subsidiaries can also offer access to the sectors and industries, where the possibility to acquire local firms is limited due to certain restrictions (Chang et al. 2012; Lee et al. 2014; Arslan and Larimo 2017). It therefore comes as a surprise that greenfield investments, as a specific establishment mode, have received far less research attention compared to cross-border M&As. The specific ownership decisions taken in the context of greenfield investments have received even less research attention.

In this study, we investigate the role of local context on the equity ownership strategy in greenfield investments undertaken in EMs. Recently Arslan and Larimo (2017), considered the role of local context by analyzing the influences of institutional distance and international trade freedom on ownership strategy in greenfield investments. Local context, however, goes beyond institutional framework and often influences the extent of resource dependency of MNEs in EMs. Related research has found that physical infrastructure is a key determinant of FDI flows as access to utilities (electricity, gas, and water), along with good transportation network and connectivity, make a location attractive to manufacturing FDI (e.g. Erdal and Tatoglu 2002; Bellak et al. 2009; Blonigen and Piger 2014; Tate et al. 2014; Lee et al. 2016). In case of greenfield investments, host country's physical infrastructure can be expected to significantly influence equity ownership strategy. As this aspect has not been addressed in earlier studies specifically, we aim to fill this gap in the literature.

We use resource dependency theory (RDT) which focuses on resource exchange and represents a political economy model of organizational and inter-organizational behavior. The primary focus of RDT is on the environment and organizational behavior is seen as a strategic reaction to perceived and potential constraints imposed by the environment. The main gist of this chapter is the notion that because organizations differ in size and experience, they may be able to reduce the resource dependence (Hutchinson et al. 2007; Leonidou et al. 2007). Hence, we argue that a relatively well-developed local infrastructure can motivate foreign MNEs to commit higher equity ownership in their EM greenfield subsidiaries, even in cases when they are of relatively small size or lack host country specific investment experience.

Furthermore, earlier research on greenfield investments has mostly analyzed equity ownership as a dichotomous/binary choice (full vs. partial ownership) (e.g. Arslan and Larimo 2017). However, the IB literature has clearly established that management dynamics varies significantly in different partially owned subsidiaries—that is, in cases of minority or majority owned ventures (e.g. Lu et al. 2014; Dikova et al. 2017). We also incorporate this aspect in our empirical analysis by considering a wider range of equity options, that is, greenfield WOS versus greenfield joint ventures (JV), and majority greenfield JV versus minority greenfield JV.

The empirical sample is based on greenfield investments undertaken by the MNEs from open and highly internationalized Nordic economies (Denmark, Finland, Norway, and Sweden) in selected EMs located in different geographical regions. The share of EMs is constantly increasing in international FDI flows, and reached to about 30% (UNCTAD 2016). Although, EMs are generally viewed as being in process development of market economy institutions (e.g. Khanna and Palepu 2010; Arslan and Dikova 2015), their infrastructures have improved significantly in last twenty-five years, and now some rank quite high in the global rankings of infrastructure (World Bank 2018; WEF 2018). A key reason for this has been the prominence of certain EMs which by increasing their attraction as a location choice for manufacturing FDI achieved economic development and growth (e.g. Gorodnichenko et al. 2014; Lee et al. 2016). Therefore, we believe that our empirical setting offers an interesting context to test the study hypotheses.

The rest of chapter is organized as follows. The next section offers theoretical discussion leading to study hypotheses development. After that, we briefly explain data sources and variable operationalization. The chapter concludes with presentation of study findings, implications, and future research directions.

Theoretical Background

Traditionally, services like telecommunications, supply and distribution of electricity and water, and construction of roads, airports, ports, and railways have been considered a public-sector responsibility. Shortages of clean water, electricity outages, traffic congestions, frequent breakdowns of telephone landlines, and insufficient transport capacity for reliable trade are common features for most EMs (Sader 2000). Regardless of the critical importance of infrastructure for economic advancement, only a limited strand of research examined the effect of infrastructure development on the inflow of FDI. Using annual data for Malaysia for the period from 1960 to 2005, Ang (2008) found that expansion of infrastructure expenditure increased the inflow of FDI into the host country. Analyzing data from 71 countries and the number of telephones per 1000 inhabitants as a measure of infrastructure development, Asiedu (2002) found that, while a better infrastructure increased the flow of FDI to non-Sub-Saharan African countries, it had no significant impact on the FDI inflow to Sub-Saharan countries. Studying 293 foreign firms that invested in Turkey in 1995, Deichmann et al. (2003) found no evidence that infrastructure development attracted multinational firms to invest in Turkey. Nourzad et al. (2014) added to this inconclusive research by reporting that the relationship between FDI and infrastructure depends on the size of the recipient's economy.

We build on this research but shift the focus away from FDI flows and focus on a specific type of FDIs, namely, greenfields or investments from scratch. We start from the widely accepted premise that greenfields are relatively risky establishment modes for several reasons. Greenfields are new firms and hence suffer from a liability of newness (Pennings et al. 1994), they entail resorting to unproven combinations of inputs and lack relationships with local stakeholders (Slangen and Hennart 2008). Given the elevated risk of greenfields in general and specifically the risk pertaining to greenfields in EMs, we consider greenfield investment ownership stake assumed by foreign investors as a means of reducing investment risk. We use resource dependency theory (RDT) to explain possible links between infrastructure and greenfield investments.

According to RDT, no organization is entirely self-sufficient hence interorganizational exchange of resources is necessary (Pfeffer and Salancik 2003). For any given organization, the need for resource acquisition creates dependencies between the organization and other organizations in its environment. Several factors would appear to exacerbate this dependence, for example, the importance of the resource(s) in question to the focal organization, the relative scarcity of the resource(s), and the degree to which the resource is concentrated in the environment (Pfeffer 2005). While an MNE making a greenfield investment is indeed able to mold the subsidiary by choosing its location and hiring its labor force (Hennart and Park 1993), greenfield investments in EMs often suffer from implementation delays, contract cancellations, drawn-out legal disputes and lack of qualified labor. In addition, infrastructure in EMs may well add additional degree of investment risk. There is often dissatisfaction with the quality and quantity of infrastructure service provision by state-owned enterprises. While public utilities struggle to maintain inadequate infrastructure systems, demand pressures in EMs continue to build (Sader

2000; Inderst and Stewart 2014). Due to technology and innovation, an increasing number of EMs have opened these sectors to private and foreign investors. In telephony for example, cellular networks created a viable alternative to fixed-wire telephony without the technological need for monopolistic market structure (Sader 2000). The extent of MNE's dependency on underdeveloped infrastructure systems in EM would determine the likelihood of the multinational involvement in the provision of infrastructure services.

RDT deals with strategies used by organizations to address and negotiate relationships of dependence. Given that MNEs seek to reduce the uncertainty surrounding the flow of needed resources in EMs, the intent of such strategies is to increase the certainty associated with this flow by linking the organization with exchange partners, competitors, and regulators. Although each strategy varies in terms of the strength and stability of the exchange relationship, several linking (bridging) strategies have been identified in the resource dependence literature (Snell 1992; Pfeffer and Salancik 2003). For example, organizations attempt to reduce dependence either partially through cooperation, that is, via JVs, contracting, the movement of executives and other personnel across organizations, resource diversification, and so on, or more completely through mergers, officer/directorate interlocks or co-optation. In this chapter, we consider greenfield JVs and different types of shared-ownership greenfields as a means of reducing the uncertainty surrounding the flow of needed resources in EMs by tackling infrastructure deficiencies. It has been established that organizations differ in size and modus operandi (Cavusgil 1984; Katsikeas and Morgan 1994). Because of these differences, some organizations may be able to reduce resource (host market) dependence (Hutchinson et al. 2007; Leonidou et al. 2007). In the next section, we develop our arguments on the relationships between host country infrastructure quality and greenfield ownership stake assumed by MNEs, considering the boundary effects of MNE size and experience.

Study Hypotheses

Host country physical infrastructure elements relevant to FDI decisions of MNEs include transport, communication (including roads, rail network, and telecommunication), energy production, and transmission (e.g. Wheeler and Mody 1992; Tate et al. 2014; Lee et al. 2016). Earlier studies have found significant correlation between amount of FDI flows received in manufacturing sectors in relation to above-mentioned infrastructure elements (e.g. Wheeler and Mody 1992; Gorodnichenko et al. 2014). Moreover, some researchers

100   A. Arslan et al.

have analyzed individual elements of infrastructure including logistics like air, rail, and road infrastructure (Deardorff 2001; Tate et al. 2014; Lee et al. 2016), and telecommunications (e.g. Leibrecht and Riedl 2010) in relation to FDI flows. Other studies have focused on aspects of energy availability and transmission (e.g. Bellak et al. 2007; Riedl 2010; Malhotra 2017), and their results also showed positive influences of these infrastructure elements on FDI inflows received in a specific country or region.

It is important to mention that even though greenfield FDIs may have different motivations (e.g. resource seeking or market seeking), they are affected by infrastructure conditions. For example, for resource-seeking FDIs, access to natural resources and transportation network (rail, road, and air) are important. On the other hand, for market seeking greenfield FDIs are influenced by opportunity to establish useful manufacturing (retail) sites, and are influenced by infrastructure elements like electricity, gas, and water as well as transportation network for transfer of manufactured goods. Earlier FDI studies have found all these infrastructure elements to influence choice and flow of FDIs (Leibrecht and Riedl 2010; Kaur et al. 2016). In case of greenfield FDIs, many western MNEs invest in manufacturing sector in EMs to not only serve local market, but also export products to other international markets (e.g. Aggarwal 2002; Mijiyawa 2017). To assure global competitiveness and well-functioning global value chain operations, MNEs often equip EM greenfields with the latest technology and machinery (which also requires training local labor accordingly). In manufacturing industries in particular, those of substantial investments that are likely protected by high-level (full) ownership. Earlier research shows that MNEs prefer control in local subsidiaries so that organizational practices and strategies can be easily transferred and implemented in the new units (e.g. Lin 2014). Good local infrastructure can facilitate meeting the productivity potential of the operation and ensure higher profitability in the long run of that greenfield manufacturing unit, without further (immediate or future) resource commitment on the side of the MNE. Hence, availability of good infrastructure in host EM is likely linked to MNEs' higher equity ownership in the greenfield subsidiary. Based on this discussion, we hypothesize that:

Hypothesis 1 Host EM physical infrastructure is positively associated with high equity ownership strategy in EM greenfield investments by the Nordic MNEs.

We also established earlier that in order to assure global competitiveness and well-functioning global operations, MNEs often equip EM greenfields with the latest technology and machinery, which are in turn protected by high-level (full) ownership. We suggested that the availability of good local infrastructure can both facilitate meeting the productivity potential of the operation and ensure higher profitability in the long run of that greenfield manufacturing unit, without further (immediate or future) resource commitment on the side of the MNE. What happens in the case of infrastructure deficiency in the EM where the MNE considers establishing a (manufacturing) greenfield subsidiary? Many MNEs may choose to invest additional resources in developing the local infrastructure to the extent necessary for the smooth operation of their subsidiary. However, investment in infrastructure development is both costly and particularly risky in EM due to inadequate institutional development to guarantee the protection of MNE's investments and interests, local government corruption or mere asymmetric information concerning such projects, which may elevate initially committed resources and raise costs substantially. We argue that the key boundary condition in the context of the link between EM quality of infrastructure and desired (high/full) greenfield ownership is MNE size. MNE size has been referred to in earlier IB studies as a key indicator of the availability of both tangible and intangible organizational resources (e.g. Bloodgood 2014). MNE size has been found to influence strategic decisions of MNEs including equity ownership in their foreign subsidiaries because it is directly linked with availability of financial resources associated with foreign market entry, which can be expensive in many cases (e.g. Ang et al. 2015; Dikova et al. 2017). In case of greenfield manufacturing investments in EMs with deficient local infrastructure, irreversibility of such investment (i.e. impossibility to divest manufacturing plant or unit without making big losses) means that investing MNE may need to commit even more financial resources than other modes under different circumstances. This would only be possible for large MNEs, while we expect MNEs of smaller size to opt for lesser equity ownership when the host EMs do not have an infrastructure of sufficient quality. Therefore, large MNE size can be expected to moderate the influences of host EM infrastructure on equity ownership strategy. Based on this discussion, we hypothesize that:

Hypothesis 2 MNE size moderates the relationship between greenfield equity ownership strategy and Host EM physical infrastructure, that is, large MNEs are likely to choose high equity ownership even in host EMs with relatively low physical infrastructure quality while small MNEs are likely to choose lower equity ownership in host EMs with relatively low physical infrastructure quality.

Investment experience of MNEs has been referred as a major resource during internationalization by a number of IB researchers (e.g. Jung et al. 2010;

Surdu and Mellahi 2016). It is important to further mention that earlier studies analyzing influences of international investment experience of MNEs have yielded conflicting results. Some studies have found general international investment experience to results in choice of high equity ownership in some international markets (e.g. Desai et al. 2004; Jung et al. 2010). However, some studies have found general international experience to be a non-significant determinant for equity ownership especially in case of EMs (e.g. Li and Meyer 2010; Arslan and Dikova 2015). Such studies have argued that specificities of EMs make them significantly differ from developed markets and as a result generic international investment experience becomes ineffective while devising strategies fitting to that context (Li and Meyer 2010; Dikova et al. 2017). Therefore, host country investment experience is significantly important for MNEs, as it enriches them with important knowledge of local institutional and market dynamics (Ascani et al. 2016; Powell and Rhee 2016) as well as of key players and networks in the industrial sectors where they operate (Vance et al. 2014; Dikova et al. 2017). In many EMs, there is a lack of firm specific information due to variance in reporting standards and information disclosure practices (e.g. Lattemann 2014; Moumen et al. 2015). In such situations, host country investment experience can further offer useful information to investing MNEs about well-established and attractive local firms (e.g. Arslan and Dikova 2015), which can be useful in situations of necessary investments in local infrastructure projects. In case of certain EMs of Africa, Asia, and Latin America, several players in key sectors of economy are still state owned (e.g. Bruton et al. 2015; Estrin et al. 2016), and can yield significant economic and political influences. However, MNEs with host country experience can opt for high equity ownership as they can manage practical contingencies associated with greenfield start-up based on their prior knowledge of both formal and informal institutional dynamics (Powell and Rhee 2016; Arslan and Larimo 2017). MNEs with high host country experience can potentially offset some disadvantages associated with low-quality physical infrastructure in certain host EMs based on their prior knowledge of good locations for manufacturing sites, as well as dealing with contingencies of energy connections and managing logistical network. Therefore, we expect host country experience to moderate the impacts of host EM physical infrastructure on equity ownership strategy in greenfield investments. Based on this discussion, we hypothesize that:

Hypothesis 3 MNE host country investment experience moderates the relationship between greenfield equity ownership strategy and Host EM physical infrastructure, that is, host country experienced MNEs are likely to choose high equity ownership even in host EMs with relatively low physical infrastructure quality while inexperienced MNEs are likely to choose lower equity ownership in host EMs with relatively low physical infrastructure quality.

Empirical Research Design and Methodology

Data Sources

The study uses Nordic MNEs' manufacturing sector FDI database that has been developed and constantly updated in the course of about 30 years by one of the authors. It has been developed using company annual reports, corporate websites and stock release information, and articles from leading business magazines (e.g. Kauppalehti, Talouselämä, Dagens Industri, Veckans Affärer, and Borsen). Moreover, historical reports published by national investment agencies like FINNFUND, SWEDFUND, and IFU (Denmark) were used in compiling and updating the dataset. The data has further been supplemented with information drawn from the Thompson One database. The database is unique and representative of the FDIs made by Nordic MNEs in the manufacturing sector.

This internal database is used for the dependent variables of the study, that is, *greenfield entry mode* (i.e. *greenfield JV* vs. *greenfield WOS and majority greenfield JV* vs. *minority greenfield JV*), as well as independent variables of study include MNE size, and MNE host country investment experience. Moreover, the control variables of the study, including industry R&D intensity, MNE international experience, and MNE product diversity, are also derived from the same internal database. Finally, the independent variable of EM physical infrastructure is operationalized using World Economic Forum's Global Competitiveness Reports, which is also a reliable data source, and used in many economics studies as explained later. The operationalization of study variables is presented in the following section.

Operationalization of Study Variables

Dependent Variable

The first dependent variable of the study is a greenfield entry mode, which is coded 0 for greenfield JVs (94% or less equity at time of investment) and 1 for greenfield WOSs (95% or more equity ownership at time of investment).

As mentioned earlier, we aim to analyze equity ownership dynamics of greenfield investments in-depth, so we use other dependent variable greenfield JV for sub-sample analysis. This variable is coded 1 for majority greenfield JV (51% to 94% equity ownership at time of investment) and 0 for minority greenfield JV (50% or less equity ownership at time of investment). For the sake of simplicity in analysis, we consider 50-50 JVs as minority JVs, as there are rather few such cases.

Independent Variables

Host EM Physical Infrastructure We use the country scores from the Global Competitiveness Reports published by World Economic Form in second pillar of rating which is infrastructure (WEF 2018). The scores in this pillar are based on both transport (road, rail, and air) infrastructure and electricity/telephony; thereby appropriately incorporating aspects of physical infrastructure being analyzed in our study. Global Competitiveness Reports are a reliable data source, which has been extensively used in IB, economics and management studies, earlier.

MNE Size We use natural log of global sales of the investing firms in the year preceding to the investment changed to Euros (e.g. Hennart and Park 1993; Arslan et al. 2015).

MNE Host Country Experience We operationalize host country experience using the number years of presence in host country calculated from the first manufacturing investment in that particular market (e.g. Hennart and Park 1993; Dikova et al. 2017).

Control Variables

In line with past literature, the study uses a number of control variables at the country, industry, and firm level, in order to enhance the validity of the study findings. We explain the operationalization of these control variables as follows.

Industry Unrelatedness We use a dummy variable where 0 means that the greenfield investment is undertaken in a related industry (the four-digit SIC code of the investment is the same as the industry where the firm already operates) and 1 which means that the greenfield investment was undertaken in an industry that is new for the firm, that is, unrelated investment (e.g. Contractor et al. 2014; Dikova et al. 2017).

Industry R&D Intensity We use a classification of various four-digit SIC industries into four categories (Low Tech, Low-Medium Tech, Medium Tech, and High Tech) based on value added figures of investing firms (e.g. Dikova et al. 2017).

MNE International Experience We measured international experience of investing MNEs by a number of earlier investments undertaken by investing firms in different international markets, as done in several earlier studies (e.g. Kaynak et al. 2007; Dikova et al. 2017).

MNE Product Diversity We use a number of four-digit SIC codes of the products in which investing firm has been operating based on the annual reports and websites of the firms (Chang et al. 2013; Dikova et al. 2017).

Host Country Ownership Freedom We operationalized host country ownership freedom based on country scores in item of foreign ownership/investment restrictions from economic freedom of the world annual reports (e.g. Arslan and Larimo 2017).

Host Country Economic Growth We use percentage of GDP growth in host country of in the preceding the investment based on UNCTAD data (e.g. Brouthers and Brouthers 2001; Arslan et al. 2015).

Host Country Risk We use *Euromoney* country risk ratings for this variable. It is operationalized by subtracting country score from 100, in the year of investment or nearest available year (e.g. Arslan et al. 2015; Dikova et al. 2017).

Sample Description

The study sample consists of 921 greenfield investments made only in the manufacturing sector by Nordic MNEs in EMs located in Africa, Asia, Europe (Central and Eastern Europe), and Latin America during 1990–2015. The main aspects of study sample are summarized in following Table 5.1.

Statistical Analysis Method

The dependent variables of this study are dichotomous (i.e. greenfield JV vs. greenfield WOS and majority greenfield JV vs. minority greenfield JV). Therefore, we use binary logistic regression analysis to analyze the impact of

Table 5.1 Sample characteristics

Sample characteristic	Description
Greenfield investments	584 greenfield JVs (63.4%) and 337 greenfield WOSs (36.6%)
Host country experience of investing firms	Average: 5.68 years. Minimum: 0 years (no earlier experience in the host country). Maximum: 37 years
R&D intensity	Low tech 286 investments (31.1%), low-medium tech 215 investments (23.3%), medium tech 331 investment (35.9%), and high tech 89 investments (9.7%)
Major investment destinations	China 275 (29.9%); Poland 135 (14.7%); Russia 124 (13.5%); India 97 (10.5%), Malaysia 46 (5%); Brazil 35 (3.8%); and Mexico 34 (3.7%)
Timing of investment	1990s: 570 (61.9%), 2000s: 351 (38.1%)

the study variables on the equity ownership strategy of Nordic MNEs. Binary logistic regression has been used as a reliable statistical analysis technique in a number of past IB studies addressing different aspects of foreign market entry strategies of MNEs. The binomial logistic regression model is formally expressed as

$$P(yi = 1) = 1/1 + \exp(-a - XiB)$$

Where yi is the dependent variable, Xi is the vector of independent variables for the ith observation, a is the intercept parameter and B is the vector of regression coefficients (Amemiya 1981). The recent version of SPSS, that is, PASW 24 is used for the binomial regression analysis in this study.

Study Results

A bivariate correlation analysis was conducted before logistic regression tests (see Table 5.2) in order to detect any multicollinearity among the independent variables. Following Pallant (2007), additional multicollinearity diagnostic tests (tolerance and variance inflation factor (VIF)) were also conducted. According to Wetherill (1986), the VIF value should not exceed 10. In the current study, the VIF values are lower than 5 and consequently, the potential collinearity among variables is not expected to influence the results of logistic regression analysis.

Table 5.3 displays the results of binomial regression analysis for the full sample of study, while Table 5.4 presents binomial regression results for subsample of greenfield JVs. The explanatory power of all the statistical models of

Table 5.2 Descriptive statistics and Pearson correlations

	Mean	Std. dev	1	2	3	4	5	6	7	8	9	10	11
1. Industry unrelatedness	0.4	0.19	1										
2. R&D intensity	2.24	0.99	−0.078	1									
3. MNE international experience	36.01	42.15	−0.152*	0.086	1								
4. MNE product diversity	9.92	11.69	0.493*	−0.147*	−0.124*	1							
5. Host country ownership freedom	6.02	1.32	−0.034	−0.028	−0.029	−0.015	1						
6. Host country economic growth	5.73	5.48	−0.083	0.121*	0.072	−0.61	−0.063	1					
7. Host country risk	56.85	13.31	−0.030	0.065	0.054	−0.038	0.085	0.508*	1				
8. Host country infrastructure	3.73	0.52	−0.042	0.043	−0.050	0.020	0.046	0.126*	0.267*	1			
9. MNE size	7.79	2.47	−0.359*	0.082	0.481*	−0.305*	−0.007	0.093	0.069	−0.067	1		
10. MNE host country experience	5.68	6.83	−0.057	0.073	0.430*	−0.121*	0.065	0.027	0.062	0.056	0.519*	1	
11. Greenfield ownership mode	0.37	0.48	0.124*	0.069	0.101	−0.143*	0.026	−0.030	−0.062	0.083	0.108*	0.112*	1

*Correlation is significant at the 0.01 level (2-tailed)

108   A. Arslan et al.

Table 5.3 Binomial logistic regression estimates full sample (greenfield WOS = 1)

Variable	Model 1: control variables	Model 2: independent variables	Model 3: moderating influences
Industry unrelatedness	−1.036	−0.909	−0.877
Industry R&D intensity	0.110**	0.100*	0.107*
MNE international experience	0.004	0.002	0.001
MNE product diversity	−0.024**	−0.025**	−0022**
Host country ownership freedom	0.054*	0.060*	0.064**
Host country economic growth	−0.006	−0.004	−0.005
Host country risk	−0.011*	−0.018***	−0.014**
Host country infrastructure		0.496***	
MNE size		0.019*	
MNE host country experience		0.023**	
MNE size × host country infrastructure			0.018
MNE host country experience × host country infrastructure			0.064**
N (greenfield WOS)	921 (337)	921 (337)	921 (337)
Model x^2	39.376***	54.765***	58.517***
−2 log likelihood	1170.341	1154.952	1151.201
Nagelkerke R^2	0.157	0.179	0.18
Correctly classified (%)	73.2%	74%	74.1%

Levels of significance: *$p \leq 0.1$; **$p \leq 0.05$; ***$p \leq 0.01$

Table 5.4 Binomial logistic regression estimates sub-sample JVs (majority greenfield JV = 1)

Variable	Model 1: control variables	Model 2: independent variables	Model 3: moderating influences
Industry unrelatedness	−0.047	−0.231	−0.186
Industry R&D intensity	0.398***	0.403***	0.408***
MNE international experience	0.010**	0.013**	0.013**
MNE product diversity	−0.020*	−0.030**	−0.029**
Host country ownership freedom	0.129*	0.132*	0.134*
Host country economic growth	0.036	0.034	0.036
Host country risk	−0.012*	−0.012*	−0.014*
Host country infrastructure		0.030**	
MNE size		−0.083	
MNE host country experience		0.884**	
MNE size × host country infrastructure			−0.018
MNE host country experience × host country infrastructure			0.013
N (majority greenfield JV)	584(227)	584(227)	584(227)
Model x^2	72.545***	74.954***	75.854***
−2 log likelihood	707.689	704.460	704.359
Nagelkerke R^2	0.158	0.163	0.167
Correctly classified (%)	76.6%	76.8%	76.9%

Levels of significance: *$p \leq 0.1$; **$p \leq 0.05$; ***$p \leq 0.01$

the study is good, as their chi-square (χ^2) values are significant at p < 0.01 level. The results show that in high R&D intensity sectors, Nordic MNEs preferred high equity ownership strategy (i.e. greenfield WOSs in the full sample and majority greenfield JVs in the sub-sample analysis). Moreover, it is further visible from the result that highly diversified MNEs preferred low equity commitment at time of market entry (like minority JVs) as they lack product specific knowledge and insights from local partner are highly useful. Host country ownership freedom is positively associated with high equity ownership strategy, while firms tended to opt for low equity commitment in host countries representing high risk at the time of entry. An important aspect visible from the results concerns influence of general international experience. It is not significant for full sample analysis but becomes significant in the sub-sample of JVs. Therefore, it can be argued that general international experience of MNEs may not offer much benefits for choice of WOSs especially in EMs as discussed earlier as well. However, it can still be useful for making decisions concerning level of equity commitment in a JV (i.e. minority vs. majority JV).

The study results show that host country infrastructure, MNE size, and host country experience are all significant determinants of equity ownership strategy in full sample. Nordic MNEs tended to prefer greenfield WOSs in host EMs with relatively good physical infrastructure, and when they had large size and host country experience. Moreover, the results also show that host country experience moderates the influences of EM physical infrastructure on equity ownership strategy. Therefore, we get support for the Hypotheses 1 and 3 in the full sample analysis. However, we do not get support for the Hypothesis 2 concerning moderating influences of MNE size. The analysis of JVs sub-sample shows that key independent variable of investing MNE size is not significant determinant of equity ownership strategy of Nordic MNEs. We do not get support for both moderating hypotheses in sub-sample analysis. These findings can be explained by referring to specificities of JV equity ownership strategy, because in specific context of EMs, mere availability of more financial resources (i.e. large MNE size) is not enough to motivate MNE for high equity ownership. Due to uncertainty caused by institutional and economic factors, investing MNEs may prefer low equity ownership strategy in greenfield investments in order to share significant costs associated with the start-up of greenfield manufacturing plant.

110   A. Arslan et al.

Discussion, Implications, and Limitations

The findings of current study offer useful implications for both managerial and academic audience. A key theoretical implication of this chapter relates to use of RDT (Pfeffer and Salancik 2003; Pfeffer 2005) in IB studies. Based on RDT, we hypothesized that use of shared-ownership greenfields (i.e. JVs) as a means of reducing the uncertainty surrounding the flow of needed resources in EMs with infrastructure deficiencies. This argument received support for both full and sub-sample analysis. Moreover, we further hypothesized that based on differences in investing MNEs size and experience, they may be able to reduce host country resource dependence including infrastructure. The results depicted partial support for boundary effects of MNE size and experience on the relationship between host country physical infrastructure and greenfield ownership strategy. The current study is one the first to perform such an analysis in context of greenfield investments, and future studies can build on it to further explore this research area using RDT as a theoretical basis.

The current study also established the importance of host EM physical infrastructure as an important determinant of equity ownership strategy of MNEs in their greenfield investments undertaken in EMs. This aspect needs attention from both managers of MNEs aspiring to internationalize to EMs, as the current debate mostly focuses on the role of institutional infrastructure, neglecting the fact that physical infrastructure is the key for establishing a successful manufacturing facility. Therefore, its different aspects including road and railways infrastructure, telecommunications, energy supply and access to required materials, should be carefully considered by the managers while deciding on an optimal site for their greenfield investment especially in EM context. The current study has further strengthened the argument presented by some earlier studies regarding the importance of host country specific investment experience for equity ownership strategy in EMs (e.g. Arslan and Dikova 2015; Dikova et al. 2017). The results showed that host country experience moderated the impact of physical infrastructure and was a significant determinant of equity ownership in the context of greenfield JV investments. MNE managers can rely on prior experience in host country while deciding on optimal equity ownership strategy for their greenfield investments. The current study showed interestingly that general international investment experience is significant determinant for equity ownership strategy in JVs sub-sample. It can be argued that general international investment experience may not offer much insights when MNEs opt for greenfield WOSs in EMs as that choice requires dealing with significant amount of resource commitment, as well as dealing with legal considerations concerning full ownership in a context where regulations have been developing slowly. However, for the choice between minority and majority JV, general international experience is useful, as prior dealing with JV partners in other international markets including EMs can equip investing MNEs with negotiation and management tools helpful to deal with complex JV relationships (e.g. Yan and Luo 2016; Hollender et al. 2017). Therefore, MNE managers can use insights from their international investment experience while devising equity ownership strategy in a collaborative venture in EMs experiencing infrastructure deficiencies.

Our study has certain limitations as well. Firstly, we address host country physical infrastructure as a holistic construct in this study. However, different components of host country physical infrastructure like roads and railways, telecommunications, access to ports and raw materials, and so on, can influence equity ownership strategy differently. It would be interesting if future studies carry forward this aspect and delve more into detailed analysis concerning influences of different elements of physical infrastructure on greenfield investments undertaken by MNEs. Moreover, this chapter focused on physical infrastructure of EMs only. However, the statistics concerning physical infrastructure reveal that even in developed economies, it is not always in best shape as well as there are significant regional differences in this aspect in both developed and emerging markets. The current study did not address this regional variance. Future studies can enrich IB research by focusing on this regional variation within large countries, as well as addressing influences of physical infrastructure in developed economies on the greenfield investments. Finally, the type of greenfield investment being undertaken (i.e. resource seeking or market seeking) can potentially result in different types of physical infrastructure elements influencing equity ownership strategy. This also remains an avenue for future studies.

References

Aggarwal, A. (2002). Liberalisation, multinational enterprises and export performance: Evidence from Indian manufacturing. *Journal of Development Studies, 38*(3), 119–137.

Ahammad, M. F., Leone, V., Tarba, S. Y., Glaister, K. W., & Arslan, A. (2017). Equity ownership in cross-border mergers and acquisitions by British firms: An analysis of real options and transaction cost factors. *British Journal of Management, 28*(2), 180–196.

Amemiya, T. (1981). Qualitative response models: A survey. *Journal of Economic Literature, 4*(4), 1483–1536.

Ang, J. B. (2008). Determinants of foreign direct investment in Malaysia. *Journal of Policy Modeling, 30*(1), 185–189.

Ang, S. H., Benischke, M. H., & Doh, J. P. (2015). The interactions of institutions on foreign market entry mode. *Strategic Management Journal, 36*(10), 1536–1553.

Arslan, A., & Dikova, D. (2015). Influences of institutional distance and MNEs' host country experience on the ownership strategy in cross-border M&As in emerging economies. *Journal of Transnational Management, 20*(4), 231–256.

Arslan, A., & Larimo, J. (2017). Greenfield entry strategy of multinational Enterprises in the emerging markets: Influences of institutional distance and international trade freedom. *Journal of East-West Business, 23*(2), 140–170.

Arslan, A., Tarba, S. Y., & Larimo, J. (2015). FDI entry strategies and the impacts of economic freedom distance: Evidence from Nordic FDIs in transitional periphery of CIS and SEE. *International Business Review, 24*(6), 997–1008.

Ascani, A., Crescenzi, R., & Iammarino, S. (2016). What drives European multinationals to the European Union neighbouring countries? A mixed-methods analysis of Italian investment strategies. *Environment and Planning C: Government and Policy, 34*(4), 656–675.

Asiedu, E. (2002). On the determinants of foreign direct investment to developing countries: Is Africa different? *World Development, 30*(1), 107–119.

Ayden, Y., Demirbag, M., & Tatoglu, E. (2017). *Turkish multinationals: Market entry and post-acquisition strategy*. Cham: Palgrave Macmillan/Springer Nature.

Bellak, C., Leibrecht, M., & Damijan, J. P. (2009). Infrastructure endowment and corporate income taxes as determinants of foreign direct investment in central and eastern European countries. *The World Economy, 32*(2), 267–290.

Bellak, C., Leibrecht, M., & Römisch, R. (2007). On the appropriate measure of tax burden on foreign direct investment to the CEECs. *Applied Economics Letters, 14*(8), 603–606.

Blonigen, B. A., & Piger, J. (2014). Determinants of foreign direct investment. *Canadian Journal of Economics/Revue canadienne d'économique, 47*(3), 775–812.

Bloodgood, J. (2014). Enhancing the resource-based view of the firm: Increasing the role of awareness. *Strategic Management Review, 8*(1), 61–75.

Brouthers, K. D., & Brouthers, L. E. (2001). Explaining the national cultural distance paradox. *Journal of International Business Studies, 32*(1), 177–189.

Bruton, G. D., Peng, M. W., Ahlstrom, D., Stan, C., & Xu, K. (2015). State-owned enterprises around the world as hybrid organizations. *Academy of Management Perspectives, 29*(1), 92–114.

Cavusgil, S. T. (1984). Differences among exporting firms based on their degree of internationalization. *Journal of Business Research, 12*(2), 195–208.

Chang, S. J., Chung, J., & Moon, J. J. (2013). When do wholly owned subsidiaries perform better than joint ventures? *Strategic Management Journal, 34*(3), 317–337.

Chang, Y. C., Kao, M. S., Kuo, A., & Chiu, C. F. (2012). How cultural distance influences entry mode choice: The contingent role of host country's governance quality. *Journal of Business Research, 65*(8), 1160–1170.

Chen, S.-F. (2008). The motives for international acquisitions: Capability procurements, strategic considerations, and the role of ownership structures. *Journal of International Business Studies, 39*(3), 454–471.

Contractor, F. J., Lahiri, S., Elango, B., & Kundu, S. K. (2014). Institutional, cultural and industry related determinants of ownership choices in emerging market FDI acquisitions. *International Business Review, 23*(5), 931–941.

Deardorff, A. V. (2001). International provision of trade services, trade, and fragmentation. *Review of International Economics, 9*(2), 233–248.

Deichmann, J., Karidis, S., & Sayek, S. (2003). Foreign direct investment in Turkey: Regional determinants. *Applied Economics, 35*(16), 1767–1778.

Desai, M. A., Foley, C. F., & Hines, J. R. (2004). A multinational perspective on capital structure choice and internal capital markets. *The Journal of Finance, 59*(6), 2451–2487.

Dikova, D., & Van Witteloostuijn, A. (2007). Foreign direct investment mode choice: Entry and establishment modes in transition economies. *Journal of International Business Studies, 38*(6), 1013–1033.

Dikova, D., Arslan, A., & Larimo, J. (2017). Equity commitment in cross-border acquisitions: The influences of distance and organizational resources. In A. Verbeke, J. Puck, & R. van Tulder (Eds.), *Distance in international business: Concept, cost and value, Progress in international business research* (Vol. 12, pp. 297–337).

Erdal, F., & Tatoglu, E. (2002). Locational determinants of foreign direct investment in an emerging market economy. *Multinational Business Review, 10*(1), 21–34.

Estrin, S., Meyer, K. E., Nielsen, B. B., & Nielsen, S. (2016). Home country institutions and the internationalization of state owned enterprises: A cross-country analysis. *Journal of World Business, 51*(2), 294–307.

Gorodnichenko, Y., Svejnar, J., & Terrell, K. (2014). When does FDI have positive spillovers? Evidence from 17 transition market economies. *Journal of Comparative Economics, 42*(4), 954–969.

Hennart, J. F., & Park, Y. R. (1993). Greenfield vs. acquisition: The strategy of Japanese investors in the United States. *Management Science, 39*(9), 1054–1070.

Hollender, L., Zapkau, F. B., & Schwens, C. (2017). SME foreign market entry mode choice and foreign venture performance: The moderating effect of international experience and product adaptation. *International Business Review, 26*(2), 250–263.

Hutchinson, K., Alexander, N., Quinn, B., & Doherty, A. M. (2007). Internationalization motives and facilitating factors: Qualitative evidence from smaller specialist retailers. *Journal of International Marketing, 15*(3), 96–122.

Inderst, G., & Stewart, F. (2014). *Institutional investment in infrastructure in emerging markets and developing economies.* Washington, DC: World Bank Publications.

Jung, W., Han, S. H., Park, H., & Kim, D. Y. (2010). Empirical assessment of internationalization strategies for small and medium construction companies. *Journal of Construction Engineering and Management, 136*(12), 1306–1316.

Katsikeas, C. S., & Morgan, R. E. (1994). Differences in perceptions of exporting problems based on firm size and export market experience. *European Journal of Marketing, 28*(5), 17–35.

Kaur, M., Khatua, A., & Yadav, S. S. (2016). Infrastructure development and FDI inflow to developing economies: Evidence from India. *Thunderbird International Business Review, 58*(6), 555–563.

Kaynak, E., Demirbag, M., & Tatoglu, E. (2007). Determinants of ownership-based entry mode choice of MNEs: Evidence from Mongolia. *Management International Review, 47*(4), 505–530.

Khanna, T., & Palepu, K. G. (2010). *Winning in emerging markets: A road map for strategy and execution.* Harvard: Harvard Business Press.

Lattemann, C. (2014). On the convergence of corporate governance practices in emerging markets. *International Journal of Emerging Markets, 9*(2), 316–332.

Lee, Y., Hemmert, M., & Kim, J. (2014). What drives the international ownership strategies of Chinese firms and quest; the role of distance and home-country institutional factors in outward acquisitions. *Asian Business and Management, 13*(3), 197–225.

Lee, I. H. I., Hong, E., & Makino, S. (2016). Location decisions of inward FDI in sub-national regions of a host country: Service versus manufacturing industries. *Asia Pacific Journal of Management, 33*(2), 343–370.

Leibrecht, M., & Riedl, A. (2010). Taxes and infrastructure as determinants of foreign direct investment in Central and Eastern European countries revisited: New evidence from a spatially augmented gravity model. *Discussion Papers SFB International Tax Coordination, 42.* WU Vienna University of Economics and Business, Vienna.

Leonidou, L. C., Katsikeas, C. S., Palihawadana, D., & Spyropoulou, S. (2007). An analytical review of the factors stimulating smaller firms to export: Implications for policy-makers. *International Marketing Review, 24*(6), 735–770.

Li, P. Y., & Meyer, K. E. (2010). Contextualizing experience effects in international business, a study of ownership strategies. *Journal of World Business, 44*(4), 370–382.

Lin, L. H. (2014). Subsidiary performance: The contingency of multinational corporation's international strategy. *European Management Journal, 32*(6), 928–937.

Lu, J., Liu, X., Wright, M., & Filatotchev, I. (2014). International experience and FDI location choices of Chinese firms: The moderating effects of home country government support and host country institutions. *Journal of International Business Studies, 45*(4), 428–449.

Malhotra, M. (2017). Foreign direct investment opportunities in infrastructure development: A Study on India. In *Handbook of research on economic, financial, and industrial impacts on infrastructure development* (pp. 302–312). Hershey: IGI Global.

Meyer, K. E., & Su, Y. S. (2015). Integration and responsiveness in subsidiaries in emerging economies. *Journal of World Business, 50*(1), 149–158.

Mijiyawa, A. G. (2017). Does foreign direct investment promote exports? Evidence from African countries. *The World Economy, 40*(9), 1934–1957.

Moumen, N., Othman, H. B., & Hussainey, K. (2015). The value relevance of risk disclosure in annual reports: Evidence from MENA emerging markets. *Research in International Business and Finance, 34*, 177–204.

Nourzad, F., Greenwold, D. N., & Yang, R. (2014). The interaction between FDI and infrastructure capital in the development process. *International Advances in Economic Research, 20*(2), 203–212.

Pallant, J. (2007). *SPSS survival manual, a step by step guide to data analysis using SPSS for windows.* Buckingham: Open University Press.

Pennings, J. M., Barkema, H., & Douma, S. (1994). Organizational learning and diversification. *Academy of Management Journal, 37*(3), 608–640.

Pfeffer, J. (2005). Developing resource dependence theory: How theory is affected by its environment. In K. Smith & M. Hitt (Eds.), *Great minds in management: The process of theory development* (pp. 436–459). Oxford: Oxford University Press.

Pfeffer, J., & Salancik, G. R. (2003). *The external control of organizations: A resource dependence perspective.* Stanford: Stanford University Press.

Powell, K. S., & Rhee, M. (2016). Experience in different institutional environments and foreign subsidiary ownership structure. *Journal of Management, 42*(6), 1434–1461.

Riedl, A. (2010). Location factors of FDI and the growing services economy. *Economics of Transition, 18*(4), 741–761.

Sader, F. (2000). *Attracting Foreign direct investment into infrastructure, Foreign Investment Advisory Services occasional paper 12.* International Finance Corporation and World Bank.

Slangen, A. H. (2011). A communication-based theory of the choice between greenfield and acquisition entry. *Journal of Management Studies, 48*(8), 1699–1726.

Slangen, A. H., & Hennart, J. F. (2008). Do multinationals really prefer to enter culturally distant countries through greenfields rather than through acquisitions? The role of parent experience and subsidiary autonomy. *Journal of International Business Studies, 39*(3), 472–490.

Snell, S. A. (1992). Control theory in strategic human resource management: The mediating effect of administrative information. *Academy of Management Journal, 35*(2), 292–327.

Surdu, I., & Mellahi, K. (2016). Theoretical foundations of equity based foreign market entry decisions: A review of the literature and recommendations for future research. *International Business Review, 25*(5), 1169–1184.

Tate, W. L., Ellram, L. M., Schoenherr, T., & Petersen, K. J. (2014). Global competitive conditions driving the manufacturing location decision. *Business Horizons, 57*(3), 381–390.

UNCTAD. (2015). *Reforming international investment governance*. Geneva: Switzerland.

UNCTAD. (2016). *World investment report 2016. Investor nationality: Policy challenges*. Geneva: UNCTAD.

Vance, C. M., Andersen, T., Vaiman, V., & Gale, J. (2014). A taxonomy of potential contributions of the host country national local liaison role in global knowledge management. *Thunderbird International Business Review, 56*(2), 173–191.

WEF. (2018). *Global Competitiveness Report 2017–2018*. Available online at https://www.weforum.org/reports/the-global-competitiveness-report-2017-2018

Wetherill, G. B. (1986). *Regression analysis with applications*. London: Chapman and Hall.

Wheeler, D., & Mody, A. (1992). International investment location decisions: The case of US firms. *Journal of International Economics, 33*(1–2), 57–76.

World Bank. (2018). *Logistics Performance Indicator*. Available online at https://lpi.worldbank.org/

Yan, A., & Luo, Y. (2016). *International joint ventures: Theory and practice*. New York: Routledge.

6

The Value of Local Externalities in Country-of-Origin Clusters: Evidence from China

Berrbizne Urzelai and Francisco Puig

Introduction

The current global environment is drawing attention to the increasing presence of multinational small-medium enterprises (SMEs) from all over the world. These firms face a number of location-specific disadvantages, as compared with national firms, when they enter a new foreign market (Hymer, 1960). This is commonly referred to as liability of foreignness (Zaheer ,1995) and is rooted in the psychological, cultural, and institutional distance between the home and the host country. Besides, these firms face other barriers linked to their size or other factors (liabilities of smallness and newness).

To surpass these liabilities one of the main strategies followed by a foreign direct investment (FDI) option is to co-locate (or collocate) and interact with other firms in specific areas to benefit from externalities and gain advantages from local institutional linkages (positive externalities). However, there are financial costs and risks associated to doing business in clusters due to rivalry, congestion or imitation (negative externalities) that discourage firms to adopt this location mode decision. In other words, the decision to co-locate and grow through networking and clustering has implications for the performance and

---

B. Urzelai
University of the West of England, Bristol, UK
e-mail: Berrbizne2.Urzelai@uwe.ac.uk

F. Puig (✉)
University of Valencia, Valencia, Spain
e-mail: Francisco.puig@uv.es

© The Author(s) 2019
A. Chidlow et al. (eds.), *The Changing Strategies of International Business*, The Academy of International Business, https://doi.org/10.1007/978-3-030-03931-8_6

118 B. Urzelai and F. Puig

survival of the subsidiary (Almodovar and Rugman, 2015; Peng and Luo, 2000).

For an effective acquisition and exploitation of these spillovers and to control negative externalities these firms need to concentrate their efforts not only on their internal development but also on the configuration and adoption of business models that best link the FDI with firms located in the same area (Lambert and Davidson, 2013). Our research analyzes the role played by the location mode by analyzing the sign and scope of the externalities that arise from country-of-origin clusters. This is approached from a multidimensional perspective and utilizing a sample of 24 FDI European SMEs localized in China. We compare subsidiaries that are located in country-of-origin clusters in a specific location (Kunshan, Jiangsu, and China) with isolated subsidiaries. China is an investment destination where European firms still face many challenges (Bao et al., 2012) and a country with high institutional distance and instability, which creates an uncertainty that firms compensate through business network knowledge (Hilmersson and Jansson, 2012).

The chapter is organized as follows. In the next section, we provide an overview of the difficulties faced by foreign investors, especially SMEs, and a brief review of agglomeration literature. The subsequent section discusses the methodology, followed by the results. The final section discusses some of the contributions and implications at different levels: academic, managerial, and political.

Theoretical Background

The Challenge of Internationalization for an SME

As various Free Trade Agreements have been implemented and new information and communication technologies have been developed, the competitive landscape of companies has become more turbulent and globalized. To face this new scenario, most companies have reconfigured their corporate, competitive, and functional strategies. SMEs, characterized for having less resources and knowledge, also have to adapt to this process of internationalization, either alone or by establishing links and collaborations with other agents (Paul et al., 2017). Successful global companies used to be large multinational corporations with many divisions and product lines but adopting a global strategy is as important for large firm as it is for SMEs or small organizations.

The Value of Local Externalities in Country-of-Origin Clusters...

SMEs are increasingly integrated into the global economy and have gone further than what is often considered the first step of internationalization, that is, exporting and importing (Puig et al., 2018). For many firms, internationalization is a challenge from which the new models (i.e. Johanson and Vahlne, 2009) go beyond the traditional gradual approach in which the company increases its resources and its involvement abroad as it gains experience in the market. In fact, nowadays we can observe different realities characterized by an accelerated internationalization, a high commitment in foreign markets and a prompt global orientation. Within the last 20 years, many SMEs have also accelerated their international commitment by investing in distant countries despite limited market knowledge, limited use of networks, and scarced international experience of the entrepreneurs and managers (Kalinic and Forza, 2012; Puig et al., 2018).

However, as Hollenstein (2005) argued SMEs have to face several barriers within their internationalization process that can be internal limitations of resources (financial, informational, managerial, etc.) and/or external barriers such as laws and regulations. According to Carlos (2011) SMEs have found new ways to deal with smallness and newness but due to their lack of experience, skills, know-how, governance structures, limited capital and management, time or information resources, SMEs are typically constrained in their efforts to reach international markets.

Which aspects drive companies to expand their activities abroad, and which ones are linked to a better international performance? According to the literature, those aspects could be linked to the membership or attachment in territorial networks (i.e. Pla-Barber and Puig, 2009). Various studies have shown that interorganizational relationships are associated with company competitiveness (Powell and Brantley, 1992; Uzzi, 1996). In fact, interorganizational relationships appear to be influential in many internationalization issues as the follows: foreign market selection, market servicing, dynamics of entry, international market development, time of internationalization, or strategic choices and performance. Generally speaking, cooperation can be considered a way to stimulate the development of enterprises in terms of reducing risk, extending markets, introducing new technologies, and so on. So, cooperation can be a strategy for SMEs not only to grow but also to enhance other types of development (Havnes and Hauge, 2004).

Due to a lack of local knowledge, foreign firms are expected to encounter the so-called disadvantage of alien status in host economies (He, 2003), so they find higher benefits from locating in existing clusters of foreign enterprises (Dunning, 1998). In this line, the identification and exploitation of opportunities, the liabilities that firms have due to their size or the lack of

120 B. Urzelai and F. Puig

market information could be better faced from being a member of a cluster (Tan and Meyer, 2011). Therefore, the relationship between investment and clusters can be seen no longer with clusters as the outcome of FDI, but as the precondition or determinant for attracting FDI (De Propris and Driffield, 2006).

Country-of-Origin Clusters and Co-location Externalities

The literature on geographic agglomeration defines agglomerations as organizational groups that interact, in an economic sector and in a geographically limited territory, where the cooperation and exchange of information and knowledge among the organizations favor growth and regional development (Porter, 1998). These interactions are fostered by the (geographical and cognitive) proximity and the active participation of the companies that are part of that social network (cluster). Therefore, industrial clusters are made up of a variety of nodes (people, institutions, and businesses) and relationships (formal and informal) that allow the generation of various synergies that increase their competitive advantage.

Since the 1980s, the phenomenon associated with clustering attracted the interest of economists, geographers, sociologists, and so on. Within this approach, different but not exclusive lines of research have studied issues such as the origin, structure, evolution, and conceptual clarification (Martin and Sunley, 2011). Business literature highlights the study of the geographical delimitation/mapping and conceptual clarification, the analysis of the effect that these agglomerations have on the strategic behavior, the performance of companies and the diagnostic of the determinants by which these territorial entities exhibit a heterogeneous performance (Molina-Morales and Martinez-Fernandez, 2004). All this has been translated into a vast scientific production that, from different research approaches, has tried to structure and characterize that literature, as shown by Gonzalez-Loureiro et al. (2018).

In today's international scenario, we can identify new organizational realities that depend on their actors and the members, where they share (a) a national sectorial platform (cluster initiatives), (b) an economic activity in a given territory (industrial clusters), or (c) a foreign territory and ethnic and cultural ties (country-of-origin/compatriot/ethnic clusters). These realities (Table 6.1) are the object of research of this chapter.

Clusters *"in origin/at home"* can serve as a platform in the early stages of internationalization of the firms, for example, to increase their exports. Cluster organizations and *initiatives* also serve as platform for the members to

The Value of Local Externalities in Country-of-Origin Clusters... 121

Table 6.1 Different types of clusters

	Cluster initiatives	Industrial clusters	Country-of-origin clusters
Belonging factors	The product and/or the market	The processes and/or knowledge of the value chain	Cultural and ethnic factors
Focus	Sectorial/multisectorial	Sectorial	Multisectorial
Objectives	Representation in the country of origin	Interrelation among firms and development and implementation of joint actions.	Lobby and negotiation power in the host country
Establishment mode	Export, alliances	Acquisitions	Greenfield
Effects	Counseling services, and access to business opportunities and entry modes	Propensity to internationalize; intensity and export diversification	Coordination of resources, knowledge and mutual support for the expatriates
Generated resource	Explicit knowledge about internationalization support and mechanisms	Access to commercial networks	Tacit market knowledge
Examples	Beauty cluster in Catalonia, Spain	Textile cluster in Alcoi-Ontinyent, Spain	Basque firms in Kunshan, China

Source: Own elaboration

cooperate and improve their internationalization. These organizations provide services in exchange for a fee, establish relationships that facilitate the creation of business opportunities with external partners, and organize trade missions, among others (Jankowska et al., 2017). Being a member of an industrial cluster could increase the firms' exports through the network that the cluster offers to position and promote those firms in foreign markets, to increase their global strategic capacity, to advise on financial support for internationalization, or to facilitate access to new business opportunities or entry modes (distributors, agents, etc.) (Pla-Barber and Puig, 2009).

On the other hand, in a more advanced phase of the internationalization process, companies invest in foreign markets through entry modes that require a higher commitment (FDI) (Shen et al., 2017). Country-of-origin clusters or groups of firms from the same or country-of-origin provide a supportive environment to, among other things, acquire legitimacy and negotiation power in the target market, reduce uncertainty and opportunism, or facilitate tacit knowledge sharing and a mutual support ecosystem (Urzelai and Puig, 2018).

Co-location and Entry Reasons

Researchers and academics have come up with different classifications that explain the reasons why firms go international and invest in foreign markets. Authors such as Dunning (1988) classified entry reasons into (1) natural resource seeking (available resources), (2) market seeking (exploit markets, follow customers, etc.), (3) efficiency seeking (availability and costs factors to gain economies of scale and scope), and (4) strategic-asset or innovation seeking (acquire technology, knowledge, etc.).

Jain et al. (2016) found that when a firm wants to exploit their resources they internationalize with a market-seeking or resource-seeking reasons, whereas they are likely to explore new resources with an asset-seeking motive. Country-of-origin cluster has been taken as a strategy-seeking choice where firms are attracted to locate nearby firms from the same country (Mucchielli and Yu, 2011). However, some empirical studies show that these types of clusters are also attractive for firms with other investment reasons. Looking at 31 Spanish firms in China, Puig et al. (2017) found that manufacturing firms were more associated with clustered locations than trading-service firms were. More specifically, Shen and Puig (2017) evidenced that smaller Chinese investors in Germany, with a state background or those that seek market expansion (market seeking) tend to co-locate with their compatriots in the host country, while investors who seek strategic assets (strategic seeking) are more likely to tap into industry clusters. Therefore, it is not clear whether firms that go into country-of-origin clusters follow a single reason when entering that host market.

The Value of Country-of-Origin Clusters

As we have argued before, the influence of clusters on the generation and development of social networks between firms is reasonable, since the social process of interfirm learning works best when partners are close enough to allow a frequent interaction and real exchange of information. Cooperation finds in clusters a proper space for its development, since it is within that context where the basic conditions for its existence are met (geographical and/or cognitive proximity). Social networks and connections are especially useful for cases in which internationalization needs a high degree of mutual trust among the partners (Chang and Park 2005). An efficient functioning of the network limits the coordination cost and minimizes the risk of opportunistic behavior. Thus, geographic proximity, along with the interaction and cooperation, makes these networks generate information and knowledge externalities for their members (Guillén 2002).

As Breschi and Malerba (2005) distinguish, agglomeration drivers for any given sector are location specific and generate agglomeration benefits due to dynamic increasing returns to concentration (e.g. ex ante "intrinsic" differences across territories and cross-sectoral spillovers that cumulatively act upon the existing concentration patters). On the other hand, agglomeration drivers that are entirely sector specific could promote concentration across all territories (e.g. thanks to economies of agglomeration forces that are intrinsically related to the way knowledge is accumulated, innovations are generated).

So, if clustering and networking are so efficient, why have some clusters disappeared and why have some initiatives based on that relational model failed? We think that this is because there are different types of clusters that can bring different types of advantages to international companies. There are *inter* and *intra*-cluster differences due to the life cycle of the sector, the absorption capacity of the companies or the characteristics of its participants, which allow to identify a wide and diverse range of combinations and evolutionary stages. For example, if we accept that a Colombian textile cluster will differ from an Italian one due to their different competitive environment (size of companies, customers, suppliers, etc.), and that, due to their differences in origin, a cluster of Chinese compatriot firms in Germany will differ from a cluster of Spanish compatriots in China, then we could accept that a cluster initiative will not have the same effect on all the member firms, as they differ in terms of their abortion capacity or experience, among other factors.

Investors who enter for the first time in a market, and on their own, experience a greater degree of marginality and face more difficulties. In addition, the more tacit the shared knowledge of the network is, the more important the geographical and cognitive proximity will be. For example, as argued by Belderbos and Zou (2009), imagine a group of Japanese companies that decide to establish in India. New investors will have a greater need for local knowledge than those already there. This need will drive them to look for a country-of-origin or ethnic agglomeration. After the initial stage of the activity, an intense social process that is fostered by a shared culture among all these companies will be developed.

In other words, proximity facilitates formal and informal interaction, facilitating the information exchange and potential collaboration (Larson 1992). The value of these networks is the differential between benefits and costs. The benefits can be related to information externalities, reduction of consumer search costs, increased reputation, knowledge and information spillovers or specialized labor and infrastructure (Tan and Meyer 2011). Costs on the other side could be derived from congestion and competition in input and output markets within the cluster (Henderson 2003). However, as we have previously argued, these aspects could be moderated by the strategic reasons of the firms when entering a new market.

Research Methodology

Data was collected through questionnaires and constant emails and visits to the companies in China from March to June 2013. The researcher also spent time with the expatriates during lunch, spare, and traveling time. This is part of a broader research where other areas were also analyzed (challenges faced in China, social capital generated in country-of-origin clusters, etc.). It is important to mention that conducted a pilot study that helped redefine the questionnaire in order to increase its validity.

The sample used for the analysis is formed by 24 subsidiaries: 12 subsidiaries in MKIP (Mondragon Kunshan Industrial Park), 4 subsidiaries in KGIP (Kunshan German Industrial Park), 3 subsidiaries to enter MKIP in 2013, and 5 Basque isolated subsidiaries located in the same city. All the subsidiaries are SMEs that established in Kunshan from 2005 to 2013. In terms of the activity, 96% of the firms are industrial, 87% are related to manufacturing, and 57% to machinery, equipment, furniture, and recycling sector. Most of the subsidiaries analyzed are subsidiaries that are or will be located in industrial parks. Most of the firms are small (62%) and 54% of the firms are on rented facilities. In terms of size, the factories/offices are of less than 5000 square meter and with more direct than indirect workers. Half of the subsidiaries of the sample entered in China due to market-seeking reasons, 21% due to resource and efficiency-seeking reasons, and the rest due to a combination of strategic, market, and resource-seeking motives. It is important to highlight that all the subsidiaries are WFOEs or greenfield investments.

To analyze the value of the country-of-origin cluster as a platform, we have used different variables related to the location, reasons of establishment in China and externalities.

Given that there is no single technique to define when a firm is located in a cluster or not (Alcácer and Zhao, 2016), we decided we could measure the firms' belonging to a cluster. Then, with visual mapping techniques, this information was contrasted. As a result of it we define the location mode as:

1. Co-located: subsidiaries that are located inside an industrial park (cluster) where they have a membership status.
2. Isolated: subsidiaries that are not members of any industrial park.

Some prior studies have shown that the reason of establishment has a significant impact on MNEs' location preference (Alcácer and Chung, 2013). Following these authors, we distinguished two types of investment motivations in the sampled firms: production/manufacturing or efficiency seekers (coded as 1) and trading/services or market seekers (coded as 2). The reason makes reference to the availability of resources or to costs factors that facilitate economies of scale and scope. The latter includes activities related to overseas market expansion, either by wholesaling or retailing products or services, and other sales-support activities. A third category was created for those firms with a mixed objective for their investments, taking the value of "3," implying the double motivation of seeking efficiency and markets. Therefore, we distinguished:

1. Firms searching for cheaper or more available productive factors (resource seeking).
2. Firms searching for market expansion or following the clients (market seeking).
3. Firms with mixed reasons for their investments, implying a double motivation of seeking efficiency as well as markets.

Given that externalities are multidimensional constructs, we have measured the cluster effect by using six areas of analysis, based on different authors in the literature. Besides, we used Cronbach's Alpha and item-total correlations to check the reliability of the scale and improve the quality of those constructs.

1. Local market knowledge and resources (LMK): this area considers factors such as the knowledge about the establishment process and to surpass country entry barriers, about how to adapt and transform the management routines and business practices to the local setting, or knowledge about the legal environment or local culture (Tan and Meyer, 2011).
2. Industry-specific knowledge and resources (ISK): this area includes factors such as the knowledge about the industrial forecast or technology trends, the suppliers' behavior, the capacity to find specialized goods and labor, or the access to productive inputs (Makino et al., 2002).

3. Legitimacy and reputation (LEG): this area considers different types of legitimacy (normative, pragmatic, and cognitive), the knowledge on how to achieve local legitimacy, or the firms' visibility and representation (Lin et al., 2009).
4. Networking and social interaction (NET): this area considers factors such as the access to tacit knowledge, the cooperation on social and professional activities, or the capacity to surpass the liability of outsidership (Chung and Tung, 2013).
5. Market conditions (MARK): this construct embraces variables related to customers, competitors, knowledge about the customers or access to new sales opportunities and business partners (Almeida and Kogut, 1997).
6. Costs (COST): this last area considers the cost of transportation, transaction costs, qualified workers, infrastructure, or financial resources among others (Tan and Meyer, 2011).

The question given to the interviewees to analyze the perceptions was: *To what extent does your localization mode (co-located or isolated) positively influence the following factors.* We used a Likert scale of 5 point to collect the responses (1 not at all/2 limited extent/3 not sure/4 certain extent/5 large extent).

As the aim was to analyze the association between the cluster effect variables and the co-location mode of the firms or their entry reasons a comparison of means was used to identify and visualize the relations between variables.

Research Findings

Table 6.2 presents the correlations between variables. The correlations between the variables were generally not lower than 0.5, which indicates that there were no serious problems of multicollinearity (Hair et al. 2006), except for justifiable reasons the ones between collocation and NET (0.56), ISK (−0.51), and COST and LEG (0.59).

Table 6.3 shows the average values and standard deviations of externalities classified by the localization mode and entry reason, as estimated with SPSS-20. The average values give us an indication of how the perceptions about those externality dimensions are evaluated, and the standard deviation values indicate the agreement level of the managers' perceptions.

The Value of Local Externalities in Country-of-Origin Clusters...   127

Table 6.2 Descriptive statistics and correlation coefficients

	1	2	3	4	5	6	7
1. Co-location	–						
2. Entry reason	−0.34						
3. LMK	0.07	−0.33					
4. ISK	−0.51*	0.08	0.13				
5. LEG	0.06	−0.37	0.47*	0.41*			
6. NET	0.56**	−0.22	0.06	−0.06	0.34		
7. MARK	−0.45*	0.20	0.00	0.37	0.32	−0.32	
8. COST	−0.07	−0.04	0.31	0.25	0.59**	0.30	0.00

Note: $*p < 0.10$; $**p < 0.05$
Source: Own elaboration

Table 6.3 Average punctuations by type of subsidiary

		Location mode		Main entry reason		
Externalities	Average	Co-located	Isolated	Market	Resource	Mix
MARK	**2.21 (1.25)**	2.03 (1.23)	**3.13 (1.01)**	1.88 (1.20)	2.50 (1.09)	2.75 (1.35)
ISK	2.26 (1.20)	2.25 (1.15)	**3.70 (1.32)**	2.34 (1.23)	**2.80 (1.60)**	2.73 (1.31)
COST	2.77 (1.19)	2.71 (1.18)	**2.97 (1.24)**	2.64 (1.29)	2.49 (0.93)	3.16 (1.14)
LMK	2.99 (1.17)	3.04 (1.16)	**3.20 (1.24)**	3.01 (1.17)	2.93 (1.31)	3.26 (1.25)
LEG	3.02 (1.24)	**3.13 (1.21)**	2.87 (1.18)	3.00 (1.24)	2.63 (1.10)	**3.52 (1.13)**
NET	**3.60 (1.11)**	3.53 (1.14)	2.12 (0.87)	**3.44 (1.30)**	2.50 (1.08)	3.40 (1.05)

Source: Own elaboration
*Standard deviations are shown in parentheses()

In general and on an average, none of the factors seems to be very relevant for the firms, which make us think that the location may not be the only factor to explain the externalities gained by the firms. The factor that, individually analyzed, has been punctuated more positively has been NET (3.60) and the lowest factors is MARK (2.21). In a context like China, this might be explained by the fact that the tacit knowledge about how to operate in the country and the support that a firm obtains from other firms and managers are more important than other market related reasons, especially when firms (in this case European subsidiaries) have not much experience in the market.

On one side, in terms of the location mode of the subsidiaries in China, we observe that the factors that were more positive and differently evaluated by two types of location mode were those related to NET (3.53). Moreover, if we analyze other values of isolated firms, we can observe that the higher values are on ISK (3.70) and MARK (3.13). It is remarkable that the isolated firms have a quite high consensus (standard deviation of 0.87) in how their isolated location does not contribute to gain externalities on networking (2.12). Figure 6.1 shows graphically these results.

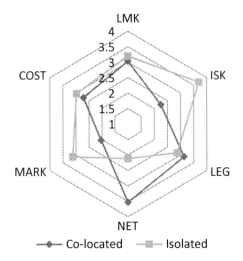

Fig. 6.1 Externalities by location mode. (Source: Own elaboration)

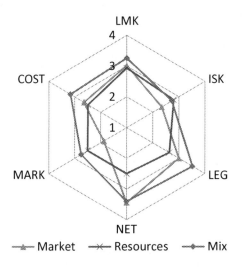

Fig. 6.2 Externalities by entry reason. (Source: Own elaboration)

On the other side, when studying the externalities by the entry reasons, we notice at least two important aspects: (1) on an average the higher values for the externalities are from firms seeking mixed reasons in China (market and efficiency) and (2) that the highest punctuations are on NET for market-seeking firms (3.44), and NET (3.40) and LEG (3.52) for mixed entry reason. Besides, it should be noted that although firms with mixed entry reasons have higher positive effects on most of the dimensions, industry-specific knowledge and resources (ISK) is higher for resource-seeking firms (Fig. 6.2).

Our results extend the previous work done on the net effect of agglomeration by nationality on innovation (Kim, 2014) by classifying the clustering effect into different and various areas such as networking, industry-specific knowledge or legitimacy. Besides, this research argues, that the co-location status or entry reasons of the firms can also influence these perceptions. Moreover, it is important to notice that firm's entry reasons also influence diverse opinions on how their location mode provides market benefits. As compared to market-seeking firms, those that enter seeking resources or have mix reasons to enter that market tend to perceive higher significant benefits on market factors. Specifically, market-seeking firms have lower benefits on legal knowledge, the speed of reaction to the market and competitors, or higher cost of qualified workers. Resource-seeking firms get less personal support but higher market knowledge or lower costs of qualified workers. On the other hand, firms with mixed entry reasons have higher benefits on legal knowledge, personal support, speed of reaction, or market knowledge. This is a remarkable finding that relates the entry reasons with externalities. Considering the current managerial concerns about the cost increase in China, cost factors could be the crucial element that makes firms prefer isolated location modes in the future. However, as firms increase their willingness to tap the local Chinese market, they would also look for areas with high connectivity, so both situations can act as centrifugal and centripetal location factors.

To summarize, we can say that co-location per se does not have a positive or negative influence on subsidiaries, but that influence depends on the strategic motives why firms entered in China and the expectations of their investments there. These factors have shown that a heterogeneity exists regarding the benefits of the country-of-origin clusters and the perceptions of the managers.

Conclusions

To face globalization and the liberalization of markets, business cooperation through clustering is essential, especially for the internationalization process of SMEs. As interactions within these clusters can be diverse in nature (formal, temporary, collaborative, etc.), pursue different objectives, and adopt different modalities, we propose that those platforms adopt different modalities: cluster initiatives, country-of-origin clusters, and sectorial clusters. In these interorganizational geographic networks firms are simultaneously interconnected productively, socially, and commercially in origin and destination, and through different types of interactions. In other words, these organizational realities act as platforms for internationalization.

In this work, we argue that country-of-origin clusters in emerging countries can be studied as a platform of relationships that provide the key resources (tangible and intangible) necessary to meet the challenge of internationalization of SMEs successfully. However, due to their origin and participants, we also believe that there is a heterogeneity in the role played for the clustering, which needs further research on organizational (the entrepreneur, the size, etc.), informational (needs), and institutional (host country) issues that characterize these clusters.

From the analysis made we can say that the country-of-origin cluster is perceived as a strategic asset that gives members access to information, resources, markets, and knowledge. Specifically, the co-location is providing the members with externalities related to market and host country knowledge, fostering information sharing about suppliers, financial conditions, HR practices, IP protection methods, legal issues or bureaucracy. They relate proximity and daily interaction (informal meetings, etc.) with the exchange of tacit knowledge (based on experience). Member companies find it important not only the geographic proximity but the social and cognitive proximity. In other words, our study suggests that the role of clustering and the value of the location on externalities are bigger in the dimensions of networking and for the companies established for mixed or various reasons (seeking efficiency as well as markets). However, opposite to what we expected, we could not validate that a general higher positive perception is associated to co-located firms. This could be due to some limitations derived from the size of the sample or the methodology used. We also need to acknowledge the limitation of collecting data from a single manager (the general manager of the subsidiary).

Summarizing, while the research on social networks and multinational SMEs is still scarce on the IB literature, our research offers a new insight suggesting that the country-of-origin cluster may contribute positively in the internationalization in distant markets (China). From a practical point of view this research helps firms to take decisions regarding the location mode that allow them reduce risks and share knowledge key in the process. At a political level, the research can enlighten the design and implementation of policies by stimulating the geographical clustering and facilitating the creation of these types of business agglomerations abroad.

References

Alcácer, J., & Chung, W. (2013). Location strategies for agglomeration economies. *Strategic, Management Journal, 35*(12), 1749–1761.

Alcácer, J., & Zhao, M. (2016). Zooming in: A practical manual for identifying geographic clusters. *Strategic Management Journal, 37*(1), 10–21.

Almeida, P., & Kogut, B. (1997). The exploration of technological diversity and geographic localization in innovation: Start-up firms in the semiconductor industry. *Small Business Economics, 9*(1), 21–31.

Almodovar, P., & Rugman, A. M. (2015). Testing the revisited Uppsala model: Does insidership improve international performance? *International Marketing Review, 32*(6), 686–712.

Bao, Y., Chen, X., & Zhou, K. Z. (2012). External learning, market dynamics, and radical innovation: Evidence from China's high-tech firms. *Journal of Business Research, 65*(8), 1226–1233.

Belderbos, R., & Zou, J. (2009). Real options and foreign affiliate divestments: A portfolio perspective. *Journal of International Business Studies, 40*(4), 600–620.

Breschi, S., & Malerba, F. (2005). Clusters, networks and innovation: Research results and new directions. In S. Breschi & F. Malerba (Eds.), *Clusters, networks and innovation* (pp. 1–26). Oxford: Oxford University Press.

Carlos, M. J. (2011). Social capital and dynamic capabilities in international performance of SMEs. *Journal of Strategy and Management, 4*(4), 404–421.

Chang, S. J., & Park, S. (2005). Types of firms generating network externalities and MNCs' co-location decisions. *Strategic Management Journal, 26*(7), 595–615.

Chung, H. F., & Tung, R. L. (2013). Immigrant social networks and foreign entry: Australia and New Zealand firms in the European Union and Greater China. *International Business Review, 22*(1), 18–31.

De Propris, L., & Driffield, N. (2006). *FDI, clusters and knowledge sourcing. Clusters and globalisation: The development of urban and regional economies* (pp. 133–158). Cheltenham: Edward Elgar.

Dunning, J. H. (1988). The eclectic paradigm of international production: A restatement and some possible extensions. *Journal of International Business Studies, 19*(1), 1–31.

Dunning, J. H. (1998). Location and the multinational enterprise: A neglected factor? *Journal of International Business Studies, 29*(1), 45–66.

Gonzalez-Loureiro, M., Puig, F., & Urzelai, B. (2018). Agglomerations, clusters and industrial districts: Evolution and opportunities for future research. In F. Puig & B. Urzelai (Eds.), *Economic clusters and globalization: Diversity and resilience*. Routledge (Taylor and Francis Group) (forthcoming).

Guillén, M. F. (2002). Structural inertia, imitation, and foreign expansion: South Korean firms and business groups in China, 1987–1995. *Academy of Management Journal, 45*(3), 509–525.

Hair, J. F., Black, W. C., Babin, B. J., Anderson, R. E., & Tatham, R. L. (2006). *Multivariate data analysis* (6th ed.). Upper Saddle River: Pearson Prentice Hall.

Havnes, E., & Hauge, P. A. (2004). *Observatory of European SMEs*. SMEs and cooperation.

He, C. (2003). Location of foreign manufacturers in China: Agglomeration economies and country of origin effects. *Papers in Regional Science, 82*(3), 351–372.

Henderson, J. V. (2003). Marshall's scale economies. *Journal of Urban Economics, 53*(1), 1–28.

Hilmersson, M., & Jansson, H. (2012). Reducing uncertainty in the emerging market entry process: On the relationship among international experiential knowledge, institutional distance, and uncertainty. *Journal of International Marketing, 20*(4), 96–110.

Hollenstein, H. (2005). Determinants of international activities: Are SMEs different? *Small Business Economics, 24*(5), 431–450.

Hymer, S. H. (1960). *The international operation of national firms: A study of direct foreign investment*. Doctoral dissertation, Massachusetts Institute of Technology.

Jain, N. K., Kothari, T., & Kumar, V. (2016). Location choice research: Proposing new agenda. *Management International Review, 56*(3), 303–324.

Jankowska, B., Götz, M., & Główka, C. (2017). Intra-cluster cooperation enhancing SMEs' competitiveness-the role of cluster organisations in Poland. *Investigaciones Regionales*, (39), 195–214.

Johanson, J., & Vahlne, J.-E. (2009). The Uppsala in internationalization process model revisited: From liability of foreignness to liability of outsidership. *Journal of International Business Studies, 40*(7), 1411–1431.

Kalinic, I., & Forza, C. (2012). Rapid internationalization of traditional SMEs: Between gradualist models and born globals. *International Business Review, 21*(4), 694–707.

Kim, H. (2014). *Should birds of a feather flock together? Agglomeration by nationality as a constraint in international expansion*. Doctoral dissertation, The University of Michigan.

Lambert, S. C., & Davidson, R. A. (2013). Applications of the business model in studies of enterprise success, innovation and classification: An analysis of empirical research from 1996 to 2010. *European Management Journal, 31*(6), 668–681.

Larson, A. (1992). Network dyads in entrepreneurial settings: A study of the governance of exchange relationships. *Administrative Science Quarterly, 37*, 76–104.

Lin, Z. J., Yang, H., & Arya, B. (2009). Alliance partners and firm performance: Resource complementarity and status association. *Strategic Management Journal, 30*(9), 921–940.

Makino, S., Lau, C. M., & Yeh, R. S. (2002). Asset-exploitation versus asset-seeking: Implications for location choice of foreign direct investment from newly industrialized economies. *Journal of International Business Studies, 33*, 403–421.

Martin, R., & Sunley, P. (2011). Conceptualizing cluster evolution: Beyond the life cycle life? *Regional Studies, 45*(10), 1300–1318.

Molina-Morales, F. X., & Martinez-Fernandez, M. T. (2004). How much difference is there between industrial district firms? A net value creation approach. *Research Studies, 33*(4), 473–486.

Mucchielli, J. L., & Yu, P. (2011). MNC's location choice and agglomeration: A comparison between US and European affiliates in China. *Asia Pacific Business Review, 17*(4), 431–453.

Paul, J., Parthasarathy, S., & Gupta, P. (2017). Exporting challenges of SMEs: A review and future research agenda. *Journal of World Business, 52*(3), 327–342.

Peng, M. W., & Luo, Y. (2000). Managerial ties and firm performance in a transition economy: The nature of a micro-macro link. *Academy of Management Journal, 43*(3), 486–501.

Pla-Barber, J., & Puig, F. (2009). Is the influence of the industrial district on international activities being eroded by globalization?: Evidence from a traditional manufacturing industry. *International Business Review, 18*(5), 435–445.

Porter, M. E. (1998). Clusters and the new economics of competition. *Harvard Business Review, 76*(6), 77–90.

Powell, W. W., & Brantley, P. (1992). Competitive cooperation in biotechnology: Learning through networks. In *Networks and organizations: Structure, form and action* (pp. 366–394). Boston: Harvard Business School Press.

Puig, F., Portero, B., & González-Loureiro, M. (2017). Clustering strategy and development of subsidiaries in China. *Economia e Politica Industriale, 44*(2), 221–243.

Puig, F., Gonzalez-Loureiro, M., & Ghauri, P. (2018). Running faster and jumping higher? Survival and growth in international manufacturing new ventures. *International Small Business Review*. https://doi.org/10.1177/0266242618777792.

Shen, Z., & Puig, F. (2017). Spatial dependence of the FDI entry mode decision: Empirical evidence from emerging market enterprises. *Management International Review, 58*(1), 171–193.

Shen, Z., Puig, F., & Paul, J. (2017). Foreign market entry mode research: A review and research agenda. *The International Trade Journal, 31*(5), 429–456.

Tan, D., & Meyer, K. E. (2011). Country-of-origin and industry FDI agglomeration of foreign investors in an emerging economy. *Journal of International Business Studies, 42*(4), 504–520.

Urzelai, B., & Puig, F. (2018). Developing international social capital: The role of communities of practice and clustering. *International Business Review* (forthcoming).

Uzzi, B. (1996). The sources and consequences of embeddedness for the economic performance of organizations: The network effect. *American Sociological Review, 61*, 674–698.

Zaheer, S. (1995). Overcoming the liability of foreignness. *Academy of Management Journal, 38*(2), 341–363.

7

Acquirer's Country of Origin and Target Firm's Performance

Jinlong Gu, Yong Yang, and Roger Strange

Introduction

An acquirer's country of origin plays an important role in enhancing a target firm's performance. For instance, the internalisation of intangible assets allows multinational enterprises (MNEs) to exploit their ownership advantage in overseas markets. The transfer of knowledge-based firm-specific advantage from the acquirer enhances the target firm's competitiveness, leading to the target firm's improved performance (Buckley and Casson 1976; Chidlow et al. 2009; Park and Ghauri 2011). Moreover, several empirical studies have documented a positive relation between acquisition and performance of target firms (Conn and Connell 1990; Cheng and Chan 1995; Ning et al. 2014).

Although the existing studies have made important contributions, one weakness of this literature is that it generally has not distinguished different acquirers' country of origin (international vs domestic) and has ignored the role of differences across the acquirer-target linkage characteristics. The cross-border acquisitions typically show remarkable heterogeneity in several variables, such as the characteristics of the acquirer-target industry and ownership linkages, which are believed to be imperative determinants of a target firm's success. In this context, one important research question for scholars and managers is whether the foreign acquisition premiums

---

J. Gu (✉) • Y. Yang • R. Strange
University of Sussex Business School, Brighton, UK
e-mail: Yong.Yang@sussex.ac.uk; R.N.Strange@sussex.ac.uk

© The Author(s) 2019

A. Chidlow et al. (eds.), *The Changing Strategies of International Business*, The Academy of International Business, https://doi.org/10.1007/978-3-030-03931-8_7

135

differ with regard to the acquirer's industry relatedness with target and ownership shares of the target. In particular, we intend to discover whether the additional performance gain from foreign acquisitions in the same industry differs from that in different industries, as well as whether this additional performance gain in high ownership mode differs from that in low ownership mode. This can be achieved by our analysis of a multi-country data set, which contains 3152 firm-year observations from 45 economies.

The acquirers may prefer to locate their acquisition investment in the same industry in order to maximise the synergies from resource similarity with the target and minimise risk of resource misallocation. This advantage tends to be magnified when the target is acquired by foreign rather than domestic acquirer; this is because the former owns stronger firm-specific advantage and resources to compete in foreign markets (Rumelt 1982; Palich et al. 2000).

Targets with high ownership shares owned by acquirers tend to have a stronger performance in the case of foreign acquisition rather than domestic acquisition. The effective transfer of knowledge-based firm-specific advantage from acquirer to target relies on the effective control and protection of the acquirer's intangible assets, such as technology. Therefore, target firms benefit more from a high ownership mode that makes the foreign acquirer more willing to and capable of transfer. For instance, due to a fear of technology leakage, in the weak institutional environment of developing countries, the foreign acquirer will prefer to transfer more to a majority owned target than to a minority owned target in order to protect its technology (Gaur and Lu 2007; Driffield et al. 2016).

In our empirical analysis, we find a positive relationship between an acquirer's country of origin (international vs domestic) and target firm performance. This is consistent with the results in prior studies (Swenson 1993; Cheng and Chan 1995; Ning et al. 2014). Importantly, we also find that the acquirer's industry relatedness with the target and ownership shares of the target positively moderate this relationship. We interpret these results as indicating that while the acquirer's country of origin would be imperative for target firm's performance, the characteristics of the acquirer-target industry and ownership linkages matter. A high industry relatedness and ownership level facilitates the transfer of knowledge-based firm-specific advantage from the acquirer to the target, thus enhancing the target's additional performance gain from foreign acquisition.

Literature Review

There are several motivations for conducting an acquisition, including managerial hubris, management's comparative advantage, and synergy effects (Balsvik and Haller 2010). While this argument does not distinguish between foreign and domestic acquisition, the acquirer's country of origin matters. Foreign acquisition is different from domestic acquisition since the former enters a new international market and faces an environment different from their home market (Zou and Ghauri 2008). Given the importance of cross-border acquisitions, as evident in the huge surge of cross-border acquisitions occurring among countries in the context of globalisation (UNCTAD 2017), it is interesting for scholars to understand why acquisition occurs and how the target performs after the acquisition.

Foreign acquisition faces various costs and benefits when the acquirers are acquiring and managing target firms across national borders. Many of these costs and benefits are different from those in domestic acquisitions. Compared with domestic acquisition, foreign acquisitions tend to offer a magnified advantage that more than compensates for the risk of doing business abroad. On the one hand, foreign acquisitions incur some costs, such as liabilities of foreignness and coordination costs. Foreign acquirers have a lack of local legitimacy and information (Zaheer and Mosakowski 1997; Shimizu et al. 2004; Majocchi and Strange 2012). These costs may be smaller in the case of domestic acquisition.

On the other hand, foreign acquisitions bring many benefits that may be larger than those of domestic acquisitions. First, foreign ownership, brought by the foreign acquisition, introduces a new management style and incentive system to the target firm. The enhanced corporate governance leads to reduced agency costs and improved performance (Heugens et al. 2009). Second, hiring existing staff in foreign acquisitions helps to overcome the liability of foreignness since these employees and managers have valuable local information and experience (Gaur and Lu 2007). Third, leveraging location advantage across country borders between acquirer and target countries, such as cheap capital and labour, is not available to domestic acquisitions but is feasible in foreign acquisitions (Dunning 1988). Fourth, the synergies are more likely to be stronger for foreign acquisitions than for domestic acquisitions. The home and host countries that have different technological environments tend to have different technological characteristics and complementary assets, leading to an increased know-how diffusion within the merging firms (Bertrand and Zitouna 2008). The recombination of resources makes target firms more valuable.

138   J. Gu et al.

Further, foreign MNEs tend to be more productive and have a stronger ownership advantage to penetrate the international market, while the counterparts that are least productive might only serve the domestic market (Melitz 2003; Yang and Martins 2011). Foreign MNEs have the opportunity of exploiting their core competitive advantage across various geographic markets through the internalisation of intangible assets (Buckley and Casson 1976; Dunning and Lundan 2008; Buckley and Strange 2011; Hassan et al. 2016). Their transfer of knowledge-based firm-specific advantage (FSA) to foreign targets could enhance the target firm's performance, particularly productivity.

Prior empirical literature has examined the relationship between foreign acquisition and performance. Particularly, some studies have tested the above relationship using firm-level data from one or two countries. However, these studies generate mixed results rather than a solid conclusion of this topic, as argued by the review article (Haleblian et al. 2009).

Our Contribution

This chapter distinguishes itself from the earlier empirical studies in three major aspects. First of all, cross-border acquisitions are important and becoming increasingly common among MNEs; this is an imperative factor driving the rebound of global foreign direct investment (FDI) flow (UNCTAD 2017). Therefore, considerable research has studied the conditions under which these acquisitions can create value. However, most studies have focused on either the acquirer firm's or the combined firms' performance. They typically examine short-term performance, such as stock return. Little is known about the target's performance. This chapter focuses on the performance of the target.

Second, those studies that concentrate on target firms provide rather mixed findings. Some studies find a positive foreign acquisition premium (Eun et al. 1996), while others find a negative or insignificant relationship between foreign acquisition and performance (Dewenter 1995; Moeller and Schlingemann 2005). These conflicting results may be in part due to the ignorance of some important variables, such as acquirer-target linkage characteristics, which may be crucial factors in the foreign acquisition-performance relationship. We aim to provide a better understanding of target firm's performance by considering the moderating effects of acquirer-target linkage characteristics, namely the characteristics of their industry linkage and ownership linkage. In particular, the industry linkage refers to the industry relatedness between acquirer and target firms, while the ownership linkage refers to the ownership level controlled by the acquirer over the target firm. Therefore, we believe this chapter contributes to this debate.

Third, most previous studies rely on a single- or two-country study. This may raise the question of the representativeness of their evidence. This chapter has a larger country coverage of 45 economies. This makes it possible to generalise our findings to a wider set of economies.

Data

Our analysis draws on the data from two data sets, namely the Orbis and Zephyr data sets. These two data sets are both made available by a large international consultancy firm called Bureau van Dijk (BvD). According to BvD, the information on Orbis and Zephyr are sourced from different information providers who are the experts in their regions and sectors, supplying detailed accounting and deal information. The Orbis data set is widely used in international business literature, while the Zephyr data set is well accepted in acquisition literature.

We select targets based on the following criteria: (1) targets who have location information in order to distinguish between foreign and domestic acquisitions; (2) targets whose minimum 10% shares are owned by the acquirers (Bureau of Economic Analysis 1999); and (3) targets who have complete information on sales, labour, capital, intermediate input, leverage, and firm age. To achieve this, we first collect parent-subsidiary ownership linkages and the corresponding financial information from the Orbis data set. The time period is 2004–13. Second, we collect deal information from the Zephyr data set. We chose Mergers and Acquisitions (M&A) transactions that occurred before 2013. These M&As should have a 'complete' and 'complete assumed' deal status. Next, using the unique BvD ID of each firm, we merge the deal information with ownership linkage information to identify the acquirer-target linkages among the parent-subsidiary linkages.

After identifying the targets that are involved in deals, by comparing the target and acquirer's location, we further distinguish between foreign acquisition (the target's country is different from the acquirer's country) and domestic acquisition (the target's country is the same as the acquirer's country). Therefore, we can calculate a dummy equal to 1 if the target is in a foreign country or 0 if the target is in a domestic country, the measure of the acquirer's country of origin used in this chapter. We then select targets that have complete information on the aforementioned financial variables. Firms with miss-

140   J. Gu et al.

ing values in any of these variables are dropped from our sample. With the above restriction, the final sample includes 3152 unique target-acquirer-year observations, corresponding to 512 acquirers and 648 acquisitions/targets from 45 countries (39 acquirers' countries and 32 targets' countries). The country-level data, such as gross domestic product (GDP) per capita and GDP growth, are collected from the World Bank database. The monetary variables are reported in US dollars.

Key Variables

Firm Performance Firm performance measures vary in the foreign acquisition premium literature. One common measure is cumulative abnormal return. However, this market-based firm performance measure is ruled out since the stock market data are lacking and not available for all economies. There would be a problem of a severely reduced sample size if we use this market-based variable. The most standard approach to measure firm performance is total factor productivity (TFP) (Bertrand and Zitouna 2008; Geluebcke 2015; Liu et al. 2017), despite its difficulty in the calculation. Following previous studies, we employ total factor productivity (PERF) as the performance measure in this chapter. TFP is often used to generate standard and precise estimates of firm performance (Levinsohn and Petrin 2003).

TFP captures the firm's ability to generate output using a given set of inputs. Holding the amount of general inputs (e.g. capital, labour, and intermediate input) constant, the difference in output for firms is usually explained by technology. Therefore, technology is likely to be embedded in total factor productivity. TFP is generally accepted as a proxy for technology efficiency. Following Levinsohn and Petrin's (2003) LP approach, we adopt the Stata command 'levpet' to calculate the total factor productivity. The production function is assumed to be Cobb Douglas. The labour input is measured by the number of employees. The capital is measured by the total fixed capital of the firm. The instrument to control for unobserved technology shock in the estimation procedure of the LP approach is the expenditure on intermediate goods.

Acquirer's Country of Origin Following prior studies (Claessens and Van Horen 2012; Liu et al. 2017), we employ a binary variable called 'foreign acquisition' as a proxy for the acquirer's country of origin. We create this independent variable to distinguish between foreign and domestic acquisitions.

Foreign acquisition (FORA) is a binary variable that is equal to 1 if the acquirer comes from a country different from the target's country, and equal to 0 if the acquirer's headquarters is in the target's country.

Acquirer's Industry Relatedness We consider two important characteristics of acquirer-target linkage, namely their industry and ownership linkage characteristics. First of all, the industry relatedness between the acquirer and target firms may affect the business performance of the target (Bebenroth and Hemmert 2015). To examine the role of the acquirer's industry linkage characteristic on the foreign acquisition-performance relationship, we create the variable 'acquirer's industry relatedness'. Acquirer's industry relatedness (RELF) is a binary variable equal to 1 if the acquirer adopts a focus strategy (sharing the same four-digit NACE Rev.2 industry code with the target) in the acquisition, and equal to 0 if the acquirer conducts the acquisition using a diversification strategy (locating in a four-digit industry different from the target) (Yang et al. 2014). We also use the first three-digit industry code as an alternative definition for industry relatedness in the robustness section (Jiménez et al. 2015).

Acquirer's Ownership Strategy To examine the role of acquirer's ownership linkage characteristics, we create the variable 'ownership'. Ownership (OWN) is the target's ownership shares controlled by the acquirer. As a robustness test, we create a binary variable 'majority owned' (Yang and Singh 2014). We show this result in the robustness section.

Control Variables Following Bebenroth and Hemmert (2015), we control for a number of target-level characteristics that are believed to affect firm performance, including firm size (SIZE), leverage (LEV), sales per worker (SALP), and age (AGET). We control for the acquirer-level characteristic 'acquirer firm age' (AGEA). Acquirers with a larger firm age may have more experience in identifying suitable targets to acquire and integrate them with the headquarters. We control for country-level characteristics (Li and Qian 2005) such as 'GDP per capita' (ECOT) and 'GDP growth' (GROT) of the target's country. To compare the performance difference of targets (i.e. subsidiaries) who share the same acquirer (i.e. parent), we control for parent fixed effects. We also control for country, industry, and time fixed effects (Yang and Martins 2011). See Table 7.1 for the definitions of the variables and corresponding data sources.

142   J. Gu et al.

Table 7.1 Operationalisation of variables

Variable	Operationalisation	Source
PERF	The natural logarithm of the target's total factor productivity (TFP)	Orbis
FORA	Equal to 1 (0) if the acquirer is in foreign (domestic) country	Orbis
RELF	Equal to 1 (0) if the acquirer operates in an industry the same as (different from) the target in four-digit NACE Rev.2 code	Orbis
OWN	The acquirer's ownership shares of the target firm	Orbis
SIZE	The natural logarithm of the target firm's number of employees	Orbis
LEV	The target firm's debt to equity ratio	Orbis
SALP	The natural logarithm of the target firm's sales divided by its number of employees (US$)	Orbis
AGET	The duration of the existence of the target firm since the date of incorporation	Orbis
ECOT	The natural logarithm of the target firm country's GDP per capita (US$)	WDI
GROT	The target firm country's GDP growth (%)	WDI
AGEA	The duration of the existence of the acquirer firm since the date of incorporation	Orbis
RELT	Equal to 1 (0) if the acquirer operates in an industry the same as (different from) the target in three-digit NACE Rev.2 code	Orbis
MAJO	Equal to 1 (0) if the acquirer owns the majority (minority) ownership of the target	Orbis

Descriptive Statistics

Descriptive statistics and a correlation matrix are shown in Table 7.2. The sample contains 648 targets and 512 acquirers in 45 economies (i.e. 39 home economies and 32 host economies), giving rise to 3152 unique target-acquirer-year observations. The left panel consists of descriptive statistics for key variables used in our analysis. We find that, on average, with regard to acquirer's country of origin, 54% of acquisitions are conducted by foreign acquirers, while 46% of acquisitions are made by domestic acquirers. With respect to the characteristics of the acquirer-target industry and ownership linkages, on average, 26% of targets are operating in industries the same (in four-digit NACE Rev.2 code) as the acquirers, while targets' 63% ownership shares are controlled by the acquirers. In terms of the target-level characteristics, we find that, on average, firm size is 4463 employees, leverage is 83%, sales per worker are US$513.69 thousand, target firm age is 30.52. We also include acquirer-level characteristics. Acquirer firm age, on average, is 50.66. The right panel presents the correlation matrix, which shows that most correlation coefficients are low.

We next separate our sample by the country of origin of the acquirers. Table 7.3 splits the sample into three groups. The first panel of the table pres-

Table 7.2 Descriptive statistics and correlations matrix

	Variable	Mean	Std. Dev	1	2	3	4	5	6	7	8	9	10	11
1.	PERF	5.60	0.50	1.00										
2.	FORA	0.54	0.50	−0.09	1.00									
3.	RELF	0.26	0.44	0.06	0.00	1.00								
4.	OWN	0.63	0.32	−0.13	0.30	−0.05	1.00							
5.	SIZE	6.36	1.92	0.36	−0.32	0.22	−0.38	1.00						
6.	LEV	0.83	1.13	0.01	−0.02	0.05	−0.01	0.11	1.00					
7.	SALP	12.60	0.99	0.55	−0.08	0.01	−0.11	−0.05	0.06	1.00				
8.	AGET	3.12	0.83	0.19	−0.26	0.03	−0.19	0.34	0.06	0.10	1.00			
9.	ECOT	10.06	0.86	0.10	−0.07	−0.13	0.07	−0.25	0.11	0.18	0.16	1.00		
10.	GROT	2.23	4.39	−0.01	0.07	0.05	−0.09	0.16	−0.09	−0.08	−0.16	−0.49	1.00	
11.	AGEA	3.59	0.93	0.04	0.00	−0.06	−0.07	0.14	0.05	0.07	0.20	0.04	−0.06	1.00

Note: Correlation coefficients with values larger than |0.15| are significant at 10% level

144   J. Gu et al.

Table 7.3 Descriptive statistics: domestic acquirers versus foreign acquirers

	Variable	N	Mean	Std. dev
All acquisitions	Acquirer's firm age	3152	50.66	40.89
	Acquirer from developed country	3152	0.84	0.36
	Acquirer's multinationality	3152	0.49	0.28
	Acquirer country's GDP per capita	3152	37.02	15.79
	Acquirer country's GDP growth	3152	1.80	3.96
	Survey year	3152	2008.94	2.34
Domestic acquisitions	Acquirer's firm age	1447	48.37	33.83
	Acquirer from developed country	1447	0.75	0.43
	Acquirer's multinationality	1447	0.32	0.23
	Acquirer country's GDP per capita	1447	31.08	14.63
	Acquirer country's GDP growth	1447	1.89	4.59
	Survey year	1447	2009.05	2.31
Foreign acquisitions	Acquirer's firm age	1705	52.60	45.96
	Acquirer from developed country	1705	0.92	0.27
	Acquirer's multinationality	1705	0.63	0.24
	Acquirer country's GDP per capita	1705	42.06	14.96
	Acquirer country's GDP growth	1705	1.73	3.33
	Survey year	1705	2008.84	2.37

Note: 'Acquirer's firm age' refers to the duration of the existence of an acquirer firm since the date of incorporation. 'Acquirer from developed country' refers to dummy equal to 1 (0) if the acquirer locates in developed (developing) country. 'Acquirer's multinationality' refers to the ratio of the acquirer's number of overseas subsidiaries to total number of subsidiaries. 'Acquirer country's GDP per capita' is in thousand US dollars. 'Acquirer country's GDP growth' is in %

ents descriptive statistics for all acquisitions, while the middle panel includes only domestic acquisition, and the third panel consists of foreign acquisitions. Unsurprisingly, foreign acquirers have more experience than domestic acquirers. For instance, on average, foreign acquirers are older than domestic acquirers (52.60 vs 48.37 years old). Moreover, foreign acquirers have 63% of subsidiaries located in foreign countries, while for domestic acquirers this figure is 32%, suggesting that foreign acquirers have more international experience.

We also find that 92% of foreign acquirers come from developed countries, while 75% domestic acquirers headquarter in developed countries. On a country level, foreign acquirers' countries have a higher GDP per capita than domestic acquirers (US$42.06 vs 31.08 thousand). However, domestic acquirers' countries have higher GDP growth than foreign ones (1.89% vs 1.73%).

The data cover 45 economies, including many OECD economies. Table 7.4 describes the country coverage of our sample, together with the key variables for acquirers and targets, including PERF, FORA, SIZE, among others.

Acquirer's Country of Origin and Target Firm's Performance 145

Table 7.4 Key variables by economy

Country	N	PERF	FORA	SIZE	N	RELF	OWN
	Target				Acquirer		
Australia					3	0.00	1.00
Austria					7	0.24	0.49
Belgium					8	0.00	0.67
Brazil	14	5.68	0.86	5017	2	1.00	0.20
Bulgaria					1	0.00	0.51
Canada					1	1.00	1.00
China	35	5.67	0.50	7998	16	0.37	0.45
Colombia	4	5.40	1.00	1830			
Czech Republic	4	5.91	0.89	3900	1	0.00	1.00
Denmark					7	0.00	0.77
Estonia	6	5.46	0.70	1315	6	0.44	0.79
Finland					15	0.53	0.99
France	9	5.51	1.00	25,506			
Germany	41	5.78	0.61	20,015	37	0.40	0.67
Greece	24	5.45	0.16	870	16	0.26	0.67
Hong Kong	7	5.73	0.42	10,968	7	0.43	0.43
Hungary	1	5.97	0.00	1145	1	0.00	0.97
India	7	5.82	0.84	4149	8	0.24	0.95
Indonesia	6	5.55	0.70	8391	2	1.00	0.59
Ireland					10	0.00	0.98
Israel	4	5.49	0.44	2602	6	0.30	0.43
Japan	109	5.83	0.02	4610	89	0.25	0.44
Latvia	9	5.39	1.00	248	1	0.00	1.00
Lithuania	20	5.24	0.94	560	3	0.00	0.50
Luxembourg					2	0.00	0.75
Malaysia	4	5.50	0.10	17,389	9	0.34	0.56
Netherlands					24	0.14	0.86
Norway					3	0.00	0.74
Peru	3	5.63	0.67	1355	1	0.00	0.18
Philippines	8	5.57	0.19	2001	5	0.17	0.53
Poland	27	5.34	0.58	448	14	0.19	0.64
Romania	2	5.90	1.00	23,660			
Russia	33	5.34	0.63	2170	12	0.16	0.72
Singapore	1	5.63	0.00	3547	6	0.12	0.66
Slovakia	1	6.22	1.00	3821			
South Africa	3	5.63	0.73	70,801	3	0.00	0.66
South Korea	12	5.36	1.00	402			
Spain					8	0.77	0.66
Sweden					19	0.20	0.80
Taiwan	27	5.44	0.23	1768	17	0.32	0.28
Thailand	3	5.85	0.33	2874	2	0.00	0.38
Turkey	12	5.85	0.60	3928	3	0.00	0.39
UK	200	5.55	0.81	1156	50	0.34	0.78
US	11	5.71	0.38	4325	87	0.20	0.68
Vietnam	1	6.21	1.00	1000			

Note: *N* is the number of firms. SIZE is not in logarithm here

146   J. Gu et al.

Unsurprisingly, most of the acquirers can be found in developed economies. The home economies include Australia, Austria, Belgium, Brazil, Bulgaria, Canada, China, Czech Republic, Denmark, Estonia, Finland, Germany, Greece, Hong Kong, Hungary, India, Indonesia, Ireland, Israel, Japan, Latvia, Lithuania, Luxembourg, Malaysia, Netherlands, Norway, Peru, Philippines, Poland, Russia, Singapore, South Africa, Spain, Sweden, Taiwan, Thailand, Turkey, UK, and US. On the other hand, the majority of targets are in some developed economies and the largest developing economies. The host economies include Brazil, China, Colombia, Czech Republic, Estonia, France, Germany, Greece, Hong Kong, Hungary, India, Indonesia, Israel, Japan, Latvia, Lithuania, Malaysia, Peru, Philippines, Poland, Romania, Russia, Singapore, Slovakia, South Africa, South Korea, Taiwan, Thailand, Turkey, UK, US, and Vietnam.

Regression Results

To examine the role of the acquirer's country of origin and important characteristics of the acquirer-target linkage on the performance of target firms, conditional on being acquired, we introduce the following equation.

$$\text{PERF}_{it} = \beta_1 \text{FORA}_{it} + \beta_2 \text{FORA}_{it}{}^* Z_{it} + \beta_3 Z_{it} + \lambda X_{it} + \gamma_t + e_{it} \quad (7.1)$$

where PERF refers to TFP of firm i in year t. The independent variable FORA measures the acquirer's country of origin. It equals to 1 if the acquirer comes from a foreign country, and equals to 0 if the acquirer's headquarters are in the target's country. Z_{it} is the key moderating variable, namely acquirer's industry relatedness with the target RELF and acquirer's ownership shares of the target OWN. The equations also include control variables X_{it}, including SIZE, LEV, SALP, AGET, AGEA, country fixed effect, industry fixed effects, and parent firm fixed effects. γ_t is the time fixed effects. The key parameter is β_2, which indicates the moderating effect of acquirer-target linkage characteristics. (For completeness, we also present results with only the main effect based on the equation: $\text{PERF}_{it} = \beta_4 \text{FORA}_{it} + \lambda X_{it} + \gamma_t + e_{it}$).

Our analysis employs multiple regression models with fixed effects estimators, following prior work (Yang and Singh 2014). The regression models include country, industry, parent firm, and time fixed effects. Table 7.5 shows our main estimates. There are 3152 observations in the final sample. The Adj R-squared is about 0.91. The F statistics are significant across all models.

Acquirer's Country of Origin and Target Firm's Performance 147

Table 7.5 Country of origin and performance: the roles of relatedness and ownership

	(1)	(2)	(3)	(4)
	Model 1	Model 2	Model 3	Model 4
FORA		0.2013**	0.1644**	0.0606
		(0.082)	(0.074)	(0.081)
FORA*RELF			0.1640***	
			(0.061)	
RELF			−0.1342***	
			(0.031)	
FORA*OWN				0.3111***
				(0.092)
OWN				−0.1851***
				(0.050)
SIZE	0.1954***	0.1978***	0.2001***	0.2054***
	(0.008)	(0.008)	(0.009)	(0.009)
LEV	−0.0427***	−0.0419***	−0.0426***	−0.0421***
	(0.004)	(0.004)	(0.004)	(0.004)
SALP	0.4115***	0.4133***	0.4143***	0.4158***
	(0.012)	(0.012)	(0.012)	(0.012)
AGET	−0.0228	−0.0226	−0.0202	−0.0130
	(0.019)	(0.019)	(0.018)	(0.019)
ECOT	−0.0169	−0.0222	−0.0239	−0.0253
	(0.023)	(0.024)	(0.023)	(0.023)
GROT	0.0004	0.0005	0.0004	0.0004
	(0.001)	(0.001)	(0.001)	(0.001)
AGEA	0.0573**	0.0581**	0.0582**	0.0565**
	(0.027)	(0.027)	(0.027)	(0.027)
Affiliate Country FE	X	X	X	X
Affiliate Sector FE	X	X	X	X
Year FE	X	X	X	X
Parent FE	X	X	X	X
Adj R-squared	0.911	0.911	0.912	0.912
No. observation	3152	3152	3152	3152
F statistics	196.157	190.976	186.550	187.782

Note: Dependent variable is target firm's TFP. All models control for affiliate country, affiliate sector, time, and parent fixed effects. Values in the parentheses are robust standard errors. Significance levels: **0.05; ***0.01

Model 1 presents results with control variables only. As can be seen, the controls have the expected size and sign. For instance, the number of employees (SIZE) has significant positive signs, indicating larger firms have better business performance. However, financial leverage (LEV) has a negative coefficient, suggesting that a high level of debt to equity ratio is detrimental to firm performance. Moreover, these signs are mostly unchanged across different specifications in Models 2–4, when the main effect and moderating effects are included.

148   J. Gu et al.

As expected, we document a significant positive relation between acquirer's country of origin (foreign/domestic dummy) and target firm performance, as Model 2 shows that FORA has a positive coefficient 0.2013, significant at 5% level. This may be because the performance enhancement brought by the acquisitions is larger when the acquisitions are conducted by foreign acquirers rather than domestic acquirers, when controlling for a full set of fixed effects, the difference in target's firm size, financial leverage, sales per worker, and age.

Importantly, when we include the moderating variables, we find from Model 3 that the interaction term between FORA and RELF is positively significant at 1% level, suggesting that the acquirer's industry relatedness with the target (RELF) positively moderates the relationship between acquirer's country of origin and target firm performance. The positive effect of a foreign acquirer's country of origin is strengthened when the acquirer's industry is related to the target's industry (i.e. sharing the same four-digit NACE Rev.2 industry code). Synergies could be derived from resource similarity between two products. When the acquirer and the target operate in the same industry (at the four-digit level), the target benefits from sharing common resources and skills with the acquirer, thus enhancing the target's performance. This suggests the imperative of the industry linkage characteristic in the target firm's performance.

Finally, in Model 4, we find that the interaction term between FORA and OWN has a positive coefficient, significant at 1% level, suggesting that the acquirer's ownership of targets (OWN) positively moderates the foreign acquisition-performance relationship. Relative to the domestic acquirer, the positive effect of a foreign acquirer's country of origin is stronger when the acquirer owns more ownership shares of the target. The reason might be that owning more ownership over the target ensures the acquirer has high control of the target, which helps to reduce the conflict in the joint venture and facilitate the knowledge transfer from the foreign acquirer to the target. This shows the importance of the ownership linkage characteristic in the target firm's performance.

From these results, we conclude that the relation between an acquirer's country of origin and target firm performance appears to be positive. When considering the moderating effects, we find that the acquirer's industry relatedness with the target and its ownership shares of the target positively moderate the foreign acquisition-performance relationship.

Robustness

To check the robustness of our previous results, we conduct several robustness tests. First, we consider alternative measures of our moderating variables, which are reported in Table 7.6. We include an alternative measure of acquirer's industry relatedness with target (RELT), which is equal to 1 if the acquirer shares the same first three-digit NACE Rev.2 industry code from the target, and equal to 0 if the acquirer has a different first three-digit code with the target. We find from Model 3 that the interaction term (FORA*RELT) between an acquirer's country of origin and an acquirer's industry relatedness (at the three-digit level)

Table 7.6 Country of origin and performance: additional robustness checks

	(1)	(2)	(3)	(4)
	Model 1	Model 2	Model 3	Model 4
FORA		0.2013**	0.1182	0.1492*
		(0.082)	(0.078)	(0.088)
FORA*RELT			0.2056***	
			(0.051)	
RELT			−0.1106***	
			(0.028)	
FORA*MAJO				0.3029***
				(0.061)
MAJO				−0.1151***
				(0.030)
SIZE	0.1954***	0.1978***	0.1935***	0.2073***
	(0.008)	(0.008)	(0.009)	(0.008)
LEV	−0.0427***	−0.0419***	−0.0421***	−0.0418***
	(0.004)	(0.004)	(0.004)	(0.004)
SALP	0.4115***	0.4133***	0.4109***	0.4196***
	(0.012)	(0.012)	(0.012)	(0.012)
AGET	−0.0228	−0.0226	−0.0165	−0.0059
	(0.019)	(0.019)	(0.018)	(0.019)
ECOT	−0.0169	−0.0222	−0.0199	−0.0247
	(0.023)	(0.024)	(0.024)	(0.023)
GROT	0.0004	0.0005	0.0005	0.0004
	(0.001)	(0.001)	(0.001)	(0.001)
AGEA	0.0573**	0.0581**	0.0585**	0.0553**
	(0.027)	(0.027)	(0.027)	(0.027)
Affiliate Country FE	X	X	X	X
Affiliate Sector FE	X	X	X	X
Year FE	X	X	X	X
Parent FE	X	X	X	X
Adj R-squared	0.911	0.911	0.912	0.913
No. observation	3152	3152	3152	3152
F statistics	196.157	190.976	187.125	187.247

Note: Dependent variable is target firm's TFP. All models control for affiliate country, affiliate sector, time, and parent fixed effects. Values in the parentheses are robust standard errors. Significance levels: **0.05; ***0.01

150   J. Gu et al.

is significantly positive. We also include an alternative measure of acquirer's ownership of the target (MAJO), which is equal to 1 if the acquirer owns majority ownership of the target, and equal to 0 if it owns minority ownership of the target. Model 4 shows that the interaction term (FORA*MAJO) is significantly positive. Our results of moderating effects are robust when we use the first three-digit instead of four-digit code in calculating industry relatedness, and when we use a majority owned binary variable rather than continuous ownership shares. The results of these robustness tests are consistent with the moderating effects presented in the main results in Table 7.5.

Table 7.7 Country of origin and performance: acquirers from manufacturing sectors

	(1)	(2)	(3)	(4)
	Model 1	Model 2	Model 3	Model 4
FORA		0.3477***	0.2214***	0.1887**
		(0.080)	(0.068)	(0.080)
FORA*RELF			0.4752***	
			(0.099)	
RELF			−0.0863***	
			(0.028)	
FORA*OWN				0.7193***
				(0.224)
OWN				−0.1869***
				(0.057)
SIZE	0.2091***	0.2114***	0.1909***	0.2282***
	(0.010)	(0.010)	(0.012)	(0.011)
LEV	−0.0382***	−0.0368***	−0.0384***	−0.0367***
	(0.006)	(0.005)	(0.005)	(0.005)
SALP	0.4164***	0.4216***	0.4167***	0.4317***
	(0.017)	(0.017)	(0.018)	(0.017)
AGET	−0.0377	−0.0403	−0.0467	−0.0075
	(0.030)	(0.031)	(0.030)	(0.032)
ECOT	−0.0216	−0.0286	−0.0217	−0.0398
	(0.030)	(0.031)	(0.030)	(0.031)
GROT	0.0022	0.0022	0.0023	0.0021
	(0.002)	(0.002)	(0.001)	(0.001)
AGEA	0.1460**	0.1502**	0.1478**	0.1484**
	(0.061)	(0.061)	(0.061)	(0.061)
Affiliate Country FE	X	X	X	X
Affiliate Sector FE	X	X	X	X
Year FE	X	X	X	X
Parent FE	X	X	X	X
Adj R-squared	0.923	0.924	0.926	0.925
No. observation	1719	1719	1719	1719
F statistics	80.726	93.440	99.462	103.223

Note: Dependent variable is target firm's TFP. All models control for affiliate country, affiliate sector, time, and parent fixed effects. Values in the parentheses are robust standard errors. Significance levels: **0.05; ***0.01

Next, we check different specifications. We re-estimate using a different sub-sample, particularly considering characteristics of these acquirers such as acquirer's industry context (Berry and Kaul 2016). Table 7.7 shows the results for a sub-sample, that is, acquirer firms from manufacturing sectors. The results in all models reaffirm that target firms obtain a larger performance gain when the acquirer comes from a foreign economy, and that acquirer's industry relatedness with the target and ownership of targets positively moderate this relationship, although the significance levels vary across an acquirer's industry context.

Discussion and Conclusions

The extant literature typically does not distinguish between foreign and domestic acquisition, and generally focus on either the acquirer firms' or the combined firms' performance. Little is known about target firms' performance. For those few papers that study the performance of the target firm, the empirical results are mixed. These conflicting results are in part due to the ignorance of some potentially important moderating variables such as the characteristics of the acquirer-target industry linkage and ownership linkage. Moreover, the existing studies mainly rely on data from particular home countries. We aim to fill these gaps and look at the post-acquisition performance of target firms by drawing an acquisition data set that covers many countries.

In this chapter, we have examined a multi-country sample of 3152 unique target-acquirer-firm observations from 45 economies for the period 2004–13. Our central finding is that the target firm's additional performance gain from foreign acquisition is strengthened when the acquirer has a stronger industry linkage and ownership linkage with the target. In other words, our analysis shows that the effect of a foreign acquisition premium is stronger when the acquirer is located in the same industry as the target, and when the acquirer owns a high level of ownership of the target.

The success of the target firm depends on the characteristic of acquirer-target industry linkage, particularly considering acquirer's industry relatedness with the target. The promising strategy in foreign acquisition is a focus strategy (acquiring the target in the same industry), since it contributes to a higher performance gain for the target firms. We argue that the foreign acquirer's transfer of knowledge-based FSA—which benefits the target firm's performance—is stronger when they are located in the same industry (e.g. at the four-digit NACE Rev.2 code). This may be because the benefits of industry relatedness tend to be magnified when the acquisition is conducted by a foreign acquirer instead of a domestic acquirer. These benefits include the target firm's access to the essential resources and capabilities possessed by the acquirer firm. The foreign acquirer tends to own stronger firm-specific advantage in order to compete in the international market, compared with a domestic acquirer. The target firm benefits more from exploiting resource similarity through the merging firms' joint utilisation of tangible (e.g. production facility and distribution centre) and intangible assets (e.g. know-how, trademark, and R&D products) (Panzar and Willig 1981; Rumelt 1982; Palich et al. 2000).

The target firm's success is also determined by the characteristic of the acquirer-target ownership linkage. The favourable strategy in foreign acquisition would be a high-level ownership strategy as it contributes to more performance gain for the target. We argue that the high ownership mode is associated with a greater transfer of a knowledge-based firm-specific advantage, contributing to the better performance of the target firm acquired by a foreign acquirer. The reason may be that the benefits of high ownership shares are magnified in foreign acquisitions rather than in domestic acquisitions. For instance, when the target is majority owned, the foreign acquirer may view it as an imperative knowledge channel for exploiting the MNE's intangible assets in overseas markets (Driffield et al. 2016), transferring more knowledge to this target (Liu et al. 2017). The greater ownership control, as reflected in the better coordination mechanism and greater power in appointing key managers, facilitates the intra-firm transaction between acquirer and target (Gaur et al. 2007). The foreign acquirer is willing to transfer more due to a lower fear of technology leakage. However, a domestic acquirer has local knowledge and relies less on ownership strategy to protect the technology (Desai et al. 2004). Therefore, target firm performance is less sensitive to the domestic acquirer's ownership strategy.

There are some limitations in this chapter. First, our estimates do not rule out some form of reverse causality. For instance, perhaps better-performing targets are identified and acquired by the acquirers. Second, knowledge seeking and knowledge exploiting acquisitions contribute to the rather different performance outcomes of the target firms. The identification of motivation relies on the interpretation of data. We do not know the actual motivations behind the acquisitions. One possible way of discovering these is to do a survey among managers who make decisions to conduct acquisitions. We leave these topics for future research.

Acknowledgements We thank comments from an anonymous referee. We also thank for comments from Mirko Benischke, Bert Jarreau, Christian Asmussen, Andreas Petrou, and conference participants at the Academy of International Business (UK and Ireland Chapter) in Birmingham, 12–14 April 2018, UK. We are responsible for all errors.

References

Balsvik, R., & Haller, S. A. (2010). Picking "lemons" or picking "cherries"? Domestic and foreign acquisitions in Norwegian manufacturing. *The Scandinavian Journal of Economics, 112*(2), 361–387.

Bebenroth, R., & Hemmert, M. (2015). Country-level antecedents of target firms' post-acquisition business performance: A study of inbound Japanese and Korean M&As. *Asian Business and Management, 14*(4), 303–325.

Berry, H., & Kaul, A. (2016). Replicating the multinationality-performance relationship: Is there an S-curve? *Strategic Management Journal, 37*(11), 2275–2290.

Bertrand, O., & Zitouna, H. (2008). Domestic versus cross-border acquisitions: Which impact on the target firms' performance? *Applied Economics, 40*(17), 2221–2238.

Buckley, P. J., & Casson, M. (1976). *The future of the multinational enterprise*. London: Macmillan and Co.

Buckley, P. J., & Strange, R. (2011). The governance of the multinational enterprise: Insights from internalization theory. *Journal of Management Studies, 48*(2), 460–470.

Bureau of Economic Analysis, US Department of Commerce. (1999). *Methodologies for direct U.S. investment abroad. International direct investment studies by the Bureau of Economic Analysis*. Washington, DC: U.S. Government Printing Office.

Cheng, L. T., & Chan, K. C. (1995). A comparative analysis of the characteristics of international takeovers. *Journal of Business Finance & Accounting, 22*(5), 637–657.

Chidlow, A., Salciuviene, L., & Young, S. (2009). Regional determinants of inward FDI distribution in Poland. *International Business Review, 18*(2), 119–133.

Claessens, S., & Van Horen, N. (2012). Being a foreigner among domestic banks: Asset or liability? *Journal of Banking & Finance, 36*(5), 1276–1290.

Conn, R. L., & Connell, F. (1990). International mergers: Returns to US and British firms. *Journal of Business Finance & Accounting, 17*(5), 689–711.

Desai, M. A., Foley, C. F., & Hines, J. R. (2004). The costs of shared ownership: Evidence from international joint ventures. *Journal of Financial Economics, 73*(2), 323–374.

Dewenter, K. L. (1995). Does the market react differently to domestic and foreign takeover announcements? Evidence from the US chemical and retail industries. *Journal of Financial Economics, 37*(3), 421–441.

Driffield, N., Love, J. H., & Yang, Y. (2016). Reverse international knowledge transfer in the MNE: (Where) does affiliate performance boost parent performance? *Research Policy, 45*(2), 491–506.

Dunning, J. H. (1988). The theory of international production. *The International Trade Journal, 3*(1), 21–66.

Dunning, J. H., & Lundan, S. M. (2008). *Multinational enterprises and the global economy*. Cheltenham: Edward Elgar.

Eun, C. S., Kolodny, R., & Scheraga, C. (1996). Cross-border acquisitions and shareholder wealth: Tests of the synergy and internalization hypotheses. *Journal of Banking & Finance, 20*(9), 1559–1582.

Gaur, A. S., & Lu, J. W. (2007). Ownership strategies and survival of foreign subsidiaries: Impacts of institutional distance and experience. *Journal of Management, 33*(1), 84–110.

Gaur, A. S., Delios, A., & Singh, K. (2007). Institutional environments, staffing strategies, and subsidiary performance. *Journal of Management, 33*(4), 611–636.

Geluebcke, J. P. W. (2015). The impact of foreign takeovers: Comparative evidence from foreign and domestic acquisitions in Germany. *Applied Economics, 47*(8), 739–755.

Haleblian, J., Devers, C. E., McNamara, G., Carpenter, M. A., & Davison, R. B. (2009). Taking stock of what we know about mergers and acquisitions: A review and research agenda. *Journal of Management, 35*(3), 469–502.

Hassan, I., Chidlow, A., & Romero-Martínez, A. M. (2016). Selection, valuation and performance assessment: Are these truly inter-linked within the M&A transactions? *International Business Review, 25*(1), 255–266.

Heugens, P. P., Van Essen, M., & van Oosterhout, J. H. (2009). Meta-analyzing ownership concentration and firm performance in Asia: Towards a more fine-grained understanding. *Asia Pacific Journal of Management, 26*(3), 481–512.

Jiménez, A., Benito-Osorio, D., & Palmero-Cámara, C. (2015). Learning from risky environments: Global diversification strategies of Spanish MNEs. *Management International Review, 55*(4), 485–509.

Levinsohn, J., & Petrin, A. (2003). Estimating production functions using inputs to control for unobservables. *The Review of Economic Studies, 70*(2), 317–341.

Li, L., & Qian, G. (2005). Dimensions of international diversification: Their joint effects on firm performance. *Journal of Global Marketing, 18*(3–4), 7–35.

Liu, Q., Lu, R., & Qiu, L. D. (2017). Foreign acquisitions and target firms' performance in China. *The World Economy, 40*(1), 2–20.

Majocchi, A., & Strange, R. (2012). International diversification: The impact of ownership structure, the market for corporate control and board independence. *Management International Review, 52*(6), 879–900.

Melitz, M. J. (2003). The impact of trade on intra-industry reallocations and aggregate industry productivity. *Econometrica, 71*(6), 1695–1725.

Moeller, S. B., & Schlingemann, F. P. (2005). Global diversification and bidder gains: A comparison between cross-border and domestic acquisitions. *Journal of Banking & Finance, 29*(3), 533–564.

Ning, L., Kuo, J.-M., Strange, R., & Wang, B. (2014). International investors' reactions to cross-border acquisitions by emerging market multinationals. *International Business Review, 23*(4), 811–823.

Palich, L. E., Cardinal, L. B., & Miller, C. C. (2000). Curvilinearity in the diversification-performance linkage: An examination of over three decades of research. *Strategic Management Journal, 21*(2), 155–174.

Panzar, J. C., & Willig, R. D. (1981). Economies of scope. *The American Economic Review, 71*(2), 268–272.

Park, B. I., & Ghauri, P. N. (2011). Key factors affecting acquisition of technological capabilities from foreign acquiring firms by small and medium sized local firms. *Journal of World Business, 46*(1), 116–125.

Rumelt, R. P. (1982). Diversification strategy and profitability. *Strategic Management Journal, 3*(4), 359–369.

Shimizu, K., Hitt, M. A., Vaidyanath, D., & Pisano, V. (2004). Theoretical foundations of cross-border mergers and acquisitions: A review of current research and recommendations for the future. *Journal of International Management, 10*(3), 307–353.

Swenson, D. L. (1993). Foreign mergers and acquisitions in the United States. In K. A. Froot (Ed.), *Foreign direct investment* (pp. 255–284). Chicago: University of Chicago Press.

UNCTAD. (2017). *World investment report.* New York: United Nations.

Yang, Y., & Martins, P. S. (2011). Multinational performance and intellectual property rights: Evidence from 46 countries. In J. Berrill, E. Hutson, & R. Sinkovics (Eds.), *Firm-level internationalization, regionalism and globalization* (pp. 96–112). Cham: Palgrave Macmillan.

Yang, Y., & Singh, D. A. (2014). *Foreign subsidiary location strategy and financial performance: A global value chain perspective.* Paper presented at the Academy of Management Proceedings.

Yang, Y., Narayanan, V. K., & De Carolis, D. M. (2014). The relationship between portfolio diversification and firm value: The evidence from corporate venture capital activity. *Strategic Management Journal, 35*(13), 1993–2011.

Zaheer, S., & Mosakowski, E. (1997). The dynamics of the liability of foreignness: A global study of survival in financial services. *Strategic Management Journal, 18*(6), 439–463.

Zou, H., & Ghauri, P. N. (2008). Learning through international acquisitions: The process of knowledge acquisition in China. *Management International Review, 48*(2), 207–226.

8

Human Rights Reporting of BRIC and Non-BRIC MNEs: An Exploratory Comparative Analysis

Stefan Zagelmeyer

Introduction

The United Nations Guiding Principles for Business and Human Rights (UNGPs), endorsed by the UN Human Rights Council in 2011, create a form of multilevel and polycentric governance system by establishing a set of global standards for business and human rights that cover companies in all UN member states. The first pillar of the UNGPs confirms the role of the state as primary duty bearer to protect human rights and its responsibility to prevent, investigate, punish and redress human rights abuses by companies. The second pillar includes the expectation that companies explicitly express their commitment to human rights by declaring their policy commitment to respect human rights, by conducting human rights due diligence and by establishing policies to remedy adverse human rights impacts of their business activities. The third pillar requires the state and companies to provide victims of human rights abuses with access to effective remedy (OHCHR 2011; Ruggie 2013).

This development in the field of business and human rights has triggered a substantive shift in the outlook on corporate social responsibility (CSR) within multinational enterprises (MNEs). Furthermore, it has encouraged corporate human rights reporting (Mehra and Blackwell 2016; Methven O'Brien and Dhanarajan 2016). However, while academic research is increasingly addressing the issues of whether and how MNEs report on compliance

---

S. Zagelmeyer (✉)
Alliance Manchester Business School, University of Manchester, Manchester, UK
e-mail: stefan.zagelmeyer@manchester.ac.uk

© The Author(s) 2019
A. Chidlow et al. (eds.), *The Changing Strategies of International Business*, The Academy of International Business, https://doi.org/10.1007/978-3-030-03931-8_8

157

issues within their supply chains (Giuliani and Macchi 2014), the focus has largely been on MNEs from the Global North (Preuss and Brown 2012). Recent work on MNEs from the Global South, particularly the phenomenon of 'rising power' firms based in BRIC countries, has not only highlighted the growing importance and economic dynamism that is attributed to firms from Brazil, Russia, India and China (BRIC) countries but also raised questions in relations to labour standards and human rights compliance (Sinkovics et al. 2014a, b, 2015).

This chapter looks at the issue of international business and human rights through the lens of non-financial, corporate reporting practices in order to better understand the similarities and divergences of human rights reporting across countries and between MNEs from BRIC and non-BRIC economies. Drawing on 240 randomly-selected MNEs from each of the four BRIC and four advanced (non-BRIC) economies, it analyses 691 company documents, including annual reports, CSR reports, sustainability reports, codes of conduct and human rights reports.

The next section introduces the research methods, including the research objectives, the sampling process, the data collection process and the development of the human rights reporting intensity score. The subsequent section reports on the empirical analysis. It first describes the corporate reporting channels of the 240 MNEs, then moves on to analyse the reporting channels with respect to communicating human rights-related information, and finally presents the findings with respect to the human rights reporting intensity scores. The last section of the chapter discusses the findings and proposes directions for future research.

Research Methods

Research Background and Research Objectives

The research interest behind this project is to explore and analyse the extent to which MNEs engage in publishing human rights-related information, focusing, among other things, on the differences between companies based in BRIC and non-BRIC countries.

Our research interest was inspired by previous work on corporate human rights reporting by Preuss and Brown (2012), who analysed publicly available information on companies included in the Financial Times Stock Exchange 100 Index (FTSE 100) in order to establish the degree of adoption of human rights policies and to identify emerging patterns of company-level engagement with human rights. Although a significant proportion of the FTSE 100 companies are based outside the United Kingdom, Preuss and Brown (2012) call for further comparative cross-country analysis as one of several potentially fruitful avenues for future research.

Sampling Process

In order to identify suitable companies for comparative analysis, we decided to draw on the Forbes Global 2000 list for 2013. The Forbes Global 2000 is published by the US-based business magazine *Forbes* on an annual basis and includes the 2000 largest public companies of the world, considering market value, sales, profits and assets (Murphy 2015). A random sample of ten companies was selected from the Forbes Global 2000 list for 2013 and included in the search for company-level documents, including annual reports, CSR reports sustainability reports, environmental reports and human rights reports. For seven of these 10 companies, we were able to retrieve human rights reports. This stage of the project involved exploratory qualitative analysis of the content of the reports, using computer-assisted qualitative data analysis software (Sinkovics and Alfoldi 2012). As a result, it was decided to quantify the human rights-related information to be able to later engage in the quantitative comparative analysis of the relationship between human rights reporting and corporate behaviour and performance.

The data collection process involved several stages. In order to link the analysis to the debates on emerging market MNEs (Ramamurti and Singh 2009; Sinkovics et al. 2014b) and to analyse the differences between emerging market MNEs and MNEs from developed economies, the number of countries covered by the project was limited to four BRIC countries and four non-BRIC countries (France, Germany, the United Kingdom and the United States).

In order to achieve appropriate cell sizes for bivariate and multivariate analysis, thirty companies were selected for each of the eight countries. In order to (1) be able to conduct a comparative cross-country analysis and (2) to improve the generalisability of the findings, the sampling strategy included a random component. The process was as follows: random numbers were assigned to the 1098 companies from the eight target countries, and then the first thirty of each country (random numbers in decreasing order)

160   S. Zagelmeyer

Table 8.1 The sample companies from the Forbes Global 2000 list (2013)

	Forbes dataset (*n*)	Forbes dataset (%)	Sample (*n*)
Brazil	31	1.6	30
China	136	6.8	30
India	56	2.8	30
Russia	30	1.5	30
SUM	299		120
France	64	3.2	30
Germany	50	2.5	30
United Kingdom	95	4.8	30
United States	542	27.1	30
SUM	799		120

Key: *n* number of companies

were selected to be included in the sample. This ultimately led to a sample of 30 MNEs for each of the eight countries, and a total of 240 companies in the dataset (Table 8.1).

Data Collection and Analysis

The data collection process then involved searching for different types of publicly available documentation for the year 2013. The search was conducted in 2014 by a research team and targeted the following stand-alone documents, published in English:

1. annual reports (excluding 10-K statements);
2. CSR reports;
3. sustainability reports;
4. codes of conduct/ethics; and
5. human rights reports.

It soon emerged that only 7 out of the 240 companies in the sample had published an explicit human rights report as a stand-alone document. As a consequence, we broadened our search strategy to also include human rights statements publicly available on the companies' webpages. The respective webpages were printed as PDF files and added to the data archive, documenting the accession date and the HTTP address. This broadening of the search strategy increased the number of companies for which human rights reports or statements were available from 7 to 59.

Measuring the Intensity of Corporate Human Rights Reporting

The qualitative analysis reported above yielded a considerable diversity of corporate disclosure in terms of coverage of human rights issues, reporting channels and content of the available material. In order to measure the extent to which a company is reporting on its human rights-related philosophy and/or policies and practices, and to be able to compare the findings across companies, countries or groups of companies and countries, a scoring system was developed and applied to all 691 documents. This scoring system involves the following elements.

The first stage included a systematic content search of all available documents for the term 'human right' in order to identify the document sections with information related to human rights. At this stage, we encountered two problems. First, it emerged that US-based companies frequently use the term 'civil right' instead of 'human right'. As a consequence, all documents were searched for the keyword 'civil right'. However, all companies from the other seven countries referred to human rights. Second, a number of documents from Chinese MNEs included the standard forms of the Global Reporting Initiative (GRI)—which include the keywords 'human right'—in the appendix without providing information in the respective report sections.

The second stage involved the analysis of the documents by a researcher. Each available document was given a score based on the following scheme:

- (−): No report available;
- (0): report available, but 'human rights' not mentioned in the report;
- (1): 'human rights' mentioned, but used without providing further information or context (e.g. in lists of policies/concepts OR in the appendix of the document, for example, in relation to the GRI or the United Nations Global Compact);
- (2): one or two short paragraphs on 'human rights' in the report, indicating that the concept of 'human rights' is linked to content and substance with respect to management policies and practices;
- (3): 'human rights' are mentioned in one or two sections of the report, and over several paragraphs; and

162   S. Zagelmeyer

- (4): 'human rights' play a prominent role in the respective report (e.g. human rights play an important role in corporate strategy).

In order to ensure the quality of the scoring process, all members of the research team analysed the same subsample of documents for ten companies. Reliability coefficients were calculated (Campbell et al. 2013; Krippendorff 2011) and discussed in order to converge on a similar scoring behaviour and to increase the degree of inter-rater reliability.

After allocating a score to each document, aggregate scores were calculated for each company by adding the individual scores of all documents published by the respective company. The possible range of values for the aggregate score ranges from a minimum value of 0 to a maximum value of 20, which would imply a maximum score of four on all five documents.

As the human rights reporting scores measure the intensity of human rights reporting of each of the five potential reporting channels separately—that is, annual report, CSR report, sustainability report, code of conduct/ethics and human rights report or statement—and on aggregate as a sum score of all available documents, a maximum of five individual reporting scores and one aggregate reporting score are available for analysing the human rights reporting intensity for each of the 240 companies. In the following sections, the individual and aggregate scores will be used to compute country-level scores as well as average scores for companies based in particular countries or groups of countries (i.e. BRIC vs non-BRIC). While the next section will introduce findings of this analysis, the table with the summary statistics (mean value, minimum value, maximum value and standard deviation) is included in the appendix.

Empirical Analysis

The following sections will describe and discuss the empirical observations and findings on the extent to which companies were using different reporting channels for disseminating information on their human rights philosophy, policies and practices. The subsequent section will introduce and discuss the human rights reporting scores for companies based in the different countries and country groupings (BRIC and non-BRIC).

At this stage, it should be noted that the structure of the presentation of the descriptive findings as well as the analysis and discussion will be organised according to the following sequence of steps. The first step will involve the presentation of information for different reporting channels. The second will distinguish between country groupings, for example, BRIC and non-BRIC countries. The third will look at aggregate information for each country. Finally, in the fourth step we will take a comparative cross-country perspective on particular types of reports.

Corporate Reporting Channels

The following section reports on the extent to which MNEs based in the eight countries covered by the project use specific channels for corporate reporting. It will provide aggregate information for all MNEs combined, as well as separately for MNEs from BRIC and non-BRIC countries.

Table 8.2 displays information on the total number of reports collected for each of the eight countries and each of the five reporting channels. In

Table 8.2 Corporate reporting channels

		AR	CSR	SUS	CoC	HR	n
Brazil	Number	30	15	18	19	8	90
	Percentage	100	50	60	63	27	
China	Number	26	15	4	3	0	48
	Percentage	87	50	13	10	0	
India	Number	30	19	16	21	0	86
	Percentage	100	63	53	70	0	
Russia	Number	30	21	12	18	6	87
	Percentage	100	70	40	60	20	
France	Number	30	24	12	16	13	95
	Percentage	100	80	40	53	43	
Germany	Number	30	18	16	24	12	100
	Percentage	100	60	53	80	40	
United Kingdom	Number	30	22	11	20	13	96
	Percentage	100	73	37	67	43	
United States	Number	30	13	10	29	7	89
	Percentage	100	43	33	97	23	
All MNEs	Number	236	147	99	150	59	691
	Percentage	98	61	41	63	25	
Average no. per country		29.5	18.4	12.4	18.8	7.4	86.4
BRIC MNEs	Number	116	70	50	61	14	311
	Percentage	97	58	42	51	12	
Average no. per country		29.0	17.5	12.5	15.3	3.5	77.8
Non-BRIC MNEs	Number	120	77	49	89	45	380
	Percentage	100	64	41	74	38	
Average no. per country		30.0	19.3	12.3	22.3	11.3	95.0

Key: *AR* annual report, *CSR* CSR report/statement, *SUS* sustainability report/statement, *COC* code of conduct/ethics, *HR* human rights report/statement, *n* number of documents, *BRIC* Brazil, Russia, India and China

164   **S. Zagelmeyer**

addition, the table shows the respective percentages of companies using by a particular reporting channel for each category. In total, the analysis covers 691 documents published by 240 companies. Almost all companies publish annual reports in English and make these annual reports available online, with the one notable exception of MNEs from China, whose annual reports may not be published online and are not always available in English.

When looking at overall reporting structures for MNEs from all countries, annual reports are the most frequently used reporting channel (98%), followed by codes of conduct (63%), CSR reports (61%), sustainability reports (41%) and human rights reports and statements (25%). This observation holds true for the group of non-BRIC MNEs, while CSR reports and codes of conduct swap position for the BRIC MNEs. Table 8.2 also indicates that the sample of MNEs from BRIC countries has—on average—a smaller total number of reports. The incidence of human rights reports/statements is far lower for BRIC MNEs (12%) compared to MNEs from non-BRIC countries (38%).

Looking at country-level information, in Brazil sustainability reports (60% of all companies) are more popular than CSR reports (50%), while coverage by human rights reports or statements is highest compared to other BRIC countries (27%). MNEs from China mainly use annual reports (87%) and CSR reports (50%), while the proportion of companies with sustainability reports (13%) and codes of conduct (10%) is relatively low. Similar to companies from India, none of the companies from China had published a separate human rights report or statement. For companies from Russia and France, CSR reports are the most important form of non-financial reporting. Germany and the United States stand out with respect to a relatively high proportion of companies publishing codes of conduct. Non-financial reporting in the United Kingdom stands out in terms of a relatively low proportion of companies covered by sustainability reports (37%), and a high proportion of companies having a human rights report or statement (43%). Ninety-seven per cent of the companies based in the United States have a code of conduct, but only one out of three companies published a sustainability report.

Comparing non-financial reporting channels across countries, France is leading with respect to CSR reports (80% of companies) and together with the United Kingdom (43%) is leading the league table for human rights reports or statements. Sustainability reports are most popular in Brazil (60%), while almost all US-based (97%) companies have a code of conduct. In terms of the total number of reports, German companies published a hundred reports, while companies based in China published 48 reports.

With respect to CSR reports, coverage ranges from 50% of Chinese companies to 83% of French companies. The respective figures for sustainability reports are 13% for Chinese companies and 60% for Brazilian companies. While 97% of US companies publish a code of ethics/code of conduct online, the respective figure for Chinese companies is 10%. In terms of human rights reports or statements, France has the largest number and proportion of companies using this reporting channel (43%), while MNEs based in China or India did not publish human rights reports or statements.

The Corporate Reporting on Human Rights Philosophy, Policies and Practices

While the previous section provided an overview of corporate disclosure and reporting channels, this section will establish the link between corporate disclosure and reporting on human rights philosophies, policies and/or practices. The first part will focus on the incidence of human rights reporting, that is, whether or not companies use the different potential reporting channels for reporting on human rights philosophy, policies and practices. The second part will focus on the intensity of human rights reporting, using the human rights reporting intensity score introduced above.

Table 8.3 provides information on the extent to which companies in the different countries make use of different reporting channels (i.e. annual report, CSR report, sustainability report, code of conduct, and/or human rights report or statement) to communicate human rights-related information. In order to identify relevant cases, each of the 691 documents was checked to ascertain whether or not it includes a reference to human rights philosophy, policies and/or practices.

For each country sample of 30 companies, columns 2–6 in Table 8.3 provide information on (i) the total number reports that include a reference to human rights policies, and (ii) the percentage of companies in that country (out of 30) or country group (BRIC and non-BRIC countries, out of 120) using the respective reporting channel for communicating human rights-related information. In addition, Table 8.3 includes aggregate information on MNEs from BRIC and non-BRIC countries, and for the entire sample of all 240 MNEs.

When looking at the overall picture of reporting channels used by the 240 companies from eight countries, annual reports are the most frequently used reporting channel (97 companies, or 40%), followed by sustainability reports (78, or 33%), CSR reports (70, or 29%), codes of conduct (69, or 29%) and

166   S. Zagelmeyer

Table 8.3 Reporting channels used to communicate human rights policies

		AR	CSR	SUS	CoC	HR	n
Brazil	Number	18	5	15	9	8	55
	Percentage	60	17	50	30	27	
China	Number	1	4	4	1	0	10
	Percentage	3	13	13	3	0	
India	Number	15	3	14	4	0	36
	Percentage	50	10	47	13	0	
Russia	Number	4	8	9	7	6	34
	Percentage	13	27	30	23	20	
France	Number	20	19	8	12	13	72
	Percentage	67	63	27	40	43	
Germany	Number	15	12	14	14	12	67
	Percentage	50	40	47	47	40	
United Kingdom	Number	21	11	10	11	13	66
	Percentage	70	37	33	37	43	
United States	Number	3	8	4	11	7	33
	Percentage	10	27	13	37	23	
All MNEs	Number	97	70	78	69	59	373
	Percentage	40	29	33	29	25	
Average no. per country		12.1	8.8	9.8	8.6	7.4	46.6
BRIC MNEs	Number	38	20	42	21	14	135
	Percentage	32	17	35	18	12	
Average no. per country		9.5	5.0	10.5	5.3	3.5	33.8
Non-BRIC MNEs	Number	59	50	36	48	45	238
	Percentage	49	42	30	40	38	
Average no. per country		14.8	12.5	9.0	12.0	11.3	59.5

Key: *AR* annual report, *CSR* CSR report/statement, *SUS* sustainability report /
statement, *COC* code of conduct/ethics, *HR* human rights report/statement,
n number of documents, *BRIC* Brazil, Russia, India and China

human rights reports or statements (59, or 25%). For the group of non-BRIC MNEs, annual reports are most frequently used (59 companies, or 49%), sustainability reports are least frequently used (36, or 30%), and coverage is around 40% for the remaining three reporting channels. In contrast to this, BRIC MNEs most frequently use the sustainability reports (42, or 35%). In general, with the exception of the sustainability reports, all other reporting channels are more frequently used by non-BRIC MNEs compared to BRIC MNEs.

Looking at country-level information, in Brazil, India, France, Germany and the United Kingdom, annual reports are the most frequently used reporting channel for disseminating human rights-related information. MNEs based in China prefer CSR and sustainability reports. For US-based MNEs, the codes of conduct/ethics represent the reporting channel most frequently used to refer to human rights issues.

While Table 8.2 provides information on whether companies use a particular reporting channel, Table 8.3 provides information on whether companies use a particular reporting channel for communicating human rights-related information. However, neither table provides information on the quality or quantity of the human rights-related information. In order to measure the intensity of human rights reporting, we analysed the content of the available documents and applied the scoring scheme described above.

Table 8.4 presents the results of the qualitative content analysis and the scoring process. Columns 2–6 show the average scores for the different reporting channels, considering the documents available in each category only. For example, the number of 1.8 for Brazil in column 4 (sustainability reports) means that all available sustainability reports published by Brazilian MNEs score on average 1.8, on a scale ranging from 0 (lowest level of intensity) to 4 (highest level of intensity). It is important to note that this average score is calculated on the basis of (and in relation to) the published reports for a particular category. Thus, the indicator measures the human rights reporting intensity in relation to existing documents.

Column 7 (Av doc) displays the average score for all available documents for a particular country or groups of countries. This score reflects the average intensity of human rights reporting for all available documents published by MNEs based in that country or group of countries. While column 7 uses available documents as a base for calculating the average score, column 8 (Av MNE)

Table 8.4 Human rights reporting intensity scores

Average scores	AR	CSR	SUS	CoC	HR	Av doc	Av MNE
Brazil	1.1	0.5	1.8	0.7	1.8	1.1	3.4
China	0.0	0.3	1.8	0.3	–	0.3	0.5
India	0.8	0.3	2.1	0.3	–	0.8	2.4
Russia	0.2	0.8	1.3	0.5	1.7	0.7	1.9
France	1.4	2.0	1.1	1.6	2.0	1.6	5.1
Germany	0.8	1.7	2.1	1.0	2.2	1.4	4.5
United Kingdom	1.3	1.0	1.6	1.0	2.5	1.4	4.4
United States	0.2	1.5	1.0	0.7	2.6	0.8	2.4
All MNEs	0.7	1.0	1.6	0.8	2.1	1.0	3.1
BRIC MNEs	0.6	0.5	1.8	0.5	1.7	0.7	1.7
Non-BRIC MNEs	0.9	1.6	1.5	1.0	2.3	1.3	4.1

Key: *AR* annual report, *CSR* CSR report/statement, *SUS* sustainability report / statement, *COC* code of conduct/ethics, *HR* human rights report/statement, *Av doc* average of the scores of existing documents for all five reporting channels, *Av MNE* average of the individual company scores

168   S. Zagelmeyer

uses all thirty companies as a base for calculating the average human rights reporting intensity score.

As far as the averages across all available documents are concerned, the intensity of human rights reporting is highest in human rights reports and statements (2.1), followed by sustainability reports (1.6), CSR reports (1.0), codes of conduct (0.8) and annual reports (0.7). This overall pattern holds true for non-BRIC MNEs. For BRIC MNEs, the score is highest for sustainability reports (1.8), followed by human rights reports (1.7), annual reports (0.6), CSR reports (0.5) and codes of conduct (0.5).

Comparing the results for reporting channels between countries, annual reports published by French MNEs score highest (1.4), closely followed by annual reports published by UK-based MNEs (1.3). French MNEs also lead the league table for CSR reports (2.0) and for codes of conduct (1.6). For human rights reports and statements, the reporting intensity score is highest for reports published by US-based MNEs (2.6), closely followed by UK-based MNEs (2.5). Reports published by Chinese MNEs score lowest with respect to annual reports (0.0), CSR reports (0.3) and codes of conduct (0.3), while human rights are more frequently referred to in sustainability reports (1.8). In Indian and German MNEs, the human rights reporting intensity score is highest for sustainability reports (2.1).

Column 7 in Table 8.4 (Av doc) displays the average score of the manual coding process considering all available publications per country. Reports published by French multinationals lead the list (1.6), followed by reports from German and British MNEs (1.4), Brazilian MNEs (1.1), Indian and American MNEs (0.8), Russian MNEs (0.7) and Chinese MNEs (0.3). Last but not least, column 8 (Av MNE) provides information on the human rights reporting intensity of companies between countries. On average, French MNEs score highest (5.1), followed by German MNEs (4.5), British MNEs (4.4), Brazilian MNEs (3.4), Indian and American MNEs (2.4), Russian MNEs (1.9) and Chinese MNEs (0.5). For both types of aggregate average scores in columns 7 and 8, MNEs from non-BRIC countries have higher scores than MNEs from BRIC countries.

Discussion and Future Research Directions

The overall research objective of this chapter was to explore the extent to which MNEs engage in reporting on human rights philosophy, policies and practices, with a specific focus on cross-country variation. Although rather descriptive in terms of empirical analysis, there are a couple of interesting issues and findings emerging from our research.

To start with, even though not directly and explicitly related to human rights reporting, the chapter identifies a considerable amount of variation with respect to financial and non-financial/social reporting channels being used across companies as well as across and within countries and country groupings. While the financial and non-financial reporting literature is currently discussing the phenomenon of integrated reporting (de Villiers et al. 2014; Vaz et al. 2016), the issue of multi-channel reporting deserves further investigation and analysis. Especially with respect to non-financial/social reporting, it would be interesting to see future research on the preferences for and drivers of different configurations of reporting channels. Why do some companies prefer CSR reports to sustainability reports, or vice versa? Why do companies have both, and in addition include non-financial information in their annual reports? Are different types of reports or reporting channels substitutes, or do they complement each other? Furthermore, what are the drivers of the publication cycles of specific types of reports? Annual reports are usually published on an annual basis, supposedly as a consequence of regulatory requirements. CSR and sustainability reports also seem to follow specific publication patterns. However, codes of conduct/ethics and human rights reports or statements seem to be published on a less regular basis.

Moving towards the coverage of human rights philosophy, policies and practices in financial and non-financial/social reporting, three observations stand out. First, despite the current discussion on human rights due diligence and human rights reporting requirements linked to the UNGPs, at least for the period around 2013, explicit and stand-alone human rights reports or statements seem to be relatively rare. Using our sampling strategy in order to get a 'more representative' impression on the incidence of human rights reporting among MNEs shows that in 2013 only one out of four companies in our sample had published a human rights report or statement, the proportion among BRIC MNEs being one out of ten. This raises interesting questions about the management relevance of the business and human rights debate, as well as about the impact of the UNGPs.

Second, our research yielded interesting results with respect to the incidence of human rights issues being mentioned in the different types of reports. This is especially true for annual reports—with 40% of the annual reports (49% for non-BRIC MNEs and 32% for BRIC MNEs) mentioning human rights. In addition, variation across and within countries with respect to human rights being mentioned in CSR and sustainability reports raises interesting questions about the definition and conceptualisation of CSR as well as sustainability. Third, and last, the observable cross-country variation in terms of using different alternative or multiple reporting channels for communicating human rights-related issues might lead us to question the determinants and drivers of this phenomenon.

With respect to the intensity of human rights-related reporting, the human rights reporting intensity score introduced and applied in this chapter is novel and innovative, but requires additional analysis and testing with respect to measurement quality. The intensity scores have been used to describe the intensity of human rights-related reporting of published documents, and the descriptive analysis shows interesting variation in terms of intensity of human rights reporting between the different reporting channels and companies, but also between and within countries or groups of countries. Future research may also elaborate on the respective properties of the scoring approach, especially compared to word count analysis and/or qualitative coding-based approaches.

It would be interesting to see a further analysis of the drivers and determinants of the intensity score. In addition, the intensity score can be used as a variable in quantitative research on the link between human rights reporting intensity and corporate behaviour, outcomes and performance. Finally, a further interesting research topic is to explore and analyse changes in human rights reporting practices over time.

While most of the suggestions made so far ask for additional empirical research, there is a strong need for additional conceptual and theoretical research. Legitimacy theory, stakeholder theory, signalling theory and institutionalist approaches may be useful starting points for analysing the determinants and implications of corporate human rights reporting. While there is a plethora of research available on the internal and external drivers of CSR reporting (e.g. Giannarakis 2014; Giannarakis et al. 2014), sustainability reporting (e.g. Kolk 2010), environmental reporting (e.g. Kolk and Fortanier 2013) and financial reporting (e.g. Tschopp and Huefner 2015), there is a definite need to discuss whether and to what extent the existing approaches can be used to also explain and analyse human rights reporting, or, if need be, can be adapted to include additional human rights-related elements in the respective analytical frameworks.

Appendix

Table 8.5 Human rights reporting intensity scores—summary statistics

		AR	CSR	SUS	CoC	HR	Av doc
Brazil	Mean	1.1	0.5	1.8	0.7	1.8	1.1
	Min	0	0	0	0	1	0
	Max	3	2	4	3	3	10
	SD	1.0	0.7	1.2	0.9	0.7	2.7
China	Mean	0.0	0.3	1.8	0.3	–	0.3
	Min	0	0	1	0	–	0
	Max	1	2	3	1	–	4
	SD	0.2	0.6	1.0	0.6	–	0.9
India	Mean	0.8	0.3	2.1	0.3	–	0.8
	Min	0	0	0	0	–	0
	Max	3	2	3	2	–	7
	SD	0.9	0.7	1.1	0.7	–	2.0
Russia	Mean	0.2	0.8	1.3	0.5	1.7	0.7
	Min	0	0	0	0	1	0
	Max	3	3	3	3	3	7
	SD	0.6	1.2	1.1	0.8	0.8	1.9
France	Mean	1.4	2.0	1.1	1.6	2.0	1.6
	Min	0	0	0	0	1	0
	Max	4	3	4	3	4	13
	SD	1.2	1.2	1.2	1.2	1.2	2.9
Germany	Mean	0.8	1.7	2.1	1.0	2.2	1.4
	Min	0	0	0	0	1	0
	Max	3	4	3	2	4	11
	SD	0.9	1.4	1.1	0.9	1.0	2.8
United Kingdom	Mean	1.3	1.0	1.6	1.0	2.5	1.4
	Min	0	0	0	0	1	0
	Max	3	3	3	3	4	13
	SD	1.0	1.2	0.8	1.1	1.0	3.3
United States	Mean	0.2	1.5	1.0	0.7	2.6	0.8
	Min	0	0	0	0	2	0
	Max	3	4	3	3	4	10
	SD	0.6	1.5	1.3	1.0	0.8	3.0
Average ALL MNEs	Mean	0.7	1.0	1.7	0.8	2.1	3.1
	Min	0	0	0	0	1	0
	Max	4	4	4	3	4	13
	SD	0.6	1.5	1.3	1.0	0.8	3.0
Average BRIC MNEs	Mean	0.6	0.5	1.8	0.5	1.7	2.0
	Min	0	0	0	0	1	0
	Max	3	3	4	3	3	10
	SD	0.9	0.9	1.1	0.8	0.7	2.2
Average non-BRIC MNEs	Mean	0.9	1.6	1.5	1.0	2.3	4.1
	Min	0	0	0	0	1	0
	Max	4	4	4	3	4	13
	SD	1.1	1.3	1.2	1.0	1.0	3.1

Key: *AR* annual report, *CSR* CSR report/statement, *SUS* sustainability report /statement, *COC* code of conduct/ethical code/statement, *HR* human rights report/statement, *Av doc* average of the scores of existing documents for all five reporting channels, *Mean* mean value for all companies in the respective category, *SD* standard deviation

References

Campbell, J. L., Quincy, C., Osserman, J., & Pederseon, O. K. (2013). Coding in-depth semistructured interviews: Problems of unitization and intercoder reliability and agreement. *Sociological Methods & Research, 42*(3), 294–310.

de Villiers, C., Charl de Villiers, P. J. P., Rinaldi, L., & Unerman, J. (2014). Integrated reporting: Insights, gaps and an agenda for future research. *Accounting, Auditing & Accountability Journal, 27*(7), 1042–1067. https://doi.org/10.1108/aaaj-06-2014-1736.

Giannarakis, G. (2014). The determinants influencing the extent of CSR disclosure. *International Journal of Law and Management, 56*(5), 393–416.

Giannarakis, G., Konteos, G., & Sariannidis, N. (2014). Financial, governance and environmental determinants of corporate social responsible disclosure. *Management Decision, 52*(10), 1928–1951.

Giuliani, E., & Macchi, C. (2014). Multinational corporations' economic and human rights impacts on developing countries: A review and research agenda. *Cambridge Journal of Economics, 38*(2), 479–517. https://doi.org/10.1093/cje/bet060.

Kolk, A. (2010). Trajectories of sustainability reporting by MNCs. *Journal of World Business, 45*(4), 367–374. https://doi.org/10.1016/j.jwb.2009.08.001.

Kolk, A., & Fortanier, F. (2013). Internationalization and environmental disclosure: The role of home and host institutions. *Multinational Business Review, 21*(1), 87–114. https://doi.org/10.1108/15253831311309500.

Krippendorff, K. (2011). Agreement and information in the reliability of coding. *Communication Methods and Measures, 5*(2), 93–112. https://doi.org/10.1080/19312458.2011.568376.

Mehra, A., & Blackwell, S. (2016). The rise of non-financial disclosure: Reporting on respect for human rights. In D. Baumann-Pauly & J. Nolan (Eds.), *Business and human rights* (pp. 276–284). Abingdon/New York: Routledge.

Methven O'Brien, C., & Dhanarajan, S. (2016). The corporate responsibility to respect human rights: A status review. *Accounting, Auditing & Accountability Journal, 29*(4), 542–567. https://doi.org/10.1108/aaaj-09-2015-2230.

Murphy, A. (2015). *2015 global 2000: Methodology* [Online]. https://www.forbes.com/sites/andreamurphy/2015/05/06/2015-global-2000-methodology/#16ea295e70f9. Accessed 28 Aug 2018.

OHCHR. (2011). *Guiding principles on business and human rights – Implementing the United Nations "protect, respect and remedy" framework.* Geneva: Office of the UN High Commissioner for Human Rights.

Preuss, L., & Brown, D. (2012). Business policies on human rights: An analysis of their content and prevalence among FTSE 100 firms. *Journal of Business Ethics, 109*(3), 289–299. https://doi.org/10.1007/s10551-011-1127-z.

Ramamurti, R., & Singh, J. V. (Eds.). (2009). *Emerging multinationals in emerging markets* (Reprinted. ed.). Cambridge: Cambridge University Press.

Ruggie, J. G. (2013). *Just business: Multinational corporations and human rights.* New York: W.W. Norton Company.

Sinkovics, R., & Alfoldi, E. (2012). Progressive focusing and trustworthiness in qualitative research. *Management International Review, 52*(6), 817–845. https://doi.org/10.1007/s11575-012-0140-5.

Sinkovics, N., Sinkovics, R. R., & Yamin, M. (2014a). The role of social value creation in business model formulation at the bottom of the pyramid – Implications for MNEs? *International Business Review, 23*(4), 692–707. https://doi.org/10.1016/j.ibusrev.2013.12.004.

Sinkovics, R. R., Yamin, M., Nadvi, K., & Zhang, Y. Z. (2014b). Rising powers from emerging markets-the changing face of international business. *International Business Review, 23*(4), 675–679. https://doi.org/10.1016/j.ibusrev.2014.04.001.

Sinkovics, N., Sinkovics, R. R., Hoque, S. F., & Czaban, L. (2015). A reconceptualisation of social value creation as social constraint alleviation. *Critical Perspectives on International Business, 11*(3/4), 340–363. https://doi.org/10.1108/cpoib-06-2014-0036.

Tschopp, D., & Huefner, R. (2015). Comparing the evolution of CSR reporting to that of financial reporting. *Journal of Business Ethics, 127*(3), 565–577. https://doi.org/10.1007/s10551-014-2054-6.

Vaz, N., Fernandez-Feijoo, B., & Ruiz, S. (2016). Integrated reporting: An international overview. *Business Ethics, 25*(4), 577–591. https://doi.org/10.1111/beer.12125.

Part III

International Small (but) Mighty Enterprises and Entrepreneurs

While individually, the economic impact small and medium enterprises (SMEs) may have on international business activities can be seen as small, collectively the aggregate mass of SMEs may exceed that of a single most large multinational company. Furthermore, as SMEs play a critical role in larger international inter-firm networks and global value chains and are characterised as being highly entrepreneurial, it is more important than ever that their business behaviour cannot and should not be ignored and that is conformed with socially responsible practises across different borders.

Based on the above and by including three chapters, the aim of the final chapter is to offer the reader a way of looking at the joint importance of SMEs and international entrepreneurship. This is because such topics matter greatly to both the international business scholars and practitioners.

The first chapter (Chap. 9), titled "The Role of Culture in Responsible Business Practice: An Exploration of Finnish and Russian SMEs" by Maria Uzhegova, Lasse Torkkeli and Maria Ivanova-Gongne, examines how environmental and socially responsible actions differ in two different national contexts, Russia and Finland, and what effect these actions may have on international activities and relationships. The main argument here relates to the fact that the social responsibility of SMEs in both Russia and Finland is highly influenced by informal institutions in the form of local social norms, society's cultural expectations and formal legal frameworks which the companies operate in. Further and according to the authors, the dilemma SMEs face, when internationalising rapidly, relates to the way they balance economic and business pressures when adopting responsible practices with limited resources. What is more, differences in responsible activities of SMEs are dictated by institutional and cultural environments of their home countries. As such, the international transferability of responsible activity to SMEs in another institutional context is unlikely and that broader ethical standards such, as transparency and a commitment to compliance, are transferred across firms in order to foster trust and build a good reputation as the basis for a strong relationship.

Chapter 10, titled "The Internationalization of Born-Digital Companies" by Ioan-Iustin Vadana, Lasse Torkkeli, Olli Kuivalainen and Sami Saarenketo, shifts the focus onto the entrepreneurial aspects of the internationalisation process. Here the authors conduct a conceptual literature review questioning how the disciplines of international business, entrepreneurship and marketing define internet-enabled companies, and the extent to which internationalisation and digitalisation can be measured. The authors successfully demonstrate that the existing literature, has not fully (yet) managed to capture the impact digitalisation has had in creating a new variety of enterprise whose international activities are shaped by the degree to which its activities in a value chain have been digitalised. The authors label those new companies as "born-digital" and classify them as companies with a high degree of value chain digitalisation making a clear thought that not all born-digitals are automatically international as the scope of their business activities is based on their geographical dispersion.

The final chapter (Chap. 11), titled "Technological Disruptions and Production Location Choices" by Lisa De Propris and Diletta Pegoraro, examines how the drivers and outcomes of the globalisation push brought by the Fourth Industrial Revolution impact production and supply chain. The authors suggest that in order to take full advantages of the de-globalisation, Western firms should look closer at the territory in which they establish their operations due to the territorial ecosystem and technological activities around them.

9

The Role of Culture in Responsible Business Practice: An Exploration of Finnish and Russian SMEs

Maria Uzhegova, Lasse Torkkeli, and Maria Ivanova-Gongne

Introduction

Changes to the global and local market pose both challenges and opportunities for firms engaged in international business (IB). The cultural and psychic distance between countries is a widely discussed topic in IB literature (Håkanson and Ambos 2010; Gerschewski 2013), often considered alongside the internationalization process of large multinational corporations (MNCs). Furthermore, in the IB domain, research on corporate social responsibility (CSR) and sustainability is also primarily conducted using an MNC as a unit of analysis (Perrini et al. 2007; Kolk and Van Tulder 2010). To correct these shortcomings, this study is set within the context of small- and medium-sized enterprises (SMEs) from two culturally distant countries while analyzing managerial understanding of responsibility within IB relationships. Our study emphasizes the often under-researched informal institutional element of national culture as it pertains to sustainability (Peng et al. 2014).

SMEs are the predominant form of enterprise in several countries, accounting for up to 99% of business, approximately 70% of jobs, and about 55% of

---

M. Uzhegova (✉) • L. Torkkeli
Lappeenranta University of Technology, Lappeenranta, Finland
e-mail: Maria.uzhegova@lut.fi; Lasse.Torkkeli@lut.fi

M. Ivanova-Gongne
Åbo Akademi University, Turku, Finland
e-mail: Mivanova@abo.fi

© The Author(s) 2019
A. Chidlow et al. (eds.), *The Changing Strategies of International Business*, The Academy of International Business, https://doi.org/10.1007/978-3-030-03931-8_9

178   **M. Uzhegova et al.**

value added in several countries (OECD 2016). Regardless of their volume, the majority of SMEs' operations are limited to their national economy. Thus, SMEs are still under-represented in international trade, although their involvement in IB is believed to enhance their contributions to economic development and social well-being (OECD 2017). SMEs are increasingly called upon to contribute to sustainable development and "to adhere to codes of conduct and <...> best practices on issues such as health and safety, labour rights, human rights, anti-corruption practices and environmental impact" (World Trade report 2016, p. 150). The role of SMEs in promoting responsible and sustainable business practices cannot be ignored since the aggregated impact of SMEs' business operations globally is significant (OECD 2013).

However, SMEs' willingness and ability to adopt sustainable practices often face size-related resource constraints, skill deficits, and knowledge limitations (OECD 2017). SMEs face similar challenges while pursuing internationalization activities since carrying out IB is often more complex than domestic operations alone (Johanson and Vahlne 2009). SMEs are particularly susceptible to such resource constraints when aiming for rapid internationalization (Knight and Cavusgil 2004).

SMEs' business ethics developed separately from the internationalization of SMEs, so despite the growing body of research we do not yet adequately understand how they align. This study aims to fill these gaps by examining the role of national cultural differences in SMEs' business responsibility and IB relationships. This informs the following research question for this study: *How and to what extent the distinctions in national cultures are reflected in the SMEs' business responsibility and IB relationships?* The empirical part of the study consists of a qualitative investigation of responsible business practices in Finnish and Russian SMEs involved in IB.

Therefore, we contribute to the literature in two ways. Conceptually, we bring the discussion of small business responsibility to internationalization literature. Empirically, we trace the differences between the SMEs from two neighboring but culturally distant countries, thus offering several insights into cultural distance and the managerial role in this context.

The remainder of the chapter is structured as follows. We begin with a discussion of small business responsibility and the role of national culture. We then present the empirical context of this study consisting of two culturally distant countries representing Western and Eastern cultures, Finland and Russia. After describing the methodology of the empirical investigation, we present its findings. The last section discusses the findings' theoretical interpretation.

Theoretical Background

Small Business Responsibility

A company's activities related to business responsibility are often referred to as corporate social responsibility and include a variety of actions. A single widely accepted definition of the concept exists neither in business practice nor in the academic research literature (Crane et al. 2013); the scope of such activities may refer to measures toward maintaining economic, legal, ethical, and philanthropic responsibilities, as defined by Carroll (1991).

However, the dynamics of, motivations behind, and strategies for responsibility are more explicit in large companies than SMEs (Perrini et al. 2007). SMEs are not just smaller versions of their larger counterparts, and thus, the CSR concept may appear misleading, only weakly capturing the approach employed by SMEs (Moore and Spence 2006). From the SME perspective, social responsibility is often associated with efficiency concerns: increasing the employee's motivation, reducing energy and raw material consumption, and supporting philanthropy lead by senior management or some voluntary desire to participate in the surrounding local community. Social responsibility may include a variety of actions to address these concerns (Larrán Jorge et al. 2016). Here we continue with the notion of the responsible business practice (RBP), wherein the owner or manager takes on the central decision-making role in regard to the firm's environmental and/or social responsibilities, in keeping with the SME context (Ryan et al. 2010). Indeed, SME managers were found to clearly differentiate between the interrelated and often overlapping concepts of CSR, sustainability, and business ethics (Fassin et al. 2011). However, perceptions differ between managers from different countries as macro-environmental factors, such as language and national culture, influence individual cognition (Fassin et al. 2015).

National Culture

The national culture, categorized as an informal institution, forms behavioral and mental models, informal business practices, and routines (Keim 2003) and can be defined as a set of shared values, beliefs, and expected behaviors (Hofstede 1980). National culture has been studied in the context of business internationalization over recent decades because of the assumption that trade between countries is determined not only by countries' physical distance but

180   M. Uzhegova et al.

also by other differentiating factors such as language, personal relationships, and national culture (Beckerman 1956).

IB literature has widely treated the dimension of cultural distance as a single construct influencing firms' international expansion (Håkanson and Ambos 2010; Gerschewski 2013). Studies suggest that firms behave differently based on home-country characteristics that support different perceptions of international markets. Cultural context influences the factors of individual global mindset and corporate global mindset, leading to differing internationalization behavior among SME managers (Felício et al. 2016). Other studies demonstrate that networks assist in overcoming the challenges associated with spreading internationalization activities to culturally distant target markets (Ojala 2009; Kontinen and Ojala 2010).

While the notion of national culture is widely used in IB studies, it also explains the differences associated with CSR between companies located in different (and culturally distant) countries utilizing the quantitative inquiry. CSR research in recent decades tends to link the different aspects of a company's responsibility with the national culture or national business systems (e.g. Ringov and Zollo 2007; Ioannou and Serafeim 2012). Being a complex concept in nature, the national culture can be described using a set of six dimensions proposed by Hofstede (1980). The six dimensions refer to (1) power distance (the extent to which people accept that power is unequally distributed within organizations); (2) individualism (the way people integrate with groups); (3) uncertainty avoidance (the extent to which a culture feels threatened by ambiguity); (4) masculinity/femininity (the emphasis that a culture puts on masculine or feminine values); (5) long-term orientation (the extent to which societal change is accepted); (6) indulgence (the extent to which people control desires and impulses). Hofstede's cultural dimensions widely accepted among management scholars (Marino et al. 2002) and despite the criticism it has met over the years (e.g. McSweeney 2002; Håkanson and Ambos 2010), it is nevertheless used in both IB and responsibility research fields for empirical enquiries.

Table 9.1 presents an overview of how the various CSR dimensions were found to interact with Hofstede's cultural dimensions.

As Table 9.1 demonstrates, empirical research found a causal link between national culture and CSR; however, no solid evidence exists, as the findings are inconsistent and contrast with each other. Furthermore, a recent study regarding corporate environmental responsibility opposes the previous studies employing Hofstede's six dimensions and has demonstrated that the latter two dimensions—long-term orientation and indulgence—affect the former four, thus limiting the previous findings' reliability (Graafland and Noorderhaven 2018).

Table 9.1 The overview of the CSR studies based on the Hofstede (1980) dimensions

Hofstede dimension/ Dependent variable	Ringov and Zollo (2007) Corporate social performance	Ho et al. (2012) Corporate social performance	Ioannou and Serafeim (2012) Corporate social performance	Peng et al. (2014) CSR engagement	Thanetsunthorn (2015) CSR performance	Graafland and Noorderhaven (2018) Corporate environmental responsibility
Power distance	− (n.s.)	+	+	−	−	−
Individualism	−	−	+	+	−	+
Masculinity	−	+	Not used	−	− (n.s.)	−
Uncertainty avoidance	+ (n.s.)	+	Not used	+	+	+
Long-term orientation	Not used	Not used	Not used	Not used	Not used	+
Indulgence	Not used	Not used	Not used	Not used	Not used	+

Effect: + positive, − negative, *n.s.* non-significant

The National Cultures of Finland and Russia

Eastern companies tend to differ from Western ones in management strategy, decision-making, business operations, and organizational culture (Buckley et al. 2005). In this study, we investigate how SMEs' RBPs reflect differences in national cultures. Although physically close, sharing a mutual national border, Finland and Russia nevertheless differ in cultural dimensions—Finland serving as a representative of Western culture and Russia as a representative of an Eastern one.

Previous research has specifically addressed the cultural differences in Finnish-Russian business relationships. The themes which emerged include the perception of time (sequential in Finland and synchronic in Russia) (Vinokurova et al. 2009), and expectations regarding the level of openness about the partner company's internal processes (a Finnish counterpart maintained nondisclosure behavior toward the partner, whereas the opposite was expected by Russian managers) (Ivanova and Torkkeli 2013). Moreover, the overall relationship orientation leans toward network form in Finland and toward dyadic form in Russia, which accordingly results in the networking process to being perceived as an organizational or interpersonal phenomenon (Ivanova-Gongne and Torkkeli 2018). Due to the relatively recent introduction of capitalism, general uncertainty, and a dynamic business environment, Russia's organizational culture operates under a shorter time span than Finland's (Vinokurova et al. 2009). The study of managerial sensemaking contrasted Russian managers' overall short-term orientation and tendency to seek high profits with the long-term strategic planning and strong customer service orientation of Finnish managers (Ivanova and Torkkeli 2013).

To illustrate the cultural differences between these two countries for the purposes of this study we provide scores for the various cultural dimensions as defined by Hofstede (2018) in Table 9.2.

Based on the Hofstede country profiles and the scores, Finnish society may be described as individualistic, feminine, uncertainty avoiding, normative, and indulgent, with a low power distance. Russian society, in turn, has a very high power distance, while it is also characterized as collectivist, feminine,

Table 9.2 Cultural profiles of Finland and Russia

	Power distance	Individualism	Masculinity	Uncertainty avoidance	Long-term orientation	Indulgence
Finland	33	**63**	26	59	38	**57**
Russia	**93**	39	**36**	**95**	**81**	20

Values from Hofstede insights (2018); the higher value is in bold

highly uncertainty avoiding, pragmatic, and restrained. To add to the comparison of the two cultures, we use the data from the World Values Survey (2017). The survey differentiates between cultures by *survival* (emphasis on economic and physical security) versus *self-expression* (emphasis on environmental protection, tolerance of foreigners, minorities, and gender equality) *values*. Another dimension used is the prevalence of either *traditional values* (emphasis on religion, parent-child ties, deference to authority; rejection of divorce, abortion, euthanasia and suicide; and high levels of national pride and a nationalistic outlook) or *secular-rational values* which are opposite to the traditional ones. On a scale from −2.5 to 2.5, from 2010 to 2014 Russia scored −1.25 in the *survival* versus *self-expression* dimension and 0.5 in the *traditional* versus *secular-rational values* dimension, while Finland scored 1.25 in both dimensions (WVS 2017). The difference in scores for the former dimension indicates the importance of survival values in Russian society, underscoring a relatively ethnocentric outlook and low levels of trust and tolerance. In Finland, in turn, self-expression values are stressed, indicating the demand for participation in economic and political decision-making. The latter dimension scores characterize Russia as a more traditional country compared to Finland, where secular-rational values prevail.

Regarding company responsibility, Finland is part of the European Union, where a European Commission's Green paper (2001) introduced the concept of CSR, defining it "as a concept whereby companies integrate social and environmental concerns in their business operations and in their interaction with their stakeholders on a voluntary basis". In the study of human resource reporting as a part of CSR reporting initiative, even for the biggest Finnish companies a disclosure of practices was new in the start of 2000s (Vuontisjärvi 2006). Despite high levels of civic engagement, only 12% of Finnish small firms were found regularly devoting resources to the social good in 2001 (Koos 2011). Finnish companies perceived CSR as "compliance with strict Finnish laws and regulations", with globalization being the most prominent driver (Panapanaan et al. 2003, p. 137).

Compared to the research in a Finnish context, insight on responsibility in Russian companies is scarce and more recent. The study by Crotty (2016) demonstrates a strong link between the practices and attitudes of managers toward CSR in Russia and its historical and cultural legacy. The managers of large Russian firms were found to diverge from Western rhetoric about the concepts and understanding of responsible practices (Kuznetsova et al. 2009).

Based on the above discussion of the national culture and organizational practices in the Finnish-Russian business context, we argue that the SMEs' RBPs are highly influenced by the cultural expectations and local social norms

184 M. Uzhegova et al.

to which they are bound. Following the differences identified between the two countries, we expect that the dissimilarities between the RBPs of their SMEs are rooted in diverging cultural backgrounds.

Methodology

Our research design implies a broad inductive exploration of the phenomenon under the study revealing how SMEs from different cultural contexts exhibit RBPs and execute IB operations. The evidence was collected from multiple data sources including primary data in the form of semi-structured interviews with the key informants accompanied by the secondary sources (press materials, company documents, and websites), as suggested by Yin (2009). The interviews with the top management (CEO, founder, or a key manager) of Finnish and Russian SMEs were conducted in June–December 2017 with each company representing one case. The case selection criteria included (1) a company must have fewer than 250 employees to comply with the European Commission definition for SMEs (EC 2003), (2) conduct B2B business, and (3) have business experience with a Finnish/Russian partner.

The Russian SMEs were first approached through the Finnish-Russian Chamber of Commerce (FRCC), a cross-national body for Finnish-Russian business promotion and assistance. The trade association newsletter emailed an invitation to FRCC members describing the interview's general topic and aim. Approaching the companies through a known and trusted body such as FRCC assisted in overcoming the high level of uncertainty avoidance in Russian society; according to Hofstede (2018): "as long as Russians interact with people considered to be strangers they appear very formal and distant". Hence, a certain level of trust between researchers and the respondents had to be established, resulting in the latter's willingness to share their opinions and stories. Out of the companies that signed up for the interview, the most suitable three have been chosen. After the reference from the Russian partner, the Finnish companies were approached. As a result, the primary data for this study consists of six interviews. Table 9.3 presents case companies' information.

Interview questions covered a variety of topics including an entrepreneur's personal background, social responsibility, environmental responsibility, and IB with the Finnish/Russian partners. All the interviews were audio recorded with permission, lasting an hour on average. To capture cultural features, the interviews were held in the researchers' and interviewees' native languages, after which the tapes were transcribed verbatim and translated into English by

Table 9.3 Case companies' information

Name	Industry	Founded	Main function	Experience with a FIN/RUS partner	Interviewee	Responsibility issues mentioned on a website	Length of the interview
Finnish SMEs							
TRANS_FI	All-road vehicles	1999	Distributing partner	2 years	Owner	No	51 min
VENT_FI	Ventilation systems	1998	Manufacturing, parent company	13 years	CEO	ISO 9001, CE marking, commitment to continuous improvement in environmental issues, and modernization of facilities for an efficient and reliable production process	1 h 11 min
HOSP_FI	Hospital equipment	1998	Manufacturing, a supplier	1 year	Sales management director	An extensive code of ethics, CE marking, ISO 9001, ISO 13485, ISO 14001	1 h 45 min
Russian SMEs							
TRANS_RU	All-road vehicles	2005	Manufacturing	2 years	Marketing director	Total quality management system and ISO 9001:2015 certification is mentioned	1 h 15 min
VENT_RU	Ventilation systems	2002	Manufacturing subsidiary	13 years	CEO	No	1 h 7 min
HOSP_RU	Hospital equipment	2007	Distributing partner	1 year	Owner	Responsibility is a part of our daily work. Each of our employees is responsible toward our client for the work performed	55 min

186 M. Uzhegova et al.

a professional service. Following this, the data were then analyzed with the respondents' opinions and management practices coded in NVivo 11, a software for coding paragraphs, sentences, or words. Codes were assigned first based on the a priori code list created based on the theory and an interview guide, complemented by careful inclusion of the topics that emerged from the data during the coding process. After the initial coding was finished, we rearranged the individual codes in the groups, united the overlapping codes, or rearranged them in the hierarchal order. As a result, several umbrella groups of codes emerged, namely "social responsibility", "environmental responsibility", and "international business relationship", with some of them subdivided into "company's actions" and "managerial opinions". After the coding, the data analysis included within-firm and cross-firm analysis within the countries and between them to identify differences and similarities, as well as patterns and implications (Miles et al. 2014).

Findings and Discussion

Responsible Business Practices

Both countries count compliance with the law and other requirements as a responsibility. For Russian SMEs, compliance with the labor code and obeying labor safety rules is of the utmost importance. The VENT_RU mentioned among the actions for compliance obtaining a workplace certification and adjusting the level of illumination to the requirements, with other respondents revealing their practices:

HOSP_ RU	We certify workplaces, since it must be done. The laws are the laws, they are everywhere, they must be respected, taxes must be paid. If it is necessary, then it is **obligatory for us to comply**
TRANS_ RU	[Social responsibility means] creating comfortable and safe working conditions, on-time payment, fulfilment of obligations, and **acting according to the terms** in the employment contract

However, in Russia, the issue of internal company responsibility toward employees was more pronounced:

VENT_ RU	I am convinced that one should receive a decent salary for decent work. I think this **social approach should be present in daily life**. Not once a year or just on holidays. Then they [employees] will stick to you. I wouldn't say that we have the highest salaries in the field. But they are stable and people know that we won't scam them here

HOSP_ RU	I try to **create the conditions** in the form of insurance policies, health insurance, a comfortable office, social packages, and the events for the team building

The reason for emphasizing these issues is that some companies still face little penalty for flouting the rules and work "in gray", paying only the minimal allowed wage (TRANS_RU). Notably, such emphasis on obeying employment contract terms, attributed to responsibility, aligns with Crotty's study (2016). In the historically contextualized study of Russian CSR, this notion was attributed to the Transition Legacy type of CSR. As the type's name suggests, it is an attribute remaining in Russian business practice from the 1990s when paying taxes and salaries was not perceived as compulsory.

Continuing to the external stakcholders mentioned by the interviewees, Russian SMEs emphasized responsibility to their partners and customer orientation, which entails building relationships as opposed to one-time deals (HOSP_FI). Another respondent opens up further:

Compliance with agreements and ethics is important for us. That means **not causing any economic or reputational damage** to partners. (TRANS_RU)

While discussing customer responsibility, the respondent from TRANS_FI refers to the noticed irresponsibility among the customers as the following quote illustrates:

I think that our society teaches that **consumers have no responsibility** for anything. If he breaks purchased equipment, he turns to me and says, "this piece has a 5-year guarantee, so fix it." If I sell a piece of equipment worth EUR 50,000, and the customer uses every possible opportunity to return it, to nullify the deal, it might be the end of my business. (TRANS_FI)

Other case SMEs' external stakeholders emerged from data are minority groups in need. VENT_RU opens up about their parent company's philanthropic activities and their own contributions to the Russian Orthodox Church and youth sports:

I think a lot here depends on the personal position of the director. I know that [VENT_FI] sponsors and helps the Lutheran community there, as well as here in Russia. As for me, I have been **connected to sport throughout my whole life.** <…> The child and youth **sport has a powerful social element**: the more kids we get off the street and put into the gym, the better it will be for the society at the end because the sport gets the stupid things out of their heads. I help them here in St. Petersburg, and even in the neighbouring countries. (VENT_RU)

188   M. Uzhegova et al.

Philanthropic intentions were identified in all Russian cases. In TRANS_RU, one of the owners, a former race-car driver, supports the university team in motor racing and a children's karting club on behalf of the company. The HOSP_RU respondent revealed that their company supports the children's oncology hospital and donates to soldiers' widows. However, none of the SMEs communicates about these activities elsewhere in public sources, as this is perceived as boasting (TRANS_RU) or an attribute needed by large companies only (VENT_RU). The following quote reflects this:

> When we went to the children hospital, the staff said: "Let's take a picture" but I do not like advertising, I have helped, and that's it. We do not publish a lot of information as **this attracts the attention of those who want to get money**. I believe that everyone who has the opportunity to help should help, and there's nothing to brag about. (HOSP_RU)

All of the Russian SMEs emphasized philanthropy but none of the Finnish managers mentioned it explicitly. This may be because the Soviet Legacy or Philanthropic type of Russian CSR is associated with the paternalistic social role companies played during the Soviet Union era (Crotty 2016).

Another dimension of RBPs in SMEs is attributed to a company's legitimacy and the wider benefit it offers to society, as reflected by the following quotes:

TRANS_RU	I would never be selling vodka because it's not very good. It is good when an interesting and a quality product is being created, and **there is a benefit to society**
HOSP_FI	I see it [social responsibility] in such a way that if a hospital gets better equipment, it can better serve the local population, offer better and more services, **so in that indirect way**

After the responsibility to the external stakeholders, responsibility toward the natural environment emerged as important to Finnish respondents, as they pointed to the lack of one in Russian SMEs:

VENT_FI	When it comes to energy and fuel spending and so on, in Russia it seems to carry **much less weight** [than here]
HOSP_FI	On the [Russians'] personal level, it's a bit like: "So what? We have a big country, we have lots of space left." That's a bit of a shame but **they've started to understand that now**

Indeed, Russian SMEs noticed a positive trend, although environmentalism is still prioritized less than responsibility to social stakeholders:

The Role of Culture in Responsible Business Practice: An Exploration... 189

TRANS_ RU	We collect the paper from the office and it is processed and disposed. It is for a year or two that everything is sorted including the plastic waste. It was initiated at the city level and because there are the conditions for processing the waste, there is **at least a minimal economic motivation** [for us to do it]
VENT_ RU	Talking about environment protection, we have a special contract with the company that processes our waste. They collect it and we pay. **The initiative was ours**: we have a waste and what's next? You can hire someone [and say:] "Here is the money, take the waste as far as possible." You can do that. Maybe once or twice but in the end, you will go to the forest and what will you see? Your own garbage. That is a no-go

Such a position, where environmental protection is not perceived as beneficial and requires additional incentives, aligns with findings by Simpson et al. (2004) which indicate that environmental responsibilities are hardly transferable to competitive advantage for the SMEs.

To summarize, a variety of RBPs exist in the cases from both countries, aimed at the SMEs' stakeholders both internally (maintaining good relationships with the employees) and externally (helping minorities in need). However, the actions undertaken and the stakeholders' groups to which the company owes responsibility differ slightly in both countries. The actions undertaken in the Russian cases varied more than those pursued in Finnish cases, which were mostly aimed at fulfilling the imposed requirements. In addition, philanthropy was a prominent attribute among Russian cases while environmental responsibility appeared to be a more important dimension for Finnish cases. The way Finnish companies market product reflects the latter difference:

TRANS_ FI	I don't think that in Russia **it carries any weight** but here in Finland I'm trying to bring it up, that these are ecological vehicles, and if you drive it anywhere, for example, you drive across a lawn, it doesn't leave any traces, you're not breaking the surface at all
HOSP_FI	In Russia, **it's not a selling point**. It's a neutral thing. They don't react to it in Russia like "wow, this is going to take things forward".

Nevertheless, the presented differences did not influence the IB activities of case SMEs. VENT_FI has expressed that social responsibility was not an issue in their relationships, while the HOSP_RU interviewee says that "neither Finnish nor other companies have asked such questions [about our responsibility]. Maybe they will, but meanwhile, these topics are not discussed."

To sum up, the RBPs in the SMEs from both countries have been found to comply with the view often referred to as Carroll's CSR Pyramid (Carroll

190 M. Uzhegova et al.

Table 9.4 The summary of RBPs in case companies

Responsibility	Finnish SMEs	Russian SMEs
Economic	Being profitable, paying taxes	Being profitable and looking for economic benefits from all actions including environmental responsibilities
Legal	Complying with all the rules and regulations, standards, and norms	Complying with the labor code, labor safety, paying employees' official salaries
Ethical	Honesty, no corruption, and "gray" practices also required from the international partners	Toward the partners—not to harm their reputation, no contracts with the competitors
Philanthropic	Toward the Lutheran church in Finland and Russia Through the product	Toward the Russian Orthodox church, youth sports, children's hospital, soldiers' widows, university racing team, and children's karting team

1991). It contains four elements: economic (making a profit for the shareholders and providing products for consumers and jobs for employees), legal (obeying the law), ethical (doing no harm), and philanthropic (contributing to society) (Carroll 1991). Table 9.4 summarizes the RBPs possessed by the case SMEs.

However, from the data emerges that it is a role of an individual manager, which is explicitly present in data that distinct the SMEs' RBPs. In Carroll's Pyramid, the economic and legal responsibilities are *required*, ethical responsibilities are *expected*, and philanthropic ones are *desired* by the society. However, the following quote offers insight into the role of a societal controlling mechanism:

> Our cultural differences are so large in terms **how the society controls certain activities**. In Finland, they check everything with a magnifying glass, and it feels that in Russia they spend a second. (TRANS_FI)

Indeed, in Russian data, evidence emerged of the owner-manager's dominant role, which goes beyond the management function accepted in Finland. Particularly, the head of the company decides if and in which part the company is to comply with legal requirements, behave ethically, and allocate resources to the philanthropy while still prioritizing economic profitability above social benefit. A perception of responsibility as emerged in data from Russian SMEs reflects the elements noted in Spence's (2016) study, which redraws Carrol's Pyramid from an ethics of care perspective, the viewpoint more suited to SMEs. In Spence's framework, economic and legal responsi-

The Role of Culture in Responsible Business Practice: An Exploration...   **191**

bilities are substituted for survival, while the ethical responsibility is replaced with ethics of care, the philanthropic category remains intact, and a new category of owner-managers' personal integrity is added.

Cultural Differences

The reasons for differences found in RBPs are also connected with their distinct historical backgrounds. Particularly, the influence of transition and Soviet legacies identified with regard to RBPs (Crotty 2016) are also reflected in business culture as the TRANS_RU respondent explains:

> Business culture in Russia is not yet formed after the transition happened in the 1990s and it is still oriented on making money. <...> It is mainly based on international standards but **does not exist on the cultural or community level: companies are trying to follow the law if there is no penalty**. The culture is being formed and in 5-10-15 years, it will be formed at some level. This will happen when people, who came to the management and owning the enterprise in the transition period – a period of capital accumulation and property privatization, will leave, then there will be a slightly different culture, and the next generation will come to management. (TRANS_RU)

A Finnish respondent brought up the same positive trend associated with the managerial generational change:

> There is a new generation coming up in Russia. I've communicated with high school graduates, and their way of thinking changes, even though their cultural background remains the same. <...> The Russian way of doing business has become a bit boring, **like in the western countries**. (HOSP_FI)

While the differences between RBPs were not found important to IB with Russian/Finnish counterparts, the cultural differences between business routines appear in data regularly. Finnish respondents agreed that the most notable distinctions regard the perception of time, respect for deadlines, and a particular price-consciousness evident in the maintenance expenses perceived as unnecessary by Russian counterparts (HOSP_FI), and are consistent with previous studies (Vinokurova et al. 2009; Ivanova and Torkkeli 2013). Despite the cultural and practical differences related to certifications (HOSP_FI, VENT_RU), customs routines (HOSP_FI, TRANS_RU), legislation (TRANS_FI), and tenders (HOSP_FI), respondents are striving toward better understanding of Russian business culture:

I think our views are largely similar. We have this new Russian coming up [to work for us] and one of the ideas behind that is that we would have somebody at our end too so that **we could get a bit deeper into their culture**. (VENT_FI)

In turn, having the international partners is not yet common for Russian SMEs, as TRANS_RU elaborates:

Small business here is less involved in international activities than in Europe. Such cases when a small company works for export are rare. It is connected with the culture and education, and with certain difficulties to access foreign markets. We will gradually come to this but it will happen when a new generation comes to business, which has the internships abroad, and who, from their childhood has travelled abroad. They do not see **the psychological or cultural barriers** entering the European markets. (TRANS_RU)

Nevertheless, for the experienced, an understanding of Finnish counterparts' business culture has not presented any major difficulties compared to dealing with partners from the Middle East, Asia (HOSP_RU), or the US (TRANS_RU). For these two SMEs, the relationships with Finnish companies were characterized by the slow trust building:

With our Finnish partner, **the trust is built gradually**. They do not offer the best contract terms from the initial contact but in general, there is a positive attitude towards us. (HOSP_RU)

Indeed, all the Finnish respondents brought up the importance of trust and personal contact especially with Russian partners:

VENT_FI	Personal relationships are important there. Also, meeting people in person, loyalty and trustworthiness, **so that you can trust the other person in the long term**
HOSP_FI	Although he has sent me the information in a written form, **personal chemistry is important to me too**. It's not companies that do business, it's people that do business
TRANS_FI	When companies are doing business mutually, it's a question of a relationship between two persons to a large extent. It's exactly about **who's at the other end and what kind of a person they are**

Placing such great importance upon trust building in IB relationships is consistent with the revisited Uppsala model, which acknowledges the important role of trust in relations during internationalization (Johanson and Vahlne 2009). However, it is apparent from the quotes of both Russian managers and their Finnish counterparts that gradual trust building and establishment of transparent and trustworthy relationships are more of the Finnish SMEs' concern. Moreover, analysis of the quotes reveals that the Finnish respondents described cultural differences in Finnish-Russian business relationships more often and in greater detail than Russian respondents. This suggests that the cultural distance is greater in the Finnish-Russian direction than vice versa. This is consistent with the notion of psychic distance and its asymmetrical nature (Ellis 2008).

Conclusions

Although visible in managerial decision-making and as opposed to what was theorized, the differences in national culture are not explicitly recognizable in SMEs' responsible business practices. The exception to this is the attitude toward environmental responsibility, reflected by the way Finnish SMEs position their products. By matching the RBPs of Russian SMEs with the CSR types (Crotty 2016), this study suggests that the historical background is one of the conditions that forms RBPs in SMEs. The business relationships between the case SMEs from the culturally distant countries are primarily characterized by a strong managerial role (Spence 2016), local legislation, and a cultural distance perception as perceived by the managers toward their counterparts (psychic distance) (Håkanson and Ambos 2010). The role of mutual trust in this study has appeared to outweigh the RBP's importance in the cross-border business relationships (Johanson and Vahlne 2009), suggesting the important role of the owner-manager and individual decision-making.

Our study theoretically contributes to the literature on SME internationalization and small business responsibility by integrating them through the national culture as an informal institution. The theoretical value of this chapter is that we apply a national cultural lens to explore if the differences in national culture are evident in the responsible business practices of SMEs and their IB relationships. We argue that studying SME RBPs in the IB context is possible through combining the firm-level considerations and national culture context, yielding more complex understanding.

This study has several limitations that further research could overcome. The purposeful inclusion of only the SMEs with an international partner constrains the generalizability such that for future research the inclusion of domestically operating SMEs from culturally distant countries could offer further knowledge about the interrelation of IB relationships and the RBPs' presence and scope. Accounting for the evidence that legislation presents a prominent burden for SMEs' IB, tracing RBPs from the institutional point of view would be especially beneficial, enabling researchers to contrast informal and formal institutions, thus comparing the SMEs and linking them to their origins in a developing, emerging, or developed economic context.

References

Beckerman, W. (1956). Distance and the pattern of intra-European trade. *The Review of Economics and Statistics, 38*(1), 31–40.

Buckley, P. J., Carter, M. J., Clegg, J., & Tan, H. (2005). Language and social knowledge in foreign-knowledge transfer to China. *International Studies of Management & Organization, 35*(1), 47–65.

Carroll, A. B. (1991). The pyramid of corporate social responsibility: Toward the moral management of organizational stakeholders. *Business Horizons, 34*(4), 39–48.

Crane, A., Matten, D., & Spence, L. J. (2013). *Corporate social responsibility: Readings and cases in a global context* (2nd ed., pp. 3–26). Abingdon: Routledge.

Crotty, J. (2016). Corporate social responsibility in the Russian federation: A contextualized approach. *Business & Society, 55*(6), 825–853.

EC. (2003). Commission recommendation of 6 May 2003 concerning the definition of micro, small and medium-sized enterprises. *Official Journal of the European Union, 46*, 36–41.

Ellis, P. D. (2008). Does psychic distance moderate the market size–entry sequence relationship? *Journal of International Business Studies, 39*(3), 351–369.

European Commission. (2001). Promoting a European framework for corporate social responsibilities. COM 366 final, Brussels.

Fassin, Y., Van Rossem, A., & Buelens, M. (2011). Small-business owner-managers' perceptions of business ethics and CSR-related concepts. *Journal of Business Ethics, 98*(3), 425–453.

Fassin, Y., Werner, A., Van Rossem, A., Signori, S., Garriga, E., von Weltzien Hoivik, H., & Schlierer, H. J. (2015). CSR and related terms in SME owner–managers' mental models in six European countries: National context matters. *Journal of Business Ethics, 128*(2), 433–456.

Felício, J. A., Duarte, M., & Rodrigues, R. (2016). Global mindset and SME internationalization: A fuzzyset QCA approach. *Journal of Business Research, 69*(4), 1372–1378.

Gerschewski, S. (2013). Improving on the Kogut and Singh metric of psychic distance. *Multinational Business Review, 21*(3), 257–268.

Graafland, J., & Noorderhaven, N. (2018). National culture and environmental responsibility research revisited. *International Business Review, 27*(5), 958–968.

Håkanson, L., & Ambos, B. (2010). The antecedents of psychic distance. *Journal of International Management, 16*(3), 195–210.

Ho, F. N., Wang, H. M. D., & Vitell, S. J. (2012). A global analysis of corporate social performance: The effects of cultural and geographic environments. *Journal of Business Ethics, 107*(4), 423–433.

Hofstede, G. (1980). Motivation, leadership, and organization: Do American theories apply abroad? *Organizational Dynamics, 9*(1), 42–63.

Hofstede, G. (2018). *Country comparison: Russia, Finland.* https://www.hofstede-insights.com/country-comparison/finland,russia/. Accessed 20 Aug 2018.

Ioannou, I., & Serafeim, G. (2012). What drives corporate social performance? The role of nation-level institutions. *Journal of International Business Studies, 43*(9), 834–864.

Ivanova, M., & Torkkeli, L. (2013). Managerial sensemaking of interaction within business relationships: A cultural perspective. *European Management Journal, 31*(6), 717–727.

Ivanova-Gongne, M., & Torkkeli, L. (2018). No manager is an Island: Culture in sensemaking of business networking. *Journal of Business & Industrial Marketing, 33*(5), 638–650.

Johanson, J., & Vahlne, J. E. (2009). The Uppsala internationalization process model revisited: From liability of foreignness to liability of outsidership. *Journal of International Business Studies, 40*(9), 1411–1431.

Keim, G. (2003). Nongovernmental organizations and business-government relations: The importance of institutions. In *Globalization and NGOs: Transforming business, government, and society* (pp. 19–34). Santa Barbara: Praeger.

Knight, G. A., & Cavusgil, S. T. (2004). Innovation, organizational capabilities, and the born-global firm. *Journal of International Business Studies, 35*(2), 124–141.

Kolk, A., & Van Tulder, R. (2010). International business, corporate social responsibility and sustainable development. *International Business Review, 19*(2), 119–125.

Kontinen, T., & Ojala, A. (2010). Internationalization pathways of family SMEs: Psychic distance as a focal point. *Journal of Small Business and Enterprise Development, 17*(3), 437–454.

Koos, S. (2011). The institutional embeddedness of social responsibility: A multilevel analysis of smaller firms' civic engagement in Western Europe. *Socio-Economic Review, 10*(1), 135–162.

Kuznetsov, A., Kuznetsova, O., & Warren, R. (2009). CSR and the legitimacy of business in transition economies: The case of Russia. *Scandinavian Journal of Management, 25*(1), 37–45.

Larrán Jorge, M., Herrera Madueno, J., Lechuga Sancho, M. P., & Martínez-Martínez, D. (2016). Development of corporate social responsibility in small and medium-sized enterprises and its nexus with quality management. *Cogent Business & Management, 3*(1), 1–21.

Marino, L., Strandholm, K., Steensma, H. K., & Weaver, K. M. (2002). The moderating effect of national culture on the relationship between entrepreneurial orientation and strategic alliance portfolio extensiveness. *Entrepreneurship Theory and Practice, 26*(4), 145–160.

McSweeney, B. (2002). Hofstede's model of national cultural differences and the consequences: A triumph of faith – A failure of analysis. *Human Relations, 55*, 89–118.

Miles, M. B., Huberman, A. M., & Saldana, J. (2014). *Qualitative data analysis: A methods sourcebook* (3rd ed.). Thousand Oaks: Sage.

Moore, G., & Spence, L. (2006). Small and medium-sized enterprises & corporate social responsibility: Identifying the knowledge gaps. Editorial. *Journal of Business Ethics, 67*(3), 219–226.

OECD. (2013). Green entrepreneurship, eco-innovation and SMEs. OECD working party on SMEs and entrepreneurship, CFE/SME (2011)9/FINAL.

OECD. (2016). *Entrepreneurship at a glance 2016*. Paris: OECD Publishing.

OECD. (2017). *Enhancing the contributions of SMEs in a global and digitalised economy*. Meeting of the OECD council at ministerial level, Paris, June 7–8. https://www.oecd.org/mcm/documents/C-MIN-2017-8-EN.pdf. Accessed 20 Aug 2018.

Ojala, A. (2009). Internationalization of knowledge-intensive SMEs: The role of network relationships in the entry to a psychically distant market. *International Business Review, 18*(1), 50–59.

Panapanaan, V. M., Linnanen, L., Karvonen, M. M., & Phan, V. T. (2003). Roadmapping corporate social responsibility in Finnish companies. *Journal of Business Ethics, 44*(2–3), 133–148.

Peng, Y. S., Dashdeleg, A. U., & Chih, H. L. (2014). National culture and firm's CSR engagement: A cross-nation study. *Journal of Marketing & Management, 5*(1), 38–49.

Perrini, F., Russo, A., & Tencati, A. (2007). CSR strategies of SMEs and large firms. Evidence from Italy. *Journal of Business Ethics, 74*(3), 285–300.

Ringov, D., & Zollo, M. (2007). The impact of national culture on corporate social performance. *Corporate Governance: The International Journal of Business in Society, 7*(4), 476–485.

Ryan, A., O'Malley, L., & O'Dwyer, M. (2010). Responsible business practice: Re-framing CSR for effective SME engagement. *European Journal of International Management, 4*(3), 290–302.

Simpson, M., Taylor, N., & Barker, K. (2004). Environmental responsibility in SMEs: Does it deliver competitive advantage? *Business Strategy and the Environment, 13*(3), 156–171.

Spence, L. J. (2016). Small business social responsibility: Expanding core CSR theory. *Business & Society, 55*(1), 23–55.

Thanetsunthorn, N. (2015). The impact of national culture on corporate social responsibility: Evidence from cross-regional comparison. *Asian Journal of Business Ethics, 4*(1), 35–56.

The World Values Survey. (2017). *Cultural map – WVS wave 6 (2010–2014)*. http://www.worldvaluessurvey.org/images/Culture_Map_2017_conclusive.png. Accessed 20 Aug 2018.

Vinokurova, N., Ollonqvist, P., Viitanen, J., Holopainen, P., Mutanen, A., Goltsev, V., & Ihalainen, T. (2009). *Russian-Finnish roundwood trade – Some empirical evidence on cultural based differences* (Vol. 129). Working papers of the Finnish Forest Research Institute. Finnish Forest Research Institute, Vantaa.

Vuontisjärvi, T. (2006). Corporate social reporting in the European context and human resource disclosures: An analysis of Finnish companies. *Journal of Business Ethics, 69*(4), 331–354.

World Trade report. (2016). Levelling the trading field for SME. Online document. Available at: https://www.wto.org/english/res_e/booksp_e/world_trade_report16_e.pdf. Accessed 20 Jan 2018.

Yin, R. K. (2009). *Case study research: Design and methods, Applied social research methods*. London/Singapore: Sage.

10

The Internationalization of Born-Digital Companies

Ioan-Iustin Vadana, Lasse Torkkeli, Olli Kuivalainen, and Sami Saarenketo

Introduction

Digital technologies provide businesses increasingly efficient ways to internationalize, by *digitalizing* parts of their value chain (Wentrup 2016). Indeed, a completely new type of company has emerged that bases its business model on the latest web and mobile technologies and the larger phenomenon of digitalization (Brouthers et al. 2016). The arrival of this type of company in almost all sectors of activity was made possible by the development of Web 2.0 (Addison 2006; Bell and Loane 2010; Lee et al. 2008; O'Reilly 2007), after the dot-com bubble (O'Reilly 2004), followed by Web 3.0 (Barassi and Treré 2012; Fuchs et al. 2010; Hendler 2009; Lassila and Hendler 2007). Even given these developments, entrepreneurship in a digitalized context is considered a distinct topic (Brouthers et al. 2016; Nambisan 2017; Wentrup 2016). Building on the research of Nambisan (2017), Wentrup (2016), and Brouthers et al. (2016), we propose that these companies (i.e. technology firms, ibusiness, and online service providers) be termed *born-digital*. However, others have also suggested the reality of born-digitals and that, indirectly, they

I.-I. Vadana (✉) • L. Torkkeli • S. Saarenketo
Lappeenranta University of Technology, Lappeenranta, Finland
e-mail: Iustin.vadana@lut.fi; Lasse.Torkkeli@lut.fi; Sami.saarenketo@lut.fi

O. Kuivalainen
Lappeenranta University of Technology, Lappeenranta, Finland

University of Manchester, Manchester, UK
e-mail: Olli.kuivalainen@manchester.ac.uk; Olli.Kuivalainen@lut.fi

© The Author(s) 2019
A. Chidlow et al. (eds.), *The Changing Strategies of International Business*, The Academy of International Business, https://doi.org/10.1007/978-3-030-03931-8_10

can impact entrepreneurship research. Therefore, we now extend this research to examine entrepreneurship from the international point of view.

Digitalization refers to the use of digital technologies to improve a business model to provide new revenue and value-producing opportunities (Acedo and Jones 2007; Brennen and Kreiss 2014; Li et al. 2009).[1] Based on our assertions and on existing research cited in our literature review, born-digitals are services or manufacturing companies in which most of the inward and outward value chains are digitalized soon after inception. This means that primary activities (inward: e.g. creating and producing; outward: e.g. delivery, marketing and sales, and support) are Internet-enabled (activated or coordinated by Internet applications and technologies). Born-digitals are companies that were digitalized early after foundation or were fully digitalized from day one (e.g. HelloFresh or Global Fashion Group). These companies are characterized by business models that facilitate a higher degree of digitalization, a development which in turn enables easier entry into global markets.[2]

In sum, since digitalization is a developing phenomenon in entrepreneurship (Brouthers et al. 2016; Nambisan 2017; Wentrup 2016), we argue that in addition to being relatively silent on the topic, the information provided by existent literature does not sufficiently describe the role of digitalization of the value chain on internationalization of born-digital companies. Thus, the main research question assessed in this study is: *How can born-digital companies be described based on the role of digitalization of the value chain on internationalization?*

The present exploratory study tackles the novelty of international digital entrepreneurship or internationalization of born-digitals. It is based on secondary literature and highlights the existence of a new phenomenon related to born-digital companies from two perspectives, digitalization of the value chain and degree of internationalization. A conceptual research framework will be used to analyze the selected sample to classify born-digital companies. The contribution of this chapter represents a framework that will guide the analysis.

The literature review, provided in the next section, presents the current research related to digitalization and internationalization, and digitalization of the value chain. Following this, the methodology and the constructs included in the proposed research model are described, and potential relationships

---

[1] Not to be confused with digitization, which is the process of converting any data into digits (1s and 0s) and represents the first step in realizing the phenomenon of digitalization (Brennen and Kreiss 2014).

[2] However, not all Internet-enabled companies are born-digital firms, because some of them are late in the process of digitalizing their activities. As this term is more holistic, readers may be confused.

The Internationalization of Born-Digital Companies 201

among variables are presented. After analyzing the obtained results and examining the findings, the article concludes with a discussion of the implications of the results, the overall contribution of this study, limitations, and potential future avenues of research.

Literature Review

Digitalization and Internationalization

In recent years, the blend of new digital technologies has highlighted the uncertainty in entrepreneurial processes and results, as well as ways of addressing such unpredictability (Nambisan 2017). These technologies include big data and analytics, mobility and pervasive computing, cloud computing, virtual networks, social media, artificial intelligence (AI), and robotics (outlined in Table 10.1).

These advances happened in stages known as Web 2.0 and Web 3.0. Web 2.0 flourished under the Internet's network effects: 'databases that get richer the more people interact with them; applications that are smarter the more people use them; marketing that is driven by user stories and experiences, and applications that interact with each other to form a broader computing plat-

Table 10.1 The utilities of digital technologies

Type of digital technology	Description
Social media platforms	Develop digital patterns
	Trail of user personalities and choices
	Help to know customer better and understand his needs
Cloud computing	Uses the power of networks
	Affordable digital resources
	Makes any company seem big, regardless of size or resources
AI and robotics	Machine learning
	Algorithms learn to understand human behavior
	Suggest next purchase in advance
Big data and analytics	Users are individualized
	Poll of data gathered from web platforms, mobile apps and sensors
	Predict future trends and serve unique customers
Mobility and pervasive computing	Internet of things
	Gathers data from any device more naturally
	Creates big tanks of data

Source: Bell and Loane (2010), Brouthers et al. (2016), Lu and Liu (2015), Nambisan (2017), and Wentrup (2016)

form' (Musser and O'Reilly 2006, p. 3). Although Web 3.0 is still a concept under development, it is essentially viewed as semantic web technologies implemented and powered into large-scale web applications (Hendler 2009; Lassila and Hendler 2007). Overall, these technologies enabled communication and information transparency as well as user collaboration (Addison 2006; Barassi and Treré 2012; Lee et al. 2008), all of which contributed to the rise of Internet-enabled companies (Nambisan 2017; Wentrup 2016). Thanks to these evolutions in web and mobile technologies, born-digital companies are present not only in the information and communications technology (ICT) sector, but in most industrial sectors, not only to software or hardware industries (Bell and Loane 2010; Brouthers et al. 2016).

Various terms are used in the literature, such as *ibusiness* (Brouthers et al. 2016), *high-tech firms* (Almor et al. 2014; Crick and Spence 2005; Li et al. 2012; Zhu and Qian 2015), *digital information goods providers* (Mahnke and Venzin 2003; Wentrup 2016), *e-commerce companies* (Hänninen et al. 2017; Luo et al. 2005; Singh and Kundu 2002), *new technology-based firms* (Bell and Loane 2010; Campos et al. 2009; Mahadevan 2000; Reuber 2016, and *accidental internationalists* (Hennart 2014). And, in general, these are Internet-enabled companies, the operations of which are based online, and which actively develop, produce, and/or commercialize products/services to customers using the web and mobile technologies or other computer-based information system technologies built on the Internet infrastructure.

The arrival of such companies has raised questions, specifically regarding the processes of internationalization. However, the existing studies (Addison 2006; Bell and Loane 2010; Berry and Brock 2004; Freeman et al. 2006; Hamill et al. 2010; O'Reilly 2007) have been restricted to arguing the advantages that digital technologies and the Internet infrastructure provide for overcoming the barriers to internationalization these firms often face (Addison 2006; Arenius et al. 2006; Berry and Brock 2004; Shaw and Darroch 2004; Sinkovics et al. 2013). These studies are based on the traditional classification of internationalizing enterprises, including born-global (low, incremental, and high committers) (Melén and Nordman 2009), born-internationals (Kuivalainen et al. 2007; Kundu and Katz 2003), committed internationalists (Bonaccorsi 1992), international new ventures (Oviatt and McDougall 1994), and micro-multinationals (Dimitratos et al. 2003). The current literature shows previous research typically concentrated on outward processes to determine how firms internationalize, and less on inward ones. The existing literature, therefore, provides only a partial picture of the functions and marketing strategies used by Internet-enabled firms and neglects the potential role of inward processes in enhancing innovation and performance.

According to Luostarinen (1979) and Hernández and Nieto (2015), firms generally internationalize using two types of processes: inward (related to international supply operations) and outward (related to serving or selling in foreign markets). These processes are related to value chain activities: inward to creating and producing, and outward to delivery, marketing, sales, and support.

Digitalization of the Value Chain

The value chain describes the full range of activities that firms perform to bring products or services from conception to end use and after support. To be successful, a company must design a distinctive value proposition to cover the needs of a market niche. In general, a firm gains a competitive advantage from how it configures the value chain, or the set of activities involved in creating, producing, marketing and selling, delivering, and supporting its products or services (Porter and Kramer 2011). Given the fragmentation and dispersion of activities around the globe, management literature has used the terms *global value chain* (Gereffi and Fernandez-Stark 2011) and *global factory* (Buckley 2011; Buckley and Ghauri 2004) when some core activities are located in other countries. We use the definition of *value chain* given by Porter (1991), in which a company's value chain is a system of value-adding activities that connect the supply part of a company to its demand part.

Creating an overview of value chain configuration is therefore an examination of the activities involved. These activities can be grouped according to various criteria, differentiating primary or core activities—creating, producing, delivering, marketing, and selling the product or service—from support activities (Hernández and Pedersen 2017; Porter 1991; Porter and Millar 1985). Core activities are those needed for sustaining profitable operations that are complementary and important for competitive advantage; non-core activities are those that can easily be outsourced (Hernández and Pedersen 2017; Oviatt and McDougall 1994).

The evolution of these activities may depend on industry dynamics and changes in the market, which also determine modifications in the structure of the value chain. Generally, firms retain the core activities they do best in-house, and allocate more resources, time, and effort to these activities (Buckley 2011; Buckley and Strange 2015; Hernández and Nieto 2015; Hernández and Pedersen 2017).

Thus, digital technologies provide online businesses increasingly efficient ways to internationalize by digitalizing parts of their value chain. Such companies tend to be new technology-based firms (Almor et al. 2014; Campos et al. 2009; Li et al. 2012) across different fields of activity and industry (Hagen and Zucchella 2011; Knight and Cavusgil 2004; Nambisan 2017; Power 2014); however, many scholars have found that fast internationalization exists only in highly technologized industries (Li et al. 2009; Luo et al. 2005; Mahnke and Venzin 2003). To survive in a dynamic environment, Internet-enabled companies must adapt very quickly (Bell and Loane 2010) and grow more rapidly than traditional firms (Brouthers et al. 2016; Wentrup 2016).

As mentions before, firms generally go international using inward and outward processes that are related to value chain activities. The extant literature shows previous research typically concentrated on outward processes to determine how firms internationalize, and less on inward ones. Therefore, the literature provides only a partial picture of the functions and marketing strategies used by Internet-enabled firms and neglects the potential role of inward processes in enhancing innovation and performance.

Classification of Born-Digital Companies

We analyze the phenomenon of born-digital companies using a framework that describes the internationalization dimension of these firms, as defined by their online-offline presence (Hennart 2014; Luo et al. 2005; Reuber 2016; Wentrup 2016). Following Lowy and Hood (2004), this was done using a 2×2 matrix for classification of digitalized (Internet-enabled) firms and for finding main patterns among these companies (Berrill and Mannella 2013; Brooksbank 1991).

Figure 10.1 illustrates the classification of born-digital companies across the two dimensions discussed above: degree of digitalization across value

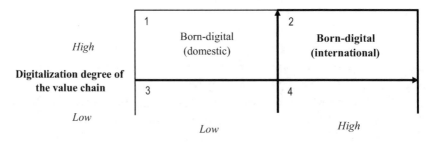

Fig. 10.1 Internationalization aspect of digitalized (Internet-enabled) firms

chain activities and degree of internationalization based on dispersion of geographic activities. To measure 'degree of internationalization,' we proposed a 'dispersion of geographical activities' measure (Brouthers et al. 2016; Li et al. 2012; Luo et al. 2005) as it is suitable for both online retailers who require a physical value chain and companies that have fewer demands for physical presence.

The internationalization dimension is expressed by the horizontal axis and comprises the number of countries in which these firms are most active (with offices), plus the number of localized websites or .com/.other domains in the country's official language(s). The first two quadrants comprise born-digital companies and the next two represent other types of companies, in different stages of digitalization, with domestic or international activities. The figure identifies two types of born-digital firms: born-digitals with more domestic activities and born-digitals with intensive international business. The third and fourth quadrants comprise those companies with a low-digitalized value chain, which have domestic, international, or global activities. According to Fig. 10.1, the more highly digitalized (Internet-enabled) a company is, the higher its degree of internationalization (Ojala and Tyrvainen 2006; Styles and Genua 2008; Su 2013). However, not all born-digital companies have intense international activities, even though they could start to sell to international customers online rather easily from inception.

At one extreme, an absolute online presence means only a digital footprint; for instance, all the value chain activities would be Internet-enabled. At the other extreme, a pure offline presence means that only physical resources, such as staff, are present (Wentrup 2016). In practice, the degrees of online and offline presence may vary over time, leading to asymmetry. Balance results from the nature of the resources that are committed to these two spatial domains (Wentrup 2016). The efficiency of the internationalization strategy overall, together with strong marketing skills and backed up by external funding, allows such ventures to 'bootstrap' into international markets (Bell and Loane 2010). To examine this classification, we applied the matrix in Fig. 10.1 to classify a sample of internationally operating firms.

Methodology

Sample Selection

This study is exploratory, based on secondary online literature. We explore this new phenomenon by describing the internationalization of born-digital companies and creating an initial model based on several variables and on a

206   I.-I. Vadana et al.

sample of firms positioned within the model. Four *shallow*[3] (Loane 2006) exploratory cases were built based on secondary sources (Bell and Loane 2010; Hänninen et al. 2017; Mahnke and Venzin 2003) to test the proposed framework.

The methodology used by *Fortune* magazine to build this list of companies is based on ranking by valuation. The list is based on a combination of data from PitchBook, CB Insights, news reports, and their investigation (Fortune Magazine 2016). The resulting sample comprises a group of 18 firms from a variety of industry sectors. All 18 companies were founded in Europe, but most of them have intensive international activities around the world. These companies are included on the so-called unicorn list, compiled by *Fortune* magazine in 2016. They are called 'unicorns' primarily due to their rapid growth and their market valuations of $1 billion or more; however, this aspect was not considered among the selection criteria.

The firms analyzed in the study are Spotify, Global Fashion Group, Delivery Hero, HelloFresh, Klarna, Adyen, Avito.ru, BlaBlaCar, Skyscanner, Blippar, Oxford Nanopore, Auto1 Group, CureVac, Avast Software, Farfetch, Funding Circle, Home24, and TransferWise (Powa, the 19th company on the list, was excluded because of the financial problems the company is facing). These firms were chosen because they were founded after 2000 (an exception was made for Avast Software), when web technologies evolved into Web 2.0 (Cearley et al. 2005; O'Reilly 2007). Other selection criteria included the sector in which these companies operate and that the firms are well known around the world so that important sources of information can be found online.

The firms and their descriptions are listed in Tables 10.2 and 10.3. Of these cases, four *shallow* (Loane 2006) exploratory cases were built based on secondary sources (Bell and Loane 2010; Hänninen et al. 2017; Mahnke and Venzin 2003). The internationalization year shown in Table 10.2 is the year in which the companies had their first international activities.

Measure Development

The firms were investigated across two dimensions: degree of digitalization and degree of internationalization. The degree of digitalization was evaluated based on the digitalization of the inward and outward (Hernández and Pedersen 2017) components of their value chain: creating, producing, selling,

---

[3] Are called *shallow* by Loane (2006) cases because are made based on secondary literature such as the World Wide Web (WWW), databases/sites, firm websites, government, and industry reports.

The Internationalization of Born-Digital Companies   207

Table 10.2 Firms in the sample

ID	Rank	Company name	Location city	Location country	Industry	Founded	Year of internationalization
1	15.	Spotify	Stockholm	Sweden	Streaming media	2006	2008
2	31.	Global Fashion Group	Luxembourg	Luxembourg	E-commerce	2011	2011
3	35.	Delivery Hero	Berlin	Germany	Food delivery	2011	2012
4	46.	HelloFresh	Berlin	Germany	Food delivery	2011	2012
5	48.	Powa	London	UK	Mobile payments	2007	
6	51.	Klarna	Stockholm	Sweden	Mobile payments	2005	2008
7	54.	Adyen	Amsterdam	The Netherlands	Mobile payments	2006	2009
8	68.	Avito.ru	Moscow	Russia	Online classifieds	2008	2008
9	75.	BlaBlaCar	Paris	France	Transportation	2006	2009
10	79.	Skyscanner	Edinburgh	UK	Flight, hotel search engine	2003	2011
11	82.	Blippar	London	UK	Augmented reality	2011	2012
12	91.	Oxford Nanopore	Oxford	UK	Biotechnology	2005	2009
13	102.	Auto1 Group	Berlin	Germany	E-commerce	2012	2015
14	104.	CureVac	Tübingen	Germany	Biotechnology	2000	2015
15	129.	Avast Software	Prague	Czech Republic	Computer security	1988	2013
16	137.	Farfetch	London	UK	E-commerce	2008	2010
17	138.	Funding Circle	London	UK	Crowdfunding	2010	2013
18	139.	Home24	Berlin	Germany	E-commerce	2012	2012
19	164.	TransferWise	London	UK	Mobile payments	2011	2015

Source: 'The unicorn list,' compiled by *Fortune* magazine in 2016

delivering, and supporting (Porter 1991; Porter and Millar 1985). Our goal was to discover how prevalent a digital basis was in these highly valued companies. Each activity of the value chain was coded with 1 if it was based or coordinated with a web technology or a non-web digital application, or with 0 if not. Subsequently, each firm's value chain was analyzed through this perspective using the information available in the secondary literature. This produced a digitalization scale of 0–5. The degree of internationalization was analyzed in line with the model illustrated in Fig. 10.2. The firms were added to the first two quadrants if the digitalization degree was 4 or greater, and to the last two if the degree was 3 or less.

The internationalization variables were analyzed based on the combined the results of localized websites or .com/.other, targeted country language, and the number of countries in which these companies are most active (besides their home country). Each variable (office or localization) was coded with 1. The highest number resulting from the sum of these two variables was 92 and the lowest was 2. The numbers were then normalized. First, every

208 I.-I. Vadana et al.

Table 10.3 Data analyzed for case comparison

ID	Company name	Total localizations and .com/.other domain with country official language	Number of countries	Total value chain Scale 0-5
1	Spotify	52	18	5
2	Global Fashion Group	24	22	4
3	Delivery Hero	32	21	4
4	HelloFresh	9	9	5
5	Powa	n/a	n/a	n/a
6	Klarna	9	17	5
7	Adyen	3	10	5
8	Avito.ru	1	1	4
9	BlaBlaCar	22	13	4
10	Skyscanner	41	7	5
11	Blippar	6	6	5
12	Oxford Nanopore	1	1	2
13	Auto1 Group	21	21	4
14	CureVac	2	2	1
15	Avast Software	52	5	5
16	Farfetch	84	8	4
17	Funding Circle	5	4	4
18	Home24	9	7	4
19	TransferWise	9	6	5

result was divided by the highest number, resulting in a scale from 0 to 1. Second, these results were multiplied by 5 to create a scale of 0–5, like that used for digitalization. The raw data is provided in Table 10.3 and a sample of the coding results for the selected cases (see sections 'Avito.ru: Domestic Born-Digital,' 'HelloFresh: International Born-Digital,' and 'Oxford Nanopore: Domestic Low-Digitalized Company') across their value chain is listed in Appendix 2.

Analysis and Findings

Figure 10.2 presents the categorization of the sample companies across a 2×2 matrix that distinguishes between the degrees of digitalization and internationalization to classify the companies according to the proposed research model.

The research framework identifies types of born-digital firms in the first three quadrants of the matrix. The first two quadrants in Fig. 10.2 represent the born-digital companies, which tend to have similar businesses. However, this is not a general rule for all the firms analyzed in this chapter. Indeed, some of these firms have intensive international activities, and some of them focus

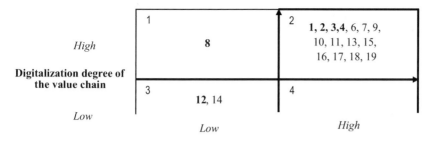

Fig. 10.2 Sample classification of the born-digital companies

more on domestic markets. All the other firms are digital from inception or soon after foundation. The difference between them is the internationalization dimension. All the firms presented in the framework have an Internet-based business model and are born-digital companies. Besides internationalization, another difference lies in the digital distribution of the final product. The first two quadrants represent the companies the value chain of which is digitalized, or at least, all five components of the value chain are coordinated by internet technologies and are conducted online. The last two quadrants are characterized by companies the value chain of which is not digitalized.

Most of the firms analyzed can, in the initial stage of internationalization, fully operate in a market without an offline presence, despite legal compliance and market-specific requirements. The length of the interval between online and offline is dependent on the business model and the sales and distribution channels used. However, as the revenues or number of users grow, even B2C-oriented firms gradually localize their offers and frequently establish an offline presence. According to Wentrup (2016), regardless of how online and digitalized a firm might be initially, the geographical impact and the localization issue become increasingly important as the firm grows. For the same reason, most of the companies establish offices in other countries. Tangible foreign assets in international markets may be used, but are often defined by business offices (UNCTAD 2017) needed more for policy issues or customer support. Furthermore, it is easier to sell ads to local companies and deal with local rights holders or to establish development offices around the world.

To analyze the firms in more detail, we selected companies from each quadrant of the initial sample, namely, Avitor.ru, HelloFresh, and Oxford Nanopore. They were chosen because they differ in the type of service they

210 I.-I. Vadana et al.

provide, their target customers, their size, and their business model. Their similarities and differences should make this sample representative of at least a part of born-digital companies. We selected the cases that can best explain the differences between the matrix cells.

Avito.ru: Domestic Born-Digital

Avito.ru, an online classified ads platform, represents a born-digital company with a value chain that was highly digitalized soon after inception. Its platforms include an online payment system; in addition, it uses online marketing campaigns based on data generated by its users. Most of its services can be delivered from headquarters. Avito.ru has its headquarters in Moscow and operations in only one foreign country. Regarding localized websites and. com/.other web domains with the country's official language(s), this firm scores one website localization with country-targeted language.

HelloFresh: International Born-Digital

HelloFresh is an online platform from which users can order a box with pre-portioned food ingredients. The company was founded in 2012. It showed growth of 90% over 2015 and closed 2016 with revenue amounting to €894 million. HelloFresh has its headquarters in Berlin and operations in more than nine countries across three continents. Regarding localized websites and .com/.other web domains with the country's official language(s), HelloFresh scores nine website localizations with country-targeted language and one website translation with a .com domain.

Oxford Nanopore: Domestic Low-Digitalized Company

Oxford Nanopore Technologies Limited develops and commercializes nanopore-based electronic systems for analysis of single molecules. Its main locations are the UK and the US.

While the secondary literature lacks detailed information about some of the firm's value chain, social media platforms and mobile apps are used for disseminating company information, organizing special events and conferences, and managing and communicating with the community of scientists all over the world. However, their business model is aligned to the industry and represents a consumer goods company. In general, companies like this spend two times more on sales and marketing than on R&D. Regarding internationalization, this company scores one website translation and has activities in another foreign country.

Summary of Cases

Born-digital companies go international faster than others, thanks to Internet technologies and the nature of their business model (see Appendix 1). These companies are designed for rapid internationalization from inception (Mäki and Hytti 2008; Saarenketo et al. 2004). According to Hennart (2014), the digitalization of their business model makes them accidental internationalists, with one key element in common—Internet technologies (Bell and Loane 2010; Hagen and Zucchella 2011).

The degree of internationalization of a born-digital company is closely related to the degree of digitalization of its value chain. Thus, to internationalize to a certain scale, these companies must digitalize their value chain. Nevertheless, it is easier to internationalize online via a controlled entry mode (Yamin and Sinkovics 2006). This could mean that a company's online presence might be an 'optical illusion,' so that the firms neglect the complexity of offline business (Wentrup 2016).

Discussion and Conclusions

In this study, we found that 16 of the 18 companies examined digitalized their value chain (inward and outward) from day one or soon thereafter. The two exceptions are the biotechnology firms, Oxford Nanopore and CureVac, which are still on the road to digital business. Thus, born-digital companies are, in general, companies that have undergone that transformation after inception (or did not have the need to). These are opposed to other companies that must, at some point, undergo the process of digital transformation process.

Theoretical Contribution

The contribution of this study is its presentation of a framework that enables classifying born-digital firms when examining their internationalization and value chain activities. By stressing the relevance of a digitalized value chain, both inward and outward, and internationalization using a balance between online and offline presence, we present a conceptual analysis arguing that born-digital companies are a distinct type of internationalizing firm with an Internet-enabled, inward-outward digitalized value chain from day one or soon after inception.

This research enables classifying companies to explain this new phenomenon of digitalization. Within this framework, four types of companies were described regarding the digitalization of their value chain activities (Porter 1985) and localized websites in the official language of the targeted country. The firm cases show that early digitalization of the value chain, translated into a stronger online presence, followed by a gradual increase of resources dedicated to the offline presence, might represent one solution for sustainable growth for born-digital firms.

We observed that the internationalization process of born-digital companies includes several steps: gradual regional expansion followed by internationalization speed, both of which are supported by Internet technologies. The rapidity of internationalization is best explained by the international venture or born-global phenomenon (Cavusgil and Knight 2015; Madsen and Servais 1997; Oviatt and McDougall 2005), ICT, and Internet-related internationalization theories (Kim 2003; Singh and Kundu 2002; Yamin and Sinkovics 2006); the gradual regional pattern, however, finds support in the Uppsala model (Johanson and Vahlne 1977). Nevertheless, not all born-digital companies operate internationally, although they could sell to international customers online rather easily from day one.

Despite expectations, our research shows that the digitalization of value chain activities is not closely related to the internationalization dimension of born-digital companies. Therefore, the degree of digitalization of the value chain activities does not significantly influence the internalization of born-digital firms. Instead, the business model influences the internationalization of born-digital companies.

Regarding this research, some internationally operating born-digital companies might represent a subset of born-global firms; however, based on Hennart's (2014) work, we might expect the behavior of born-digitals to be determined largely by their business models as well. The novel business models used by digital companies generate revenues from a very early stage (Bell and Loane 2010). These companies are perceived as rapidly internationalizing because of the degree of digitalization integrated into their business model from inception (Brouthers et al. 2016; Wentrup 2016). This could be a topic for further research.

The Internationalization of Born-Digital Companies   213

Overall, this study brings a suitable framework to make sense of the spread discussion on digitalization in the context of international entrepreneurship and business. This chapter represents a conclusive work of a new concept defined as *born-digital*. The concept explains a new phenomenon through a new perspective, analyzing the digital value chain activities correlated with internationalization across two dimensions: online and offline activities. The study brings together several concepts that are critical for international business and international entrepreneurship in general; this is an integrative work. Going forward, classification helps to develop the theory by analyzing the internationalization patterns of these companies.

Managerial and Social Implications

This research has several implications for management, such as examples of digitalized business strategies by which traditional companies can go international more efficiently. The internationalization strategies of various types of companies could become important for the future of most companies. These goals recognize that digitalization based on Internet technologies can aid global development by connecting neglected and underserved communities of customers around the world. Companies from almost any industry can use the example of born-digitals as a set of best practices in their own process of digitalization.

We observed that most of the companies we studied organize their business around online platforms; this generally transforms the logic of any industry sector, making transactions between buyers and suppliers easier and more dynamic. Through services provided by digital platforms, digital firms create consumer value. They provide value-adding services, such as loyalty programs, online personal customer support, and a last-mile delivery system; such services can convince customers to focus their purchases on one platform. We also noticed that after a certain point in their growth, these companies can transform their platform into large marketplaces due to the network effects that allow suppliers to handle the actual transaction of goods with consumers on the platform.

Wentrup (2016) claims that the company sample analyzed in his research cannot fully operate in a market without being present offline. Thus, companies are limited in how long or at what size they can operate fully online without needing a physical presence. The importance of offline entry also seems to increase with time (Hennart 2014; Mahnke and Venzin 2003; Reuber 2016; Wentrup 2016). The outcomes of these studies suggest that born-digitals are more frequently born at home rather than born-global (Hennart 2014). Our sample did not behave differently.

Limitations and Future Research

This exploratory study has several limitations. Its scope is to discover theoretical conceptualizations and empirical findings regarding the internationalization of digitalized companies. However, it should be remembered that available information about the subject is limited. We also acknowledge that other measures may be used to measure the degree of internationalization.

Sample selection represents an important limitation. A case can be made for selection bias, since the firms were selected especially because of their year of inception, activity sectors, and information available online. Market valuation was not a criterion. Also, we could have selected companies founded more recently.

Another potential limitation is the measurement used for the value chain digitalization. This is no trivial matter, since most of the activities are Internet-related and the amount of information available can make it difficult to track where in their value chain the companies have their activities. This is especially true when those activities exist in a digital format.

Future research should further explore corresponding themes. For instance, the born-digital phenomenon has been analyzed through studying large firms; other perspectives are also needed on how the value chain structure and digitalization, country of origin, and the dynamism of the industry may influence the evolution of born-digital companies. Also, future studies could empirically examine the kind of internationalization strategy that born-digital companies use, the role of internationalization strategy on international performance, or the customers' view regarding the companies' international performance.

A worldwide shift marked by technology is changing the balance of information in favor of customers. Digital firms create this shift by collaborating with consumers to not only develop new products and services, but also to enable more effective buyer interactions and optimize the customer experience (Cavusgil and Knight 2015). Digital technologies foretell the next era in both local and international entrepreneurship. This is a time in which the traditional ways and processes of following entrepreneurial opportunities will be increasingly questioned and reworked (Nambisan 2017). These firms represent the beginning of a new era in how internationalization will occur in the years to come.

Appendix 1: Some of the Digitalization Advantages of the Value Chain

Value chain	Description
Creating	Optimized inventory planning based on demand forecasting
	Data-based preventive asset maintenance
	Integration with partners in digital ecosystem to optimize service delivery
	Virtual organizations enabled by mobility and seamless cooperation
Producing	Creates new digital products, services, and offerings
	Rapid prototyping with customer interaction
	Integrates products and services into solutions that have digital components
	Convergence of products enabled by digital technologies
Selling and marketing	Analytics-driven and dynamic customer segmentation or Customer relationship management (CRM) platforms
	Faster time to market with targeted offerings
	New earnings (subscription, licensing, credit, 'freemium,' etc.) models
Delivering	Digitalized and automated delivering processes
	Efficiency of the transportation planning using 'last mile' logistics
	Coordination between storage, stocks, and delivering
Supporting	Systematic management of customer management services
	Digital manuals with instructions powered by augmented reality apps
	Forums, e-chat, Frequently asked questions (FQA), virtual assistant, social media

Source: Data sample

Appendix 2: The Sample Coding of the Results of the Empirical Sample

Value chain	Avito.ru—B2C and B2B	HelloFresh—B2C	Oxford Nanopore
Creating	R&D—technology; relationships with entrepreneurs for eShops	R&D—technology; supplier relationships; taste clustering; hyper-personalization	R&D; supplier relationships; storing and distributing the raw materials, inputs, components, and parts used in the production process
Producing	E-commerce fashion platform (core business) for classified ads and online shops	Food box (core business), recipes, complex web platform; web apps	Nanopore DNA sequencer (core business), the MinION; website; online shop

Value chain	Avito.ru—B2C and B2B	HelloFresh—B2C	Oxford Nanopore
Selling and marketing	Online payment system; online/offline marketing campaigns	Online payment system; online/offline marketing campaigns; ambassador marketing	Online payment system; online/offline marketing (lack of info)
Delivering	Software product. No need of delivery system; services/products can be delivered from headquarters; doesn't help with distribution costs	Operated warehouse facilities; logistics partners; local couriers; own last mile	Logistics partners
Supporting	Online customer care/operated call centers	Online customer care/customer care agents	Online customer care/customer care agents
Business model	Marketplace (fee based); SaaS model	Subscription model	Pharmaceutical products model

References

Acedo, F., & Jones, M. (2007). Speed of internationalization and entrepreneurial cognition: Insights and a comparison between international new ventures, exporters and domestic firms. *Journal of World Business, 42*(3), 236–252.

Addison, C. (2006). Web 2.0: A new chapter in development in practice? *Development and Practice, 16*(6), 623–627.

Almor, T., Tarba, S. Y., & Margalit, A. (2014). Maturing, technology-based, born-global companies: Surviving through mergers and acquisitions. *Management International Review, 54*(4), 421–444.

Arenius, P., Sasi, V., & Gabrielsson, M. (2006). Rapid internationalization enabled by the Internet: The case of a knowledge intensive company. *Journal of International Entrepreneurship, 3*(4), 279–290.

Barassi, V., & Treré, E. (2012). Does Web 3.0 come after Web 2.0? Deconstructing theoretical assumptions through practice. *New Media & Society, 14*(8), 1269–1285.

Bell, J., & Loane, S. (2010). 'New-wave' global firms: Web 2.0 and SME internationalisation. *Journal of Marketing Management, 26*(3–4), 213–229.

Berrill, J., & Mannella, G. (2013). Are firms from developed markets more international than firms from emerging markets? *Research in International Business and Finance, 27*(1), 147–161.

Berry, M. M. J., & Brock, J. K.-U. (2004). Marketspace and the internationalization process of the small firm. *Journal of International Entrepreneurship, 2*(3), 187–216.

The Internationalization of Born-Digital Companies **217**

Bonaccorsi, A. (1992). On the relationship between firm size and export intensity. *Journal of International Business Studies, 23*(4), 605–635.

Brennen, S., & Kreiss, D. (2014). Digitalization and Digitization. Retrieved from Culture Digitally, http://culturedigitally.org/2014/09/digitalization-and-digitization/. Accessed October 10th, 2017.

Brooksbank, R. (1991). Defining the small business: A new classification of company size. *Entrepreneurship & Regional Development, 3*(1), 17–31.

Brouthers, K. D., Geisser, K. D., & Rothlauf, F. (2016). Explaining the internationalization of ibusiness firms. *Journal of International Business Studies, 47*(5), 513–534.

Buckley, P. J. (2011). International integration and coordination in the global factory. *Management International Review, 51*(2), 269–283.

Buckley, P. J., & Ghauri, P. N. (2004). Globalisation, economic geography and the strategy of multinational enterprises. *Journal of International Business Studies, 35*(2), 81–98.

Buckley, P. J., & Strange, R. (2015). The governance of the global factory: Location and control of world economic activity. *Academy of Management Executive, 29*(2), 237–249.

Campos, H. M., del Palacio Aguirre, I., Parellada, F. S., & de la Parra, J. P. N. (2009). Technology strategy and new technology based firms. *Journal of Technology Management & Innovation, 4*(4), 42–52.

Cavusgil, S. T., & Knight, G. (2015). The born global firm: An entrepreneurial and capabilities perspective on early and rapid internationalization. *Journal of International Business Studies, 46*(1), 3–16.

Cearley, D., Fenn, J., & Plummer, D. (2005). Gartner analyzes hottest topics of 2005: Open-source, voice/data convergence, service-oriented architecture, it utility and global sourcing. Gartner Special Report.

Crick, D., & Spence, M. (2005). The internationalisation of 'high performing' UK high-tech SMEs: A study of planned and unplanned strategies. *International Business Review, 14*(2), 167–185.

Dimitratos, P., Johnson, J., Slow, J., & Young, S. (2003). Micro-multinationals: New types of firms for the global competitive landscape. *European Management Journal, 21*(2), 164–174.

Fortune Magazine. (2016). The unicorn list. http://fortune.com/unicorns/

Freeman, S., Edwards, R., & Schroder, B. (2006). How smaller born-global firms use networks and alliances to overcome constraints to rapid internationalization. *Journal of International Marketing, 14*(3), 33–63.

Fuchs, C., Hofkirchner, W., Schafranek, M., Raffl, C., Sandoval, M., & Bichler, R. (2010). Theoretical foundations of the web: Cognition, communication, and co-operation. Towards an understanding of Web 1.0, 2.0, 3.0. *Future Internet, 2*, 41–59.

Gereffi, G., & Fernandez-Stark, K. (2011). *Global value chain analysis: A primer.* Durham: Duke University.

Hagen, B., & Zucchella, A. (2011). A longitudinal look at the international entrepreneurship dimensions: Cases and predictions. *International Journal of Management Cases, 13*(3), 484–504.

Hamill, J., Tagg, S., Stevenson, A., & Vescozi, T. (2010). Editorial. *Journal of Marketing Management, 26*(3–4), 181–186.

Hänninen, M., Smedlund, A., & Mitronen, L. (2017). Digitalization in retailing: Multi-sided platforms as drivers of industry transformation. *Baltic Journal of Management. 13*(2), 152–168.

Hendler, J. (2009). Web 3.0 emerging. *Computer, 42*, 111–113.

Hennart, J.-F. (2014). The accidental internationalists: A theory of born globals. *Entrepreneurship Theory and Practice, 38*(1), 117–135.

Hernández, V., & Nieto, M. J. (2015). Inward-outward connections and their impact on firm growth. *International Business Review, 25*(1), 296–306.

Hernández, V., & Pedersen, T. (2017). Global value chain configuration: A review and research agenda. *Business Research Quarterly, 61*, 1–14.

Johanson, J., & Vahlne, J. (1977). The internationalization process of the firm—A model of knowledge development and increasing foreign commitments. *Journal of International Business Studies, 8*(1), 23–32.

Kim, D. (2003). The internationalization of US internet portals: Does it fit the process model of internationalization? *Marketing Intelligence & Planning, 21*(1), 23–36.

Knight, G., & Cavusgil, S. T. (2004). Innovation, organizational capabilities and the born-global firm. *Journal of International Business Studies, 35*(2), 124–141.

Kuivalainen, O., Sundqvist, S., & Servais, P. (2007). Firms' degree of born-globalness, international entrepreneurial orientation and export performance. *Journal of World Business, 42*(3), 253–267.

Kundu, S. K., & Katz, J. H. (2003). Born international SMEs: Bi-level impacts of resources and intentions. *Small Business Economics, 20*(1), 25–49.

Lassila, O., & Hendler, J. (2007). Embracing "Web 3.0". *IEEE Internet Computing, 11*, 90–93.

Lee, S. H., DeWester, D., & Park, S. R. (2008). Web 2.0 and opportunities for small businesses. *Service Business, 2*(4), 335–345.

Li, J., Merenda, M., & Venkatachalam, A. R. (2009). Business process digitalization and new product development: An empirical study of small and medium-sized manufacturers. *International Journal of E-Business Research, 5*(1), 49.

Li, L., Qian, G., & Qian, Z. (2012). The performance of small and medium-sized technology-based enterprises: Do product diversity and international diversity matter? *International Business Review, 21*(5), 941–956.

Loane, S. (2006). The role of the internet in the internationalization of small and medium sized companies. *Journal of International Entrepreneurship, 3*(4), 263–277.

Lowy, A., & Hood, P. (2004). *The power of the 2×2 matrix: Using 2×2 thinking to solve business problem and make better decisions.* San Francisco: Jossey-Bass.

Lu, Q., & Liu, N. (2015). Effects of e-commerce channel entry in a two-echelon supply chain: A comparative analysis of single- and dual-channel distribution systems. *International Journal of Production Economics, 165*(C), 100–111.

Luo, Y., Hongxin Zhao, J., & Du, J. (2005). The internationalization speed of e-commerce companies: An empirical analysis. *International Marketing Review, 22*(6), 693–709.

Luostarinen, R. (1979). *Internationalization of the firm: An empirical study of the internationalization of firms with small and open domestic markets with special emphasis on lateral rigidity as a behavioral characteristic in strategic decision making.* Helsinki: The Helsinki School of Economics.

Madsen, T., & Servais, P. (1997). The internationalization of born globals: An evolutionary process. *International Business Review, 6*(6), 561–583.

Mahadevan, B. (2000). Business models for internet-based E-commerce: An anatomy. *California Management Review, 42*(4), 55–69.

Mahnke, V., & Venzin, M. (2003). The internationalization process of digital information good providers. *Management International Review, 43*(1), 115–142.

Mäki, K., & Hytti, U. (2008). *"Pitching out the lost cases"—A longitudinal study of the precedents of non-growth of recent incubator graduates.* ICSB world conference proceedings, Washington, DC.

Melén, S., & Nordman, E. R. (2009). The internationalisation modes of born globals: A longitudinal study. *European Management Journal, 27*(4), 243–254.

Musser, J., & O'Reilly, T. (2006). *Web 2.0 principles and best practices.* San Francisco, Sebastopol: O'Reilly Media. http://repo.mynooblife.org/.priv8/Ebook/Web%20 2.0%20Principles%20and%20Best%20Practices.pdf

Nambisan, S. (2017). Digital entrepreneurship: Toward a digital technology perspective of entrepreneurship. *Entrepreneurship Theory and Practice, 41*(6), 1029–1055.

O'Reilly, T. (2004). Web 2.0 conference.

O'Reilly, T. (2007). What is Web 2.0: Design patterns and business models for the next generation of software. Retrieved from MPRA, http://www-public. imtbs-tsp.eu/~gibson/Teaching/Teaching-ReadingMaterial/OReilly07.pdf. Accessed October 10th, 2017.

Ojala, A., & Tyrvainen, P. (2006). Business models and market entry mode choice of small software firms. *Journal of International Entrepreneurship, 4*(2), 69–81.

Oviatt, B., & McDougall, P. (1994). Toward a theory of international new ventures. *Journal of International Business Studies, 25*(1), 45–64.

Oviatt, B., & McDougall, P. (2005). Defining international entrepreneurship and modeling the speed of internationalization. *Entrepreneurship Theory and Practice, 29*(5), 537–554.

Porter, M. E. (1985). *Competitive advantage: Creating and sustaining superior performance* (Vol. 1). New York: Free Press.

Porter, M. E. (1991). Towards a dynamic theory of strategy. *Strategic Management Journal, 12*(S2), 95–117.

Porter, M. E., & Kramer, M. (2011). The big idea: Creating shared value. How to reinvent capitalism—And unleash a wave of innovation and growth. *Harvard Business Review, 89*(1–2), 62–77.

Porter, M. E., & Millar, V. E. (1985). How information gives you competitive advantage. *Harvard Business Review, 63*(4), 149–160.

Power, B. (2014). How GE applies lean startup practices. Retrieved from Culture Harvard Business Review, https://hbr.org/2014/04/how-ge-applies-lean-startup-practices. Accessed October 10th, 2017.

Reuber, R. (2016). *Multilingualism and the internationalization of firms in digital markets*. 43rd AIB-UKI, Department of Management Birkbeck, University of London, London.

Saarenketo, S., Puumalainen, K., Kuivalainen, O., & Kyläheiko, K. (2004). Dynamic knowledge-related learning processes in internationalizing high-tech SMEs. *International Journal of Production Economics, 89*(3), 363–378.

Shaw, V., & Darroch, J. (2004). Barriers to internationalisation: A study of entrepreneurial new ventures in New Zealand. *Journal of International Entrepreneurship, 2*(4), 327–343.

Singh, N., & Kundu, S. K. (2002). Explaining the growth of E-commerce corporations (ECCs): An extension and application of the eclectic paradigm. *Journal of International Business Studies, 33*(4), 679–697.

Sinkovics, N., Sinkovics, R. R., & "Bryan" Jean, R.-J. (2013). The internet as an alternative path to internationalization? *International Marketing Review, 30*(2), 130–155.

Styles, C., & Genua, T. (2008). The rapid internationalization of high technology firms created through the commercialization of academic research. *Journal of World Business, 43*(2), 146–157.

Su, N. (2013). Internationalization strategies of Chinese IT service suppliers. *MIS Quarterly, 37*(1), 175–200.

UNCTAD. (2017). World investment report. Investment and the digital economy. United Nations conference on trade and development. Geneva.

Wentrup, R. (2016). The online–offline balance: Internationalization for Swedish online service providers. *Journal of International Entrepreneurship, 14*(4), 562–594.

Yamin, M., & Sinkovics, R. R. (2006). Online internationalisation, psychic distance reduction and the virtuality trap. *International Business Review, 15*(4), 339–360.

Zhu, H., & Qian, G. (2015). High-tech firms' international acquisition performance: The influence of host country property rights protection. *International Business Review, 24*(4), 556–566.

11

Technological Disruptions and Production Location Choices

Lisa De Propris and Diletta Pegoraro

Introduction

The last three decades have seen an acceleration of the interconnectedness of the global economy at the economic, productive, financial, social, and cultural levels. This coincided with what Friedman (2000) referred to as turbo-charged globalisation, since not only had it been multi-faceted, but it had moved faster than at any time before. The 2008 financial crisis has somewhat pushed to the fore the undesirable implications of such global linkages, especially in advanced economies where de-industrialisation, joblessness, and imbalances in the national and regional economies were reducing the responsiveness and resilience of economic systems to face external shocks. This led to the emergence of bottom-up resentment that has shaken political establishments in both the United States and Europe; consider the election of Trump in the United States, the emergence of populist parties in Europe and Brexit. A dislike for the consequences of globalisation (generally speaking in the populist narrative) has been rendered with a political discourse around 're-balancing the economy' and 'job creation'. Protectionists and insular approaches to trade have surfaced with worrying consequences. The geography of the global economy is changing as new players and new dynamics are reshaping global markets and global production.

In this work, we acknowledge such backdrop and explore a very recent debate that looks at the relationships between firms' location choices and the

L. De Propris (✉) • D. Pegoraro
University of Birmingham, Birmingham, UK
e-mail: L.depropris@bham.ac.uk; DXP622@student.bham.ac.uk

© The Author(s) 2019
A. Chidlow et al. (eds.), *The Changing Strategies of International Business*, The Academy of
International Business, https://doi.org/10.1007/978-3-030-03931-8_11

emergence of new technologies that are expected to alter the organisation of production inside the firm and along the value chain, as well as creating new pathways for value creation. A wave of disruptive new technologies are becoming available, and these are somewhat captured by the umbrella term of Industry 4.0: this is changing firms' production strategy, both in advanced and emerging economies.

In this chapter, we will first recap the drivers and the outcomes of the globalisation push that occurred between 1990s and early 2000s in the section 'Globalisation: 1990s–2000s'. We cannot really understand what is driving firms' location choices today, however, without discussing the impact that the new technologies brought in by the Fourth Industrial Revolution (FIR) will have on production and supply chain. There is a large literature on Industry 4.0 and we will start shedding some light on the link between the relocation of the production in advanced economies and the implementation of Industry 4.0 (section 'Technological Change and Industry 4.0'). This will be followed by a critical survey of the current debate on de-globalisation in the section 'De-globalisation' and evidence of a 're-bundling' of tangible and intangible activities via reshoring in the section 'Reshoring as Strategy to Re-bundle Innovation with Production'. The section 'Case Study on Shorter and Proximate Value Chain: The Automotive Ecosystem in San Jose Economic Area' will present the case study of the San Jose Economic Area (SJEA) where there is an automotive cluster adopting frontier technologies; we will argue that its success hinges on the fact that it is an ecosystem of complementary technologies and competences with crucially shorter and proximate value chains that have re-bundled manufacturing with research and design. Some concluding remarks will end the chapter.

Globalisation: 1990s–2000s

Globalisation has allowed an increasingly seamless movement of people, goods, and capital across the world. The outcomes have been greater talent mobility, more intense international trade, and better integrated global finance which has fostered the growth of the global economy at the turn of the 2000s (Gilpin and Gilpin 2001). Indeed from a world where countries mostly traded with each other final goods produced domestically, since the 1990s, we have seen the creation and thickening of global value chains connecting in particular what Dicken (2015) calls the global triad, namely Asia, North America, and Europe. Growth has not been, however, widespread both in advanced and emerging economies. The globalisation of production in the 1990s and

Technological Disruptions and Production Location Choices   **223**

2000s has been driven by American and European multi-national firms adopting efficiency-seeking strategies to reduce labour costs to compete in price-sensitive markets. The opening of Asian economies to the world as destinations for offshoring strategies has enabled Western multi-national firms to create complex outsourcing chains strategies (Cantwell and Narula 2001) by locating production functions in different 'places' depending on their internal strategic division of value via green- or brownfield investments, as well as mergers and acquisitions operations. The globalisation of production activities resulted in 'de-territorialised' production choices.

The globalisation strategies of multi-national firms were highly supported by the neo-liberal approach that dominated the late 1980s and 1990s which took the form of the so-called Washington Consensus (Marangos 2008). This pushed for free market, free trade, deregulations, and convenient currency exchanges, creating a global business environment where Western multi-national enterprises (MNEs) could operate and flourish (ibid.). World Bank and International Monetary Fund were instrumental in this respect (Williamson 1990) whilst through the World Trade Organisation (WTO), an unprecedented number of free trade agreements and trade liberalisation were concluded (Nachum 2000). As American multi-national firms were looking to China in the first instance for achieving cost-efficiency in production (Hansen-Kuhn 1997), in Europe in the 1990s, the European Commission also endorsed an outward-looking policy that promoted European competitiveness by supporting the emergence national champions in the global markets via investment in high-tech industries and cost-efficiency (Gilpin and Gilpin 2001).

The socio-economic costs and benefits of globalisation have been not evenly spread in advanced economies nor in fact in emerging economies (Barrientos et al. 2016). In roughly 20 years, trade in intermediate product doubled, the number of subsidiaries increased exponentially, the movement of young people to learn Western managerial techniques was significant, and, of course, the global economy grew continuously (Miroudot et al. 2009). The entrance of China in the WTO accelerated the fragmentation of production allowing multi-national firms to be headquartered in the North to be brains of production, while subsidiaries were moved to the global South to be the brawns. In the early years, China and South-East Asia along with Mexico in the Americas become the so-called factory of the world (Xiangguo 2007).

In the meantime, advanced countries saw a reduction in their manufacturing output and an increase in service output. This geographical cleavage between tangible assets and intangible assets coincided with what Baldwin (2006) calls the second 'great unbundling': this caused the de-industrialisation and the depopulation of declining urban areas (Essletzbichler 2004), for instance, with production shifting from the snowbelt to the sunbelt states in the United States and the decline of industrial activities in traditional manufacturing regions in Western Europe (Rodrik 2016). US manufacturing employment peaked in 1979 with 20 million jobs, followed by a steady decline since. The downward trend of manufacturing employment in the United States accelerated in the early 1990s, but slowed down in the mid-2010s driven mainly by changes in the production system towards a more technological upgrading.

The decision to outsource low-value activities in foreign countries implies also a location decision choice. Regardless of the mode of entries, the firm is intrinsically bounded with the host location once chosen (Buckley and Casson 1999). The first wave of manufacturing delocalisation was oriented towards neighbouring countries, as geography proximity reduces transportation costs and cultural proximity reduces coordination cost: Mexico, China, and Eastern Europe (ex URSS) became the prime destination respectively for American and European firms (Caraveli 2016; Fukao et al. 2004; Feenstra and Hanson 1996). The choice of these newly available destinations facilitated by the creation of North America Free Trade Agreement (NAFTA) for the United States as American MNEs relied on foreign direct investment (FDI) or offshored outsourcing in Mexico creating the so-called maquiladora in a way of establishing a hierarchical or caption relationship with them (Bair and Gereffi 2001). For European economies, the opportunity to have proximate destinations for cost-saving strategies came with the fall of the Berlin Wall in 1989; this opened up access to a large pool of relatively cheap, albeit unskilled labour, via FDI or outsourcing especially in automotive, fashion, and footwear sectors. Japanese automotive industries also heavily delocalized to China to maximise economies of scale and cost reduction to be more competitive in the European market.

Thanks to the work of Gereffi et al. (2005), the fragmentation and vertical disaggregation of production orchestrated by MNEs that spread from advanced economies to emerging economies started to be represented as a global value chain. Every single part contributes differently to the final value of production with high value-added 'tasks' being distinguished from low value-added one. Less value creating tasks were typically more labour-intensive and were ridden by the firm via outsourcing, while high value creating tasks were kept in-house, under strict management control. These are low value creating tasks that started to be offshored and scattered abroad creating indeed global value chains. The Global Value Chains (GVC) framework allows to highlight that value is not only embodied in a specific task performed along the chain, but the value is also associated with the location in which the task takes place. That is the main reason why location matters (Buckley and Casson 1999). In the 2000s, an increase in the research on GVCs resulted in a better understanding of the maps of the global production as an intersection between global connections managed by MNEs and local systems (De Propris et al. 2008) sustained by a network of stakeholders such as firms, trade associations, workers, education system, policy-makers, and local and national governments (Gereffi and Fernandez-Stark 2016).

The mushrooming expansion of global production in the period 1980–2010 was mainly driven by increasing the productivity by reducing the labour cost. This was a profitable solution until the main goal was to pursue economies of scale over a large quantity of tradeable goods (Livesey 2018). Recently, new trends in the consumer market (e.g. sustainability, customisation, and amazon effect) and new forms of the production process (e.g. automation, robotics, cloud, and remote control) usher a novel era of globalisation, in which chasing the cheapest manufacturing location could be a wane strategy (Lund and Tyson 2018).

Technological Change and Industry 4.0

There is an emerging debate that is starting to unpack the transformative impact that the current wave of technological change will bring about. De Propris (2018) argued that we are going through the FIR with a host of new technologies, started being developed in the mid-1980s, which is driving the emergence of a new techno-economic paradigm that will impact on production, consumption, and ways of life. These include biotech, nanotech, neuro-technologies, green and renewables, information and communication technology (ICT) & mobile tech, cloud technology, big data, 3D printing, artificial intelligence, internet of things (IoT), robotics, sensoring, space technology, and drones.

Applications of these new technologies have already started in some industries such as automotive where the adoption of digital technology and automation is expected to revolutionise the organisation of production inside the factory and along the supply chain. Indeed, the first translation of these new technologies in tangible change can be witnessed in the German's launch of the Industry 4.0 model of production, which describes the impact that the IoT and robotics can have on the organisation of production thanks to a new interplay between humans and machines. This has kicked a lively debate on the new Industry 4.0 model of production. The latter term has been indeed adopted widely first by think-tanks, business leaders, international organisations, and then more recently by policy-makers.

Captured by a business-focused narrative, Industry 4.0 started being celebrated for the impact that technologies such as IoT, artificial intelligence, robotics, and automation are expected to have in the production of goods by bringing efficiency, productivity, responsiveness, flexibility, and ultimately seamless integration of the supply chain in manufacturing production (Deusche Bank 2014; KPMG 2016, 2017; PWC 2016; McKinsey 2015; Berger 2013). Efficiency is mostly understood as cost-efficiency, energy efficiency, and labour efficiency, often summed up by the futuristic idea of 'light out factories' with no lights and no heating (WSJ 2002; Heng 2014). Increased productivity would come from automation enabling more flexible processes, short lead times, better control of the value chain flow, and better control of quality. Responsiveness would be greatly enhanced by the data collected thanks to cloud computing. Data can be collected during production on site and along the supply chain, as well as from consumers and users. Data provides information and feedback to be used to enhance processes and responses. Linked to the above, automation and data feed into firms' ability to maximise its flexibility, by producing in smaller batches: this is often referred to as mass customisation. Amongst many of the changes, Siemens (2015) mentions the 'integration of value chains with seamless engineering' and a combination of cloud technology and data analytics. Such smart factories and connected factories adopt IoT, robotics, sensoring, space technology, and mobile technology to enable machine-to-machine communications that will allow the coordination of complex production operations via a seamless integration of functions (KPMG 2016, 2017)

The truth is that the impact that the FIR should be—and can be—much more disruptive than designing a 'lights out factory'. De Propris (2018) argues that a broader definition of Industry 4.0+ must be considered to allow the deployment of all the technologies of the FIR to trigger a transformational shift in the techno-socio-economic paradigm attuned to a green economy and society. Industry 4.0+ only can be a key part of an effort to deliver an inclusive socio-economic growth. Indeed information technology, mobile technology, 3D printing, artificial intelligence, robotics, sensors, space technology, and drones are all new technologies that allow for small-scale production, and personalised and customer-centred innovation and applications.

Industry 4.0+ will, therefore, unfold with the creation of a new customer-centred innovation, where consumer, innovator, and producer work attuned to create disruptive and radically new products. The presence of niche and even customer-centred markets where frontier technologies can be explored via applications and adoption afford a different reorganisation of production, one that requires a tighter and better dove-tailed interaction between the innovation and production phases of the value chain. Small scale productions can be efficient and coupled with experimentation of frontier technologies in markets that are on the frontier of innovation development and adoption. This implies that both the 'making of things' and innovation are associated with high value creation; after 'the great unbundling' of the 1990–2000 (Baldwin 2006), this calls for a strategic re-bundling of innovation and production.

It will be a while before we can fully appreciate the impact that the adoption of FIR technologies will have across manufacturing and the economy more widely; however, technological change is only one of the factors that are already reshaping the organisation of production globally. Indeed, the Great Recession (van Bergeijk 2018) that followed the 2008 financial crisis has profoundly changed the general perception of globalisation: from being inevitable and desirable, globalisation has more recently pointed to as the cause of socio-economic malaise in advanced economies, wider income inequalities (Piketty 2014), and crucially wider intra-countries socio-economic disparities. Has the global economy reached 'peak globalisation'?

De-globalisation

The financial contagion that kicked off in 2008 and led to the Great Recession across advanced economies and the shock it caused to the real economy was a wake-up call especially for the 'average person in the street' of the extent to which single economies were interconnected globally (Van Bergeijk 2018). Globalisation and the integration of global markets, for the first time, were seen as undesirable. Instrumental to capitalism, globalisation was nevertheless deemed to be the only route possible to growth. However, a more critical narrative about globalisation was also emerging especially in relation to the price that regions and cities across advanced economies had paid due to the delocalisation of production overseas. The de-industrialisation, deskilling, and marginalisation of entire communities who lost jobs and identity were for the first time scrutinised and in the United Kingdom, for instance, a large debate on 'Re-balancing the economy' (Bailey and De Propris 2014a) attempted to unpack such sore issues.

At the macro level, evidence is also emerging that since 2008 the global economy is de-globalising. Global trade and the internationalisation activities of multi-national enterprises show signs of decelerating. As discussed in the Organisation for Economic Co-operation and Development (OECD) (2017), data on global trade and gross domestic product (GDP) growth rate show that after the big dip in 2008 in correspondence with the financial crisis, GDP growth rate returned to pre-crisis level relatively quickly but dropped afterwards below 3% (Fig. 11.1). At the same time, trade recovered between 2009 and 2011 but plateaued after to drop after 2014. OECD (2017) claims that the slow and weak trade recovery has been a sign of a still fragile global economy unable to pick up the pace of growth pre-crisis. Still looking at the trend of the KOF Swiss Economic Institute (Konjunkturforschungsstelle) globalisation index (Gygli et al. 2018), the hypothesis that the globalisation is slowing down is taking shape (see Fig. 11.2).

If some form of de-globalisation (Martin et al. 2018; Livesey 2017, 2018) is occurring, what are the signs? Is there some evidence for it? We are considering two amongst many: one is FDI trends and the other is global value chains' activities. Outward FDI has gone through peaks and troughs since its big drop in 2008–09 as described in Fig. 11.3, with the latest figures suggesting a contraction. Changes in FDI trends can signal tensions in the global organisation of production. Evidence compiled by the OECD (2017, p. 46) shows

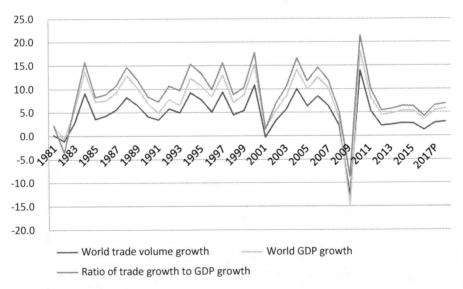

Fig. 11.1 GDP and trade (annual percentage change and ratio). (Source: Our elaboration from WTO statistics)

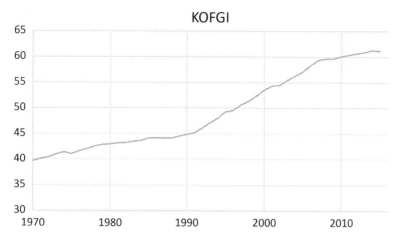

Fig. 11.2 Trend of the KOF globalisation index. (Source: Our calculation with KOF data (Gygli et al. 2018))

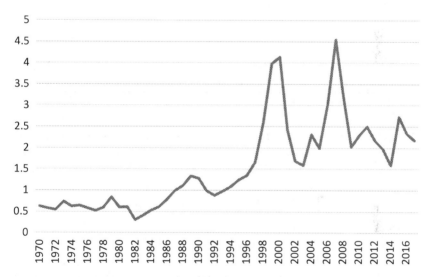

Fig. 11.3 Developed economies: FDI outflows, annual 1970–16 (as percentage of GDP). (Source: Our elaboration from UNCTADSTAT)

that between 2011 and 2015 GVC activities have dropped for G7 economies (both simple GVC and complex GVC) whilst the production-to-export has increased. This has been particularly the case for the manufacturing sector which experienced positive growth for pure domestic production (mode evidence is needed to extrapolate if this is some form of export substitution) and production-to-export, with negative growth for both simple and complex GVC activities (OECD 2017).

There are many possible explanations for this de-globalisation drive: there are political forces advocating more protectionist approaches; the global competitive environment has changed with the emergence of attractive markets to an untapped pool of consumers where before there was an untapped pool of labour; multi-national firms' internationalisation strategies are moving away from cost-saving to being close-to-market and finally, new technologies are changing the nature of products, processes, and therefore the essence of their competitive advantage. We are focusing here on the latter.

The wave of new technologies that is unfolding has the potentials to disrupt all sectors and markets; often defined as key enabling technologies (Corradini and De Propris 2017) they have wider applicability and transferability. The adoption of new technologies in products will occur through discovery and experimentation in markets that are yet to be created, but which start taking embryonic form thanks to the curiosity of a small demand. These frontier markets tend to be top end, they realise small quantity and are relatively price inelastic and can, therefore, afford high prices. In these frontier markets, firms' competitive advantage is measured by their ability to create value through adoption.

The capacity of such frontier producers to embody new technologies in existing products or to create new products shapes what we can call their 'translational readiness' which requires tight and thick synergies between innovation and production. Research and Development (R&D), design, product development, and prototyping are at this stage technology pushed but their applications will require engaged inputs from demand as product specifications are developed almost in response to customers' experimentation with such frontier products. The constant and crucial feedback loops between innovation and production call for a re-bundling of the intangible and tangible stages in the value creation chain. This does not imply a return to greater integration of production through internalisation, but rather a smoother and rimless interaction between highly specialised component designer and makers, as well as service providers. Such frontier products are likely to have very short life cycles since technological applications are continuously updated and upgraded driven both by advancements in technology pushed translations and by streams of feedback from demand.

Disruptive technological change is, therefore, creating a new competitive environment in some markets where value creation hinges on a technology-innovation-production-market continuum. We have tried to argue that two are therefore the consequences of this. One is that innovation and production are pulled together and functionally re-bundled, and the other consequence is that such re-bundling can be eased by the co-location of the two. Small-scale productions, short product life cycles, low price elasticity, all suggest that such frontier products can be produced in high-cost economies, eliminating the need for efficiency-driven offshoring. On a larger scale, technological change is reducing the need for cross-continental transactions resulting in a form of de-globalisation.

Reshoring as Strategy to Re-bundle Innovation with Production

According to the theory of international business *'the possibilities of economies of scale in certain activities, the complexities of the activities, the extent of their integration, the type of market structure and the extent of Government intervention will all influence location strategy'* (Buckley and Casson 1999, p. 57). As the theories of firms' location choices are well understood, we draw on them to shed some light on recent trends that have seen manufacturing activities being relocated from low-cost economies to advanced economies due to a new geography of production shaped by a re-bundling of tangible and intangible functions is an increasing complex model of technological adoption that is reshaping the competitiveness of advanced economies.

Indeed, firms' strategic decision to relocate manufacturing activities in the home economy has so far been studied by Supply Chain Management scholars pinpointing to factors that have made long and complex supply chains risky and costly. Long and complex supply chains were found inflexible, difficult to manage, and logistically frail, whilst long-distance transactions resulted in delivering lags, large inventory, and quality control problem (Ellram et al. 2013). At the same time, raising wages in China made the cost opportunity increasingly less attractive (Bailey and De Propris 2014b). This new trend was documented in several report from international organisations (e.g. OECD) and consultancy firms such as PwC and Boston Consulting, as well as in local and national magazines with specific company case studies (e.g. *The Economist, The Wall Street*, the *Financial Times*). Terms such as reshoring and back-shoring were increasingly used to capture firms' strategic decision leading to the *'return [home] of a previous delocalized activity'* (Gray et al. 2013).

Framed in a broader narrative about de-globalisation, both reshoring and back-shoring suggested that firms' location choices were no longer driven by an internationalisation rationale. However, to fully understand their drivers and dynamics more in-depth analysis was necessary. Indeed, further questions

232 L. De Propris and D. Pegoraro

need to be addressed to have a better understanding of the phenomenon of reshoring:

* Who are the stakeholders engaged in the process? Does the local or national government in the domestic economy play a key role?
* What is the value of the activity brought back? Is that activity strategic to the competitiveness of the firm? Will the activity brought back be the same as the one that was previously offshored or will be it upgraded? Will the manufacturing process be the same or will be it upgraded?
* How the activity has been or will be bought back? Greenfield/Brownfield investments or partnership with suppliers?
* Where the activity will be located? In the same territory of the HQ or in another part of the country?

These questions have been addressed partially by Supply Chain Scholars and by few Economic Geographers, suggesting that a holistic approach is preferred when exploring the feasibility of investments in manufacturing in advanced economies (Ellram et al. 2013; Gray et al. 2013). Since reshoring deals also with firms' location decisions, a valuable contribution on the subject could be offered by International Business theories.

Reshoring and the Role of Extra-Firm Stakeholders

As pointed out by Ellram et al. (2013) and Kinkel (2014), institutions play a critical role in fostering reshoring decision. This has been investigated by Srai and Ané (2016), who argued that institutions should have a primary role in supporting those companies which decide to reshore a manufacturing activity. The results highlight the relevance of local brands and quality features as drivers for reshoring strategy. The importance of an institutional participation has been also documented by Bailey and De Propris (2014b). The surveyed research outcome is the plea for a policy agenda, which should benefit those companies which are reshoring. In the United States, Tate (2014) stresses that leveraging the US public policy could foster reshoring strategies, even if more attention should be placed on fully understand the term reshoring. In addition, Tate (2014) argues that the 2008 financial crisis can be seen as the starting point of the current trend towards developing repatriation manufacturing strategies. In the paper (ibid), proximity to the final market is argued to be delivered by greater flexibility in the manufacturing processes partly delivered through shorter supply chains.

Reshoring and Industry 4.0

In the literature on reshoring, some studies are emerging that consider the adoption of Industry 4.0 technologies and the importance of the territorial context as drivers for shortening value chains.

The role that new technologies will have in 'reindustrialising' advanced economies is still embryonic (Fratocchi 2018). Several studies highlight that a narrowing in the labour cost's gap between advanced and developing economies is a push factors (Bailey et al. 2018; Tate and Bals 2017; Moradlou and Backhouse 2016; Srai and Ané 2016; Stentoft et al. 2016; Ancarani et al. 2015; Bailey and De Propris 2014b; Kinkel 2012), but few studies are looking at the role played by new technologies as substitute for workers to increase production efficiency. Other studies acknowledge a lack of skilled workers in host country (Foerstl et al. 2016; Canham and Hamilton 2013;) but still, there is no reference to skills related to the adoption of technologies in production process: for instance, in relation to digital and coding skills.

Some initial work looked at the adoption of additive manufacturing as a driver of reshoring (Fratocchi 2018; Moradlou and Tate 2018) In particular, Fratocchi (2018) analysed through secondary data the magnitude of the adoption of additive manufacturing technologies in bringing the manufacturing process back to the domestic economy; results seem to confirm a positive link between the two. Moradlou and Tate (2018) also endorse these results and according to their study, the adoption of additive manufacturing following reshoring strategies resulted in shorter lead time, better firm's responsiveness to market shifts, lean inventory, low emission due to reduction in road transportation, and less risk of misunderstandings with suppliers. Such finding confirms as initial study by Stentoft et al. (2016) where it was found that the more firms invest in automation in the manufacturing process, the more they are likely to bring production back home. At the same time, Marfia and Degli Esposti (2017) investigated the role of blockchain technology to increase a firm's reputation and products' emotional value for the end consumers. Outside the academic debate, MNEs—such as Adidas in Germany—have already started implementing robot-sourcing strategy in order to reduce production costs and increase labour productivity (O'Connor 2016). Investing in new technologies therefore could reduce the complexity of too extensive global value chain by focusing on in-house innovation and closeness to the final market.

Case Study on Shorter and Proximate Value Chain: The Automotive Ecosystem in San Jose Economic Area

The adoption of digital technology, automation, and IoT in manufacturing processes and product design, tighter control of the supply chain thanks to blockchain technology, and a stronger ecological logic are just some of the new disruptive technologies that are shaking the automotive sector. The convergence between robust data analysis and IoT has initiated a shift towards a more engaged ecosystem, whereby the manufacturing activity is becoming way more interwoven and embedded with other activities of the chain, such as R& or Logistic & Distribution, because of its high value creation contribution. To unleash the potential of this value creation, new skills and new type of jobs are needed. Hence, the education and training system has also to keep up such changes. Firms have to design and map out all the digital changes emerging along the value chain (from design to distribution); so that the focus is not on the adoption of one technologies or another, but on how to integrate all the relevant technologies in the process and in the product. By creating a more connected network, where people, assets, and processes share the same system of information, the feedback loop could be shorter, the sourcing more controlled, and the diffusion of new ideas easier (Mason 2018). Hence, a reorganisation of the manufacturing process has to take place if firm wants to benefit from technological adoption.

An example of this integrated digital manufacturing ecosystem in the automotive sector in California. In 2016, California was ranked first for hosting 108 headquarters of large (1000 Fortune) firms, mostly in the sectors of Information Technology, Biopharma and Defence. In particular, the functional economic area of San Jose (including San Francisco and Oakland) ranks third in terms of innovation and number of job creation with respect to the rest of the United States. Innovation is driven by companies (top-three for patents) such as Google, Apple, and IBM, while job creation is led by firms in Business Services, Marketing and Design, and Education & Knowledge sectors. At first sight, the SJEA is not manufacturing driven, although food-related industries and automotive rank respectively seventh and eighth in terms of the number of jobs created. However, beyond any forecast, the automotive industry has grown significantly. In 2016, according to the sector national growth forecast, the automotive sector in San Jose should have decreased its job creation unit of 4292. Instead, it created more than 7400 new jobs in the same year, bringing the economic area as one of the most dynamic in the automotive sector.[1]

---

[1] See data in this link http://clustermapping.us/

Technological Disruptions and Production Location Choices 235

Automotive is a sector which is disrupted by new technologies but where incumbents are only slowly upgrading their value chains, at least in the United States. Although the final product is still a car, the new technologies that can be adopted and embedded in the processes and in the products are such that they require completely different competences from before. The need to incorporate high-tech options in the production process requires the use of high-tech skilled workers and the proximity with the research and development department. These are the main motives why in Silicon Valley, in the SJEA, the automotive sector is booming (He 2017). In the SJEA, there are already 64 automotive companies operations mainly R&D oriented (Coren 2017). Established car makers brands have a facility there such as the BMW Group Technology office in Mountain View, General Motors Advanced Technologies in Palo Alto, Honda Research Institute in Mountain View, Volkswagen Electronics Research Lab in Belmont, and Nissan Research Centre in Sunnyvale (Coren 2017). New players such as Apple and Google entered in this sector for developing driverless cars, Tesla as established electronic car makers and Ubers which is revolutionising the transportation system.

The automotive sector in SJEA is very different from the one in Detroit Area, as in the last one there is the bulk of the entire industry. The peculiarity of the Californian hub is its connection with the technological ecosystem that the area offers. An ecosystem pervaded by an interdependence between industries and overlapping sectors. Examples are Apple, which granted the permission to test self-driving car tech and Tesla, which acquired SolarTech in order to become a supplier of solar energy (Della Cava 2018). These strategies are leading the green-tech revolution, the first by transforming the auto performance from miles per hour to data per minutes, the second by hocking the opportunity to supply its own fuel (electric energy) to its product and create a fully integrated loyalty experience.

The technology is leading towards an ecosystem in which the single firm's strategy is not competitive anymore (Engel 2015). Its strategy has to be developed in parallel with the innovations available in the ecosystem, in order to create compatible solutions to complement other players. Players comprise firms from different sectors (e.g. BMW and IBM), local and regional policy-makers and education institutions (such as the Centre for Automotive Research at Stanford University).

In order to generate this value, the ecosystem cannot be globally spread, each ecosystem is unique to its territory. The automotive companies established in Silicon Valley are operating in an ecosystem different from those operating in the Midlands or Oxford in United Kingdom or Emilia Romagna in Italy. In today's scenario, the global value chain of a frontier automotive firm is less global and cost concerned, but instead more local and technology driven. As reshoring underpins a strategic location choice, manufacturing or sourcing activities should be located where there is the opportunity for greater value creation and access to frontier technologies. This explains that many companies have reshored to Silicon Valley those activities previously performed overseas (Reshoring Institute 2017).

This case study on automotive sector in the SJEA shows that the adoption of frontier technologies in the automotive sector is linked to connected mobility and greening automotive emission; disruptive change is driven by innovators and producers that are co-located in the same space, allowing a functional re-bundling that is speeding up the process of technology exploration and adoption.

Conclusion

This chapter conceptually exposes the idea that a shorter global value chain, with focus on the territorial ecosystem, may be a strategy to follow for competing in today's economic scenario. De-globalisation is not the reverse of globalisation, as people, trade goods, and financial capital will continue to travel across borders, but we would like to stress the point that the value of tangible assets is decreasing in favour of intangible assets. In line with this, as the manufacturing is becoming more valuable because of Industry 4.0, its location could be changed from a low-cost labour force country to a high-cost labour force country. This follows the concept offered by the theory of international operation.

Another point is the topical role of extra-firm actor for creating an ecosystem in which the firm can prosper. Policy-makers should orient policies towards a more technological goal, promoting the development of technical skills job and collaborate with the education system of the territory.

To conclude, to take full advantages of de-globalisation, Western firms are starting to look closer at the advantages embedded in the territorial ecosystems where they are located and to collaborate with public and private stakeholders in particular in relation to the adoption of new technologies and the derived adjustments at the firm and system levels.

Acknowledgements The writing of this chapter has been supported by the EU Horizon 2020 project MAKERS—Smart Manufacturing for EU Growth and Prosperity is a project funded by the Horizon 2020 Research and Innovation Staff Exchange Programme, which is a Research and Innovation Staff Exchange under the Marie Skłodowska-Curie Actions, grant agreement number 691192.

References

Aart, J. (2000). *Globalization: A critical introduction*. Houndmills: Palgrave Macmillan.

Ancarani, A., Di Mauro, C., Fratocchi, L., Orzes, G., & Sartor, M. (2015). Prior to reshoring: A duration analysis of foreign manufacturing ventures. *International Journal of Production Economics, 169*, 141–155.

Bailey, D., & De Propris, L. (2014a). Recession, recovery and resilience? *Regional Studies., 48*(11), 1757–1760.

Bailey, D., & De Propris, L. (2014b). Manufacturing reshoring and its limits: The UK automotive case. *Cambridge Journal of Regions, Economy and Society, 7*(3), 379–395.

Bailey, D., & De Propris, L. (2017). What does Brexit mean for UK automotive and industrial policy. In *The political economy of Brexit*. Newcastle: Agenda Publishing.

Bailey, D., Corradini, C., & De Propris, L. (2018). 'Home-sourcing' and closer value chains in mature economies: The case of Spanish manufacturing. *Cambridge Journal of Economics, 42*(6), 1567–1584.

Bair, J., & Gereffi, G. (2001). Local clusters in global chains: The causes and consequences of export dynamism in Torreon's blue jeans industry. *World Development, 29*(11), 19.

Baldwin, R. (2006). Globalisation: The great unbundling(s). *Economic Council of Finland, 20*, 5–47.

Barrientos, S., Gereffi, G., & Pickles, J. (2016). New dynamics of upgrading in global value chains: Shifting terrain for suppliers and workers in the global south. *Environment and Planning A, 48*(7), 1214–1219.

Berger, S. (2013). *Making in America: From innovation to market*. Cambridge: Mit Press.

Buckley, P. J., & Casson, M. (1999). A theory of international operations. In *The internationalization process of the firm: a reader* (2nd ed., pp. 55–60). London: International Business Thomson.

Canham, S., & Hamilton, R. T. (2013). SME internationalisation: Offshoring, "backshoring", or staying at home in New Zealand. *Strategic Outsourcing: An International Journal, 6*(3), 277–291.

Cantwell, J., & Narula, R. (2001). The eclectic paradigm in the global economy. *International Journal of the Economics of Business, 8*(2), 155–172.

Caraveli, H. (2016). Global imbalances and EU core-periphery division: Institutional framework and theoretical interpretations. *World Review of Political Economy, 7*(1), 29–55. https://doi.org/10.13169/worlrevipoliecon.7.1.0029.

Cava, D. (2018, August 22). Siri, please bring my iCar around now: Is Apple making a cool new ride or just dabbling with the techie parts? *USA Today*.

Coren, M. J. (2017). *All of the car companies, suppliers, and auto startups in Silicon Valley*. Retrieved from https://qz.com/1072873/all-of-the-car-companies-suppliers-and-auto-startups-in-silicon-valley/

Corradini, C., & De Propris, L. (2017). Beyond local search: Bridging platforms and inter-sectoral technological integration. *Research Policy, 46*(1), 196–206.

De Propris, L. (2018). Disruptive Industry 4.0, MAKERS report. Report to the EU Commission.

De Propris, L., Menghinello, S., & Sugden, R. (2008). The internationalisation of local production systems: Embeddedness, openness and governance. *Entrepreneurship and Regional Development, 20*(6), 493–516.

Deusche Bank. (2014). *Industry 4.0 upgrading of Germany's industrial capabilities on the horizon.* Deusche Bank Research. Available at SSRN: https://ssrn.com/abstract=2656608

Dicken, P. (2015). *Global shift: Mapping the changing contours of the world economy.* London: Sage.

Ellram, L. M., Tate, W. L., & Petersen, K. J. (2013). Offshoring and reshoring: An update on the manufacturing location decision. *Journal of Supply Chain Management, 49*(2), 14–22.

Engel, J. S. (2015). Global clusters of innovation: Lessons from Silicon Valley. *California Management Review, 57*(2), 36–65.

Essletzbichler, J. (2004). The geography of job creation and destruction in the US manufacturing sector, 1967–1997. *Annals of the Association of American Geographers, 94*(3), 602–619.

Feenstra, R. C., & Hanson, G. H. (1996). *Globalisation, outsourcing, and wage inequality* (No. w5424). National Bureau of Economic Research.

Foerstl, K., Kirchoff, J. F., & Bals, L. (2016). Reshoring and insourcing: Drivers and future research directions. *International Journal of Physical Distribution & Logistics Management, 46*(5), 492–515.

Fratocchi, L. (2018, April). *Additive manufacturing as a reshoring enabler considerations on the why issue.* In 2018 workshop on metrology for Industry 4.0 and IoT (pp. 117–122). IEEE.

Friedman. (2000). *The Lexus and the olive tree: Understanding globalization.* New York: Random House.

Fukao, K., Inui, T., Kawai, H., & Miyagawa, T. (2004, June). *Sectoral productivity and economic growth in Japan, 1970–98: An empirical analysis based on the JIP database.* In Growth and productivity in East Asia, NBER-East Asia seminar on economics (Vol. 13, pp. 177–228). University of Chicago Press.

Gereffi, G., Humphrey, J., & Sturgeon, T. (2005). The governance of global value chains. *Review of International Political Economy, 12*(1), 78–104. https://doi.org/10.1080/09692290500049805.

Gilpin, R., & Gilpin, J. M. (2001). *Global political economy: Understanding the international economic order.* Princeton: Princeton University Press.

Gray, J. V., Skowronski, K., Esenduran, G., & Johnny Rungtusanatham, M. (2013). The reshoring phenomenon: What supply chain academics ought to know and should do. *Journal of Supply Chain Management, 49*(2), 27–33.

Gygli, S., Haelg, F., & Sturm, J.-E. (2018). *The KOF globalisation index – Revisited.* KOF working paper, no. 439.

Technological Disruptions and Production Location Choices 239

Hansen-Kuhn, K. (1997). Clinton, NAFTA and the politics of US trade. *NACLA Report on the Americas, 31*(2), 22–26.

He, E. (2017). *How Silicon Valley is inventing the future of cars*. Retrieved from https://www.paloaltoonline.com/news/2017/07/28/how-silicon-valley-is-inventing-the-future-of-cars

Heng, S. (2014). *Industry 4.0: Upgrading of Germany's industrial capabilities on the horizon*. Available at SSRN: https://ssrn.com/abstract=2656608

Kinkel, S. (2014). Future and impact of backshoring – Some conclusions from 15 years of research on German practices. *Journal of Purchasing and Supply Management, 20*(1), 63–65.

KPMG. (2016). *The factory of the future. Industry 4.0 – The challenges of tomorrow*. KPMG AG Wirtschaftspruefungsgesellschaft.

KPMG. (2017). *Beyond the hype. Separating ambition from reality in Industry 4.0*. KPMG International.

Livesey, F. (2017). *From global to local*. London: Profile Books.

Livesey, F. (2018). Unpacking the possibilities of deglobalisation. *Cambridge Journal of Regions, Economy and Society, 11*(1), 177–187.

Lund, S., & Tyson, L. (2018). Globalisation is not in retreat: Digital technology and the future of trade. *Foreign Affairs, 97*, 130.

Marangos, J. (2008). The evolution of the anti-Washington consensus debate: From 'post-Washington consensus' to 'after the Washington consensus'. *Competition & Change, 12*(3), 227–244.

Marfia, G., & Degli Esposti, P. (2017). Blockchain and sensor-based reputation enforcement for the support of the reshoring of business activities. In *Reshoring of manufacturing* (pp. 125–139). Cham: Springer.

Martin, R., Tyler, P., Storper, M., Evenhuisd, E., & Glasmeier, A. (2018). Globalization at a critical conjuncture? *Cambridge Journal of Regions, Economy and Society, 11*, 3–16.

Mason, B. (2018). A tale of two automotive industries. *US blogs*. Retrieved from http://usblogs.pwc.com/industrialinsights/2018/01/30/a-tale-of-two-automotive-industries/

McKinsey. (2015). *Industry 4.0. How to navigate digitalization of the manufacturing sector*. McKinsey Digital. Available at: https://www.mckinsey.com/business-functions/operations/our-insights/industry-four-point-o-how-to-navigae-the-digitization-of-the-manufacturing-sector

Miroudot, S., Lanz, R., & Ragoussis, A. (2009). *Trade in intermediate goods and services* (OECD trade policy papers, Vol. 93). Paris: OECD Publishing. https://doi.org/10.1787/5kmlcxtdlk8r-en.

Moradlou, H., & Backhouse, C. J. (2016). A review of manufacturing re-shoring in the context of customer-focused postponement strategies. *Proceedings of the Institution of Mechanical Engineers, Part B: Journal of Engineering Manufacture, 230*(9), 1561–1571.

Moradlou, H., & Tate, W. (2018). Reshoring and additive manufacturing. *World Review of Intermodal Transportation Research, 7*(3), 241–263.

Nachum, L. (2000). World investment report 1999: Foreign direct investment and the challenge of development. United Nations Conference on Trade and Development (UNCTAD): United Nations, New York and Geneva, 1999, ISBN 92-1-112440-9.

O'Connor, S. (2016). Robots may cut off the path to prosperity in the developing world. *The Financial Time*. Retrieved from https://www.ft.com/content/5d0b1206-36f2-11e6-a780-b48ed7b6126f

OECD. (2017). *Measuring and analysing the impact of GVCs on economic development, global value chain development report*. Paris: OECD.

Piketty, T. (2014). *Capital in the twenty-first century*. Cambridge, MA: The Belknap Press of Harvard University Press.

PWC. (2016). *Industry 4.0: Building the digital enterprise*. 2016 global industry 4.0 survey.

Reshoring Institute. (2017). *California, state economic survey and incentive comparison*. Retrieved from https://reshoringinstitute.org/wp-content/uploads/2017/07/state-economic-profile-california.pdf

Rodrik, D. (2016). Premature deindustrialization. *Journal of Economic Growth, 21*(1), 1–33.

Siemens. (2015). *On the way to Industrie 4.0 – The digital enterprise*. Siemens AG. Available at: https://www.siemens.com/press/pool/de/events/2015/digitalfactory/2015-04-hannovermesse/presentation-e.pdf

Srai, J. S., & Ané, C. (2016). Institutional and strategic operations perspectives on manufacturing reshoring. *International Journal of Production Research, 54*(23), 7193–7211.

Stentoft, J., Olhager, J., Heikkilä, J., & Thoms, L. (2016). Manufacturing backshoring: A systematic literature review. *Operations Management Research, 9*(3–4), 53–61.

Tate, W. L. (2014). Offshoring and reshoring: US insights and research challenges. *Journal of Purchasing and Supply Management, 20*(1), 66–68.

Tate, W. L., & Bals, L. (2017). Outsourcing/offshoring insights: Going beyond reshoring to rightshoring. *International Journal of Physical Distribution & Logistics Management, 47*(2/3), 106–113.

van Bergeijk, P. A. G. (2018). On the brink of deglobalisation…again. *Cambridge Journal of Regions, Economy and Society, 11*, 59–72.

Williamson, J. (Ed.). (1990). *Latin American adjustment: How much has happened*. Washington, DC: Institute for International Economics.

WSJ. (2002, November 19). Workers aren't included in lights-out factories. *The Wall Street Journal*.

Xiangguo, C. H. E. N. (2007). Is China the factory of the world? Ritsumeikan Center for Asia Pacific Studies (RCAPS). Occasional paper, *7*(4).

Index[1]

B

Barriers to knowledge sharing, 73–78, 87
Born-digital, 176, 199–215
Born-global, 202, 212
Bounded rationality, 6, 21
Brazil, Russia, India and China (BRIC) countries, 72, 157–171
Brexit, 1, 2, 27–44, 221
Business
  ethics, 178, 179
  models, 2, 29, 118, 200, 209–212

C

Clusters, 72, 117–130, 222
Co-location externalities, 120–122
Competitive advantage, 2, 29–36, 75, 120, 138, 189, 203, 230
Contextual barriers, 71, 74–78, 80, 83, 85–87
Corporate reporting, 72, 158, 163–168
Corporate social responsibility (CSR), 22, 157–160, 162, 164–166,
168–170, 177, 179–181, 183, 187–189, 193
Corruption, 12, 33, 34, 56, 101, 190
Country of origin, 72, 117–130, 135–153, 214
CSR Pyramid (Carroll 1991), 189
Cultural distance, 56, 178, 180, 193

D

De-globalisation, 176, 227–231, 236
De-industrialisation, 221, 223, 227
Delocalisation, 227
Digitalization/digitalisation, 176, 199–208, 200n1, 211–215
Digital technologies, 199–203, 214, 215, 225, 234
Dynamic capabilities, 29–33

E

Eclectic paradigm (OLI), 29–34, 37–39, 41
Economic integration, 39–42

---

[1] Note: Page numbers followed by 'n' refer to notes.

© The Author(s) 2019

A. Chidlow et al. (eds.), *The Changing Strategies of International Business*, The Academy of International Business, https://doi.org/10.1007/978-3-030-03931-8

242 Index

Entry mode, 50, 55, 103, 121, 211
Equity ownership, 72, 95–111
Externalities, 51, 72

F

Firm-specific assets (FSAs), 29–33, 151
Foreign acquisitions (FORA), 54, 58, 72, 135–152
Fourth industrial revolution (FIR), 176, 222, 225–227

G

Global factory, 203
Globalisation/globalization, 129, 137, 176, 183, 221–225, 227–229
Global value chain (GVC), 60, 100, 175, 203, 222, 224, 228, 229, 233, 235, 236
Governance, 4, 7–10, 12, 20–23, 29, 31–33, 35, 36, 52, 59, 119, 137, 157
Greenfield investments, 42, 53, 54, 72, 95–111, 124

H

Hofstede's cultural dimensions, 180, 181
Human rights (HR), 72, 130, 157–171, 178

I

Industry 4.0, 222, 225–227, 233, 236
Informal institution, 30, 102, 175, 177, 179, 193
Innovation, 14, 39, 73–76, 78, 79, 85, 87, 99, 122, 123, 129, 202, 204, 226, 227, 230–235
transfer, 71, 73–87
Institutional

distance, 76, 96, 117, 118
environment, 3–5, 7, 11, 22, 54, 76, 136
governance, 1, 3–23
theory, 1, 4
Internalization/internalisation, 32, 33, 38, 72, 135, 138, 212, 230
International entrepreneurship, 175, 213, 214
Internationalization/internationalisation, 39, 50–54, 57, 58, 101, 118–121, 123, 129, 130, 176–180, 192, 193, 199–215, 228, 230, 231

J

Joint ventures (JVs), 53–55, 74, 97, 99, 103–106, 108–111, 148

K

Knowledge-based view, 31
Knowledge sharing, 71, 73–78, 87

L

Legitimacy, 1, 3–23, 72, 121, 126, 129, 137, 170, 188
Liability of foreignness, 55, 117, 137
Location-specific advantages, 31–32, 38

M

Mergers and acquisitions (M&As), 39, 43, 55–58, 95, 96, 139, 223

N

National culture, 177–180, 182–184, 193
Networks, 31, 33–36, 72, 74, 75, 77, 96, 99, 100, 102, 117–123, 127,

Index 243

129, 130, 175, 180, 182, 201, 213, 225, 234

O

Ownership-specific advantages, 30–31
Ownership strategy, 72, 95–111, 152

P

Physical infrastructure, 72, 96, 99, 101–104, 109–111
Political
 instability, 16
 risk, 1–23, 56
Property rights, 7, 8, 30
Protectionism, 8
Psychic distance, 57, 177, 193

R

Relational assets, 31, 33–34
Reshoring, 231–233
Resource-based theory, 29
Resource dependence theory (RDT), 54, 72, 96, 98, 99, 110
Responsible business practices, 175, 177–194
Risk management, 56–57

S

Social
 capital, 33, 34, 36, 43, 74, 77–78, 86, 87, 124

interaction, 7, 71, 73–87
network, 74, 120, 122, 130
Spillovers, 35, 118, 123, 124
State-owned enterprises (SOEs), 2, 49–59, 98
State-owned multinational enterprises (SOMNEs), 49–59
Sustainability, 158–160, 162–170, 177, 179, 225
 reporting, 170

T

Tacit knowledge, 77, 81, 122, 126, 127, 130
Tariffs, 27, 28, 40, 53
Technological change, 225–227, 230, 231

U

Uppsala model, 57, 192, 212

V

Value chain, 121, 175, 176, 199, 200, 203–215, 222, 226, 227, 233–236

W

Washington Consensus, 223

Printed in the United States
By Bookmasters